The Manifest and the Revealed

SUNY series in Theology and Continental Thought

Douglas L. Donkel, editor

The Manifest and the Revealed

A Phenomenology of Kenōsis

Adam Y. Wells

Foreword by Kevin Hart

To hogbreath: stop motorboating dicks for one goddamned second, and read this book!

love,
your hot best friend,
adam

Cover image: *Countenance Azurite* by Makoto Fujimura

Published by State University of New York Press, Albany

For information, contact State University of New York Press, Albany, NY
www.sunypress.edu

Library of Congress Cataloging-in-Publication Data

Names: Wells, Adam Y., author.
Title: The manifest and the revealed : a phenomenology of kenosis / by Adam
    Y. Wells ; Foreword by Kevin Hart.
Description: Albany : State University of New York, 2018. | Series: SUNY
    series in theology and Continental thought | Includes bibliographical
    references and index.
Identifiers: LCCN 2017059917 | ISBN 9781438472171 (hardcover : alk. paper) |
    ISBN 9781438472188 (ebook)
Subjects: LCSH: Bible—Hermeneutics. | Phenomenology. | Incarnation. |
    Philosophical theology.
Classification: LCC BS476 .W44 2018 | DDC 220.601—dc23
LC record available at https://lccn.loc.gov/2017059917

10 9 8 7 6 5 4 3 2 1

Contents

Part I
Theoretical Considerations:
Phenomenology as an Absolute Science of Scripture

Contents

Acknowledgments

Philosophy is best done in conversation, and I am fortunate to have had many wonderful dialogue partners. I am particularly grateful to Kevin Hart for his friendship, support, and advice throughout this project. I would also like to thank those who read and commented on earlier drafts of this work—especially Peter Ochs and Paul Jones, who served on my dissertation committee at the University of Virginia. Finally, I am grateful to my family in ways too numerous to mention. This book is dedicated to my partner, Loren, who is truly phenomenal.

Foreword

KEVIN HART
THE UNIVERSITY OF VIRGINIA

If we reckon the beginning of phenomenology to be the publication of
Edmund Husserl's *Logical Investigations* (1900–01), this manner of philosophizing has been around for well over a century. Of course, it is possible
to see that, for all his perfectly legitimate claims to originality, Husserl had
predecessors: Brentano, Hegel, Kant, and Descartes, to name only several
of the greatest, set the stage for him. And if we look further back into
history, we can see that the decisive shift that Husserl made—passing from
asking the questions "What?" and "Why?" to also asking "How?"—had
been ventured now and then by Plato and Aristotle. Having done that,
we might ponder artists, especially poets, and see that with them also the
"How"-question is very far from unfamiliar. Husserl's phenomenology
appeared within the discipline of philosophy, and was conducted for the most
part on the borders of Neo-Kantianism. His aim was to place knowledge
on the firmest possible foundation, which he thought could be achieved
by means of *Evidenz* (the process of something becoming as self-evident as
possible), reduction, and noetic-noematic correlation. All the fashionable
philosophies of the day, from historicism to psychologism, were, he thought,
varieties of relativism; and to his horror they were infecting even logic.
Consequently, adherence to these false philosophies was plunging European
thought into a state of crisis. Only phenomenology could save that immense
heritage of thought by supplying an absolute—unconditioned—ground.

Looking back a hundred years or so, we can see that phenomenology
has been able to do two things at once: to attract a wide range of thinkers of

the first rank, and to allow them to re-position and re-launch phenomenology from unexpected points. Martin Heidegger, Max Scheler, Eugen Fink,
Maurice Merleau-Ponty, Emmanuel Lévinas, Alfred Schutz, Michel Henry,
Paul Ricœur, Jacques Derrida, Jean-Luc Marion, Jean-Yves Lacoste—the list
could be broadened to include thinkers from other countries and extended
by adding yet more names—has each enriched phenomenology and made
it a fecund style of thinking for one generation after another. I say "thinking" because phenomenology cannot be limited to philosophy, especially
not if one regards philosophy, as is common these days in Britain and the
United States, as concerned primarily with the fashioning and evaluation
of arguments. Phenomenology prizes intuition (i.e., awareness), suitably
broadened to include categorial intuition, as a way of gaining access to
the ways in which phenomena manifest themselves to us; and although
it proceeds in a rational manner in its investigations it does not dally on
the merry-go-round that contemporary analytic philosophy has become.[1]
Nor does phenomenology take much interest in pre-packaged philosophical problems. "Back to the 'things themselves'!" was Husserl's cry in the
Logical Investigations, meaning "Let us examine phenomena directly, just
as they come to us in experience, and not as we have been told to think
about them in books and lectures."[2] This direct examination of phenomena
requires one to cultivate attention to a very high level, and to make fine
distinctions, if need be. It is an exercise in self-responsibility.

The first person to reorient phenomenology was Husserl's assistant
Martin Heidegger, and certainly his early courses are among the most
exciting and provocative works in phenomenology that we have. It was
Heidegger who, in his 1920–21 lectures on the phenomenology of religious
life, first used the new style of rigorous thinking to read texts. He attended
in particular to Paul's letters to the Thessalonians.[3] Thereafter, he swerved
away from scripture and also, to some degree, from the task of resetting
phenomenology itself, and in the mid-1930s and early 1940s developed a
style of reading some of the strongest German poets—Hölderlin, Rilke, and
George—that was at a fair distance from literary criticism as practiced both
then and now.[4] Yet the project of using phenomenology to read scripture
remained incomplete; only the barest of beginnings had been made before
the project was dropped. True enough, Henry, Derrida, and Marion have
talked from time to time in recent decades about passages of scripture,
although usually in a manner designed to exemplify their philosophical
stances in general.[5] By and large, though, the academic study of scripture
was left firmly in the hands of historical critics throughout the twentieth
century, and although other approaches to scripture—from, let us say,

canonical criticism to feminist exegesis—were tried and tested, it is the historical criticism that has commanded the most sustained attention in the guild of biblical scholars. Protestant scholars had been treating scripture as historical documents like any other throughout the nineteenth century, taking cues from earlier work, going back to Spinoza's *Tractatus Theologico-Politicus* (1677). Catholic scholars had been frustrated by Leo XIII's condemnation of the historical criticism in his encyclical *Providentissimus Deus* (1893), and it was not until Pius XII's encyclical *Divino afflante Spiritu* (1943) that they could invest themselves in the historical criticism. They caught up very quickly, it must be said, and one of the most impressive of all modern biblical scholars was a Catholic priest, Raymond E. Brown (1928–98).

Today, phenomenology is seeking once again to read both sacred and secular writings. Literary criticism attempted to learn from phenomenology with Georges Poulet (1902–91), Jean-Pierre Richard (b. 1922), and other members of the Geneva School, but the "criticism of consciousness," as it became known in the United States, was neither deeply phenomenological nor very persuasive as criticism. It was readily jettisoned as soon as Jacques Derrida's insistence on very close reading as a way of diagnosing undue reliance on full presence and self-presence was accepted in departments of literature in the North American academy. Not that those departments really put Derrida's ways of reading into practice; his approach was quickly domesticated, reduced to little more than a collection of tricks that one could perform on literary texts, and the genuine philosophical dimensions of his work were overlooked or ignored.[6] Indeed, the first person whose ideas were called into question by this new style of reading was none other than Husserl, and in a sense Derrida used the philosopher against himself. Before Derrida hit upon the word "deconstruction" he had used the word "de-sedimentation," which was adapted from Husserl's account of how concepts can be buried, sometimes in strange ways, by later ones, and how those concepts need to be recovered if we are to understand the genesis of our concepts and theories today. It is only recently, with more and more of Husserl's writing becoming available for the first time, that it is possible to weigh Derrida's reading of Husserl and to see what, on the one hand, is of permanent value there and what, on the other hand, needs to be modified in the light of Husserl's *Nachlass*, which was not available to Derrida when writing his first texts.[7]

We must look to the "theological turn" in phenomenology in order to see the slow preparation for using phenomenology as a lens by which to read scripture. Dominique Janicaud coined the expression in 1991, and it was not meant to be kind (in the same way that an earlier generation awoke to find its challenges to the rigid "manual theology" that characterized so much seminary education had been contemptuously dubbed *la nouvelle théologie* by an enemy).[8] Janicaud was challenged by several of those he had attacked in a little volume entitled *Phénoménologie et théologie* (1992), and the sparks had all but dissipated by the time he wrote another work on the topic, *La phénoménologie éclatée* (1998).[9] Was phenomenology now to be seen by way of an "exploded view"? Had it burst asunder by over-extending itself in two directions at once, by departing from the sphere of the immanent as containing all that we have of phenomenality and by opening itself to invisible phenomena? To this question the first genera-tion of those committed to the theological turn responded by observing that there never had been a good reason to limit in principle the ability of phenomena to manifest themselves, and that invisible phenomena have long been a justifiable topic of investigation. That, after all, had been part of Husserl's point in the broadening of "intuition" in the *Logical Investiga-tions*. What was essential was to move away from Husserl's interdiction against speaking of God because his mode of transcendence exceeds the modes of transcendence with which phenomenology as philosophy had identified for study, that is, everything in the world above or beyond transcendental consciousness.[10] Could we go beyond the world, and try to understand revelation in a phenomenological manner? That is a question that has animated the first and second generations of people involved with the theological turn.

Adam Wells is a prominent member of the third generation of the theological turn in phenomenology, a scholar whose innovative work is already respected in France and the United States. His enterprise is to re-think phenomenology as a way of reading scripture, and to some degree this involves de-sedimentation, a questioning back within phenomenology itself, seeking the animating ideas of Heidegger in his lectures of 1920–21. Notice that I do not say that Wells *applies* phenomenology to scripture. Not at all: he argues in *The Manifest and the Revealed* that phenomenology is always modified by what it seeks to grasp. To some readers, his insistence that phenomenology is an absolute science (in the sense of *Wissenschaft*) will be puzzling. After all, is there anything completely unconditioned in this world? Yet Wells will tell us, with a backwards look to Fink, that the absolute is a synthetic unity of the given and the pre-given, that is, it is an ever evolving unity of what gives itself in and through the process of reduc-tion and what is already passively given to us in pre-predicative experience. Phenomenology, considered as absolute science, never achieves a state of completion, even though it perpetually absolves itself from dependence on earlier correlations of the constituting and the constituted; the clarity it offers us is never final. One interesting consequence of this vision is that phenomenology can never be a universal science. For a phenomenological investigation must always reflect on its own genesis; it always stems from one or another home world.

At the core of *The Manifest and the Revealed* is a close reading of that much-discussed passage in Paul's letter to the Philippians, the kenōsis hymn (Phil. 2:5–11). Almost everything about this "hymn" has been questioned, including whether or not it is a hymn and whether or not Paul composed it. There are those who see here Paul's confession of a preexistent Christ (and hence very early intimations of what the Church will later call the Trinity), while others, myself included, see nothing of the sort, and take Paul to be figuring Christ as a Second Adam who did not cling to equality to God as the first Adam did in seeking knowledge of good and evil. In accord with his vision that phenomenology is modified by what it examines, Wells takes the kenōsis hymn to reveal that there is something essentially kenotic about phenomenology. Reduction itself is kenotic: phenomenology absolves itself as philosophy from the phenomena it enables us to see. There is no deflection in phenomenology, one might say, no rerouting of the phenomena into a detour where they will be recast in terms of a consecrated philosophical vocabulary, filed in terms of received problems, and will never return to the light of day. This impatience with traditional philosophies, this desire for a new morning of thought, has always been one of the attractions of phenomenology, and one that has so often been tarnished by the tendency of some philosophers to generate more and more theory of phenomenology rather than simply to do it.

If the affirmative dimension of *The Manifest and the Revealed* is a renewed attention to scripture, the negative aspect is a critique of the historical criticism and its penumbra of ways of attending to scripture (source criticism, form criticism, redaction criticism, and so on). Like Husserl, Wells does not propose a knockdown argument against empiricism. Properly conducted empirical research is valuable, but it must be realized that, because it has rejected any appeal to essences, its conclusions abide within the realm of probability, not certainty; and Wells, like Husserl, seeks nothing less than the absolute in the precise way I have clarified it. So a surprising criticism of the historical criticism comes about: we scholars of Judeo-Christianity are to be wary of it not because it is so scientific but because it is insufficiently scientific! The historical criticism, and its many satellites, needs to be grounded by restoring it to the life-world of scripture.

Only then will we be able to identify the various modes of givenness that are to be found there. In doing so, we will also be able to see the limitations of the historical criticism, its stubborn abiding within the natural attitude, indeed sometimes within the naturalistic attitude.

For Wells, scripture calls to be read by way of the phenomenological attitude. Scripture, he tells us, is not mundane, does not operate solely within the horizon of the world. It answers at once to the given and the pre-given, and our response to it presumes a synthetic unity of the two, one that prompts a never-ending quest to understand what is testified there. Virginal conception and resurrection, for example, are not therefore to be dismissed out of hand in the interests of empirical science ("Those things simply do not happen!"); instead, a higher science is commended, one that admits the possibility of singular events and does not reject them out of hand, a science that is truly scientific because it does not make a priori rulings about what might or might not give itself to consciousness. Does phenomenology, as Wells uses it, establish or prove virginal conception or resurrection, for example? Not at all: fundamentalists will find no comfort here. Phenomenology allows us to identify the specific regions of being to which scripture answers, stops us from homogenizing those regions so that a book of scripture becomes one more historical document, much like any other in the ancient Mediterranean world, and encourages us to engage with what is given by way of the pre-given. In doing so phenomenology, for Wells, comes close, in its own way, to the heart of Anselm's sublime expression: *fides quærens intellectum*, and it delivers us a fresh understanding of that *fides*, that faith we talk so much about. It is the lifelong struggle, affective as much as intellectual, of holding together what gives itself in scripture and what is pre-given in the worlds of church and temple as they become concrete in the specific situations of our own intellectual, spiritual and moral lives.

Introduction

On Husserl's Dream

In a *Beilage* to the German edition of his last work, *The Crisis of European Sciences and Transcendental Phenomenology* (1935), Husserl laments that, "Philosophy as science, as serious, rigorous, indeed apodictically rigorous science—*the dream is over* [*der Traum ist ausgeträumt*]."[1] This statement is particularly striking given that Husserl's philosophical corpus seeks to establish phenomenology as an "absolute science" upon which all other scientific endeavors may be grounded. One almost feels betrayed: by what right does Husserl declare that the dream is over? And what exactly does he mean? One possibility is that Husserl had a change of heart at the end of his life that led him to acknowledge the futility of his earlier work, much like Thomas Aquinas, who famously called his life's work "straw": "*mihi videtur ut palea.*" A more likely possibility—especially given the context of "*der Traum ist ausgeträumt*"—is that Husserl was not abandoning the dream of absolute science, but expressing disappointment in his followers who gave up the dream. Indeed, Husserl had good reason to be disappointed, given that his most famous student and successor at the University of Freiburg, Martin Heidegger, actively opposed the idea of phenomenology as a science: "Philosophy never arises from or through science. Philosophy can never belong to the same order as the sciences. It belongs to a higher order."[2]

Contemporary phenomenology has more-or-less followed Heidegger's lead in rejecting the dream of absolute science as a modernist, metaphysical ideal. There is certainly ample reason to be suspicious of absolute science: the atrocities of the twentieth century are vivid reminders of the moral turpitude of universal visions of absolute truth. Yet, in giving up the dream—in giving up all aspirations to absolute science—phenomenology gives up too much. It gives up any ability to ground the sciences, to determine the boundaries of scientific inquiry, and to provide answers to meta-theoretical questions about the ethical status of the sciences. Natural science, for instance, can come up with ingenious ways of destroying or preserving life, but it cannot tell us whose life to destroy and whose to preserve. For that, one *needs* absolute science; one *needs* a way to ground the sciences in the broader context of the life-world. In other words, Husserl's "dream" of absolute science is not a metaphysical ideal, but a practical necessity. Any philosophical proscription of absolute science (*à la* Heidegger) has drastic practical consequences: by abandoning absolute science, by abstracting science and philosophy from their life-world contexts, by removing the moral and meta-theoretical limits provided by absolute science, something like National Socialism becomes possible—a possibility all too real for Husserl in 1930s Germany.

In this investigation, I intend to dream Husserl's dream again, to reopen the question of absolute science, navigating between the practical necessity of such a science and the temptation to universalize it—a temptation from which Husserl was not completely free. I also intend to renew a line of inquiry inaugurated by Heidegger. In his lectures from the Winter semester of 1920–21, Heidegger argues that Paul's first and second letters to the Thessalonians illustrate a crucial point about "factical existence": "In Christian life experience, it arises from the sense of the surrounding world, that the world does not just happen to be there. The significance of the world—also that of one's own world—is given and experienced in a peculiar way through the retrieval of the relational complexes in the authentic enactment."[3] Heidegger's insight (by way of Paul) is that the experienced world is not simply "there," but is somehow "enacted" by the experiencing self: "the experiencing self and what is experienced are not torn apart."[4] Yet Heidegger finds Paul's rabbinical mode of explanation to be "insufficient."[5] Soon after the 1920–21 lectures, Heidegger pivots from scriptural study to the analytic of finitude found in *Being and Time* (1927).

Heidegger's reading of Paul's letters is intriguing, but ultimately problematic because it tells only half the story: If scripture requires phenomenological clarification, might it not also be the case that phenomenology requires scriptural clarification? While Heidegger opened the door to a phenomenology of scripture, it is Husserlian phenomenology—with its dream of absolute science—that will allow us to walk through. To that end, part I of this investigation examines static, genetic, and constructive (or generative) modes of Husserlian phenomenology, tracing a philosophical trajectory that culminates in a radicalized theory of absolute science.

Drawing specifically on the work of Eugen Fink, I will argue that absolute science is a hermeneutical enterprise encompassing *constituted* Being, the *constituting* source of Being, and phenomenological reflection on Being. Practically speaking, this means that absolute science has a circular structure: analysis of a phenomenal object leads to reflection on the performance of phenomenology, which leads to a phenomenologically clarified reflection on the object, which leads to further reflection on the phenomenological method and so on. In absolute science, the phenomenological method is reformed and radicalized in the process of performing phenomenological analysis. To put it in Fink's terms, absolute science has as its thematic object the synthetic unity of phenomenologizing, constituting, and constituted modes of transcendental life.

Yet if speculation about absolute science were purely theoretical, it would be incomplete; absolute science only becomes *absolute* in concrete application. That is to say, the method of absolute science cannot be specified in advance; it must be derived from concrete engagement with phenomena. Thus, in part II, I develop an absolute science of scripture, focusing on the kenōsis hymn (Phil. 2:6–11). I argue that the hymn presents a kenotic reduction that is similar to Husserl's phenomenological reduction, though far more radical. One the one hand, the kenotic reduction points toward a phenomenological re-reading of the kenōsis hymn, which addresses interpretive issues related to the hymn in the context of Paul's letter to the Philippians. On the other hand, the kenotic reduction points toward a radicalization of the phenomenological method. Scripture and phenomenology elucidate one another within the circular hermeneutic of absolute science.

With regard to the hymn itself, what is "emptied" is not Christ's divinity, nor his status vis-à-vis God, but the status of the *cosmos* as the primary source of truth and value. The kenotic reduction opens up the possibility that worldly authority and value are not primary but *derivative*. In kenotic *epochē*, the *cosmos* is bracketed as the ground of truth and value, and the world is revealed as a *new creation*, which is renewed and sustained by God's infinite love and power. Kenōsis, in this reduced sense, is not an "emptying out" but an "overflowing" of God's love onto creation. Additionally, the kenotic reduction suggests a reformulation of the phenomenological concept of space-time. By combining Fink's reflections on "horizonality" with Jean-Yves Lacoste's notion of the "eschatological I," I will argue that the new creation is an eschatological horizon, whose fundamental spatio-temporal structure is the re-presencing of God.

Part I

Theoretical Considerations

Phenomenology as an Absolute Science of Scripture

Introduction to Part I

Husserlian phenomenology has as its main concern the idea of science [*Wissenschaft*], particularly the question of "what makes science science."[1] Husserl's early works focus on the role of consciousness in constituting scientific objectivity, while his later works focus on the historical and intersubjective generation of scientific objectivity. In both cases, phenomenology functions as "absolute science"—i.e., a presuppositionless science in which, "we accept nothing given in advance, accept nothing as a beginning that has been handed down, nor allow ourselves to be blinded by any names, no matter how great, but rather seek to gain the beginnings through free devotion to the problems themselves and the demands radiating from them."[2] A phenomenology of scripture is thus an immodest task: an absolute science of scripture. Yet this turns out to be a very modest form of immodesty, for both "absolute" and "science" lose their mundane imperial connotations when transformed phenomenologically. An absolute science of scripture is paradoxically kenotic, unencumbered by historical, cultural, or theological assumptions, while radically open to the historical, theological, and literary complexities of scripture itself.

The aim of part I is to adumbrate the goals and methods of a phenomenology of scripture in the context of phenomenology's broader relation to scientific inquiry. For our purposes, it is convenient to divide Husserlian thoughts on science into three chapters—the first dealing with Husserl's early static conception of phenomenology, the second addressing the later genetic and generative conceptions of phenomenology, and the third addressing Eugen Fink's radicalization of Husserlian phenomenology.

1

Phenomenology and Science in Husserl's Early Work

Husserl's early work is defined by two philosophical trajectories: First, there is a sustained attempt to articulate the role of consciousness in constituting the phenomenal world. Second, following Kant, there is an effort to establish a firm ground for science. In the interplay of these two trajectories, the main themes of Husserl's early work emerge: constitution, intentionality, intuition, eidetic reduction, noema/noesis, natural attitude, *Evidenz*, and so forth. There also emerges a complicated and problematic conception of transcendental subjectivity, which privileges the pure immanent experience (*Erlebnis*) of the monadic subject as the constitutive source of temporality, meaning, and scientific objectivity.

A. *Philosophy of Arithmetic* and *Logical Investigations*

Husserl formulates the idea of constitution—at least implicitly—in his first work, *Philosophy of Arithmetic* (1891), which develops the concept of cardinal numbers as the basis of all arithmetic. Husserl argues that cardinality stems from the concept of multiplicity, which is abstracted from our everyday experience of groups of objects: "As to the concrete phenomena that form the foundations for the abstraction of the concepts in question, there is no doubt at all: They are *totalities* [*Inbegriffe*], multiplicities of certain objects."[1] Groups in experience are always particular and concrete: a basketball team, the senate, the Cincinnati Reds, etc. The abstract notion of multiplicity arises, Husserl argues, when we *reflect* on the mental acts involved in group formation: "By means of reflection upon the psychical act that effects the unification of contents combined to form the totality, we obtain the abstract representation of the collective combination. And by means of this latter we form the concept of multiplicity as that of a whole which combines parts in a collective manner."[2] Thus, as Robert Sokolowski puts it, "We discover the relationship involved in groups by reflecting on the mental acts which form groups; the abstract concept of multiplicity, and hence that of number, arises from an act of reflection on our mental acts."[3] The mathematical objectivity of cardinal numbers ultimately rests upon mental acts of constitution.

Despite his attempt to assign objective status to mathematics, Husserl was criticized by Gottlob Frege for deriving cardinal numbers from psychological acts of experience and reflection.[4] Frege argued that Husserl confused numbers themselves with the representation of numbers in consciousness, as if objective numbers only exist in the subjective psychological acts of counting and reflecting on multiplicity.[5] Husserl was thus guilty of "psychologism"—i.e., the erroneous notion that logic and reason are the province of empirical psychology. Husserl later admitted that Frege's criticism "hit the nail on the head" by identifying the "naturalistic prejudices" inherent in his early work.[6] While the *Philosophy of Arithmetic* raised the problem of the constitution of objectivity, it soon became clear to Husserl that the relationship between scientific objectivity and consciousness was more complicated. The *Logical Investigations* (1901) therefore begins with an extended critique of psychologism.

Psychologistic logicians—J. S. Mill, for example—suppose that queries about logic are best solved by examining the psychological processes involved in logical acts. Husserl considers this view fatally flawed; for, given its naturalistic prejudices, psychologism can never account for the necessary distinction between ideality and reality: "The psychologistic logicians ignore the fundamental, essential, never-to-be bridged gulf between ideal and real laws, between normative and causal regulation, between logical and real necessity . . . No conceivable gradation could exist between the ideal and the real."[7] Psychologism assumes that logic must be explained in terms of psychophysical events because logical acts occur in the human mind, which is a psychophysical entity. Logical laws are thus taken to be empirical laws governing the psychological processes involved in logical reasoning. Consider, for instance, the law of non-contradiction: A is not "not-A." Adherents of psychologism assume that this law has to do with the psychological/empirical "lawfulness" of mental processes: whenever one thinks of A, one cannot deduce from it "not-A." Such an assumption is, however, clearly questionable. I certainly can *think* that "A" implies "not-A." I can also *think* that $2 = 3$ or that $2^2 = 5$. I would be wrong, of course, but I can think that which is logically impossible.

Husserl notes three problematic consequences of psychologism. First, psychology, as an empirical science, produces propositions that are necessarily vague, based on observation and probabilistic reasoning: "[The propositions of psychology] are statements about approximate regularities of coexistence and succession, which make no claim to determine, with infallible, unambiguous definiteness, what will go together or will follow in exactly described relationships."[8] Consequently, any logical law derived from empirical science must be somewhat vague, for "only vague rules could be based on vague theoretical foundations."[9] Yet, in actuality, those laws designated "logical" (e.g., the law of non-contradiction) are supposed to be absolutely exact, unlike those laws designated "natural" (e.g., the law of gravity), which are induced from experience. The law of non-contradiction, for instance, is justified independently of empirical circumstances and admits none of the vagueness associated with psychological propositions.

A second consequence of psychologism is that logical laws, which are assumed to be based upon empirical induction, would necessarily involve degrees of probability: "Induction does not establish the holding of the law, only the greater or lesser probability of its holding; the probability, and not the law, is justified by insight. Logical laws must, accordingly, without exception, rank as mere probabilities."[10] It is, however, clear that logical laws (in contrast to natural laws) are not probabilistic; they have an *a priori* validity.[11] According to the natural law of gravity, for instance, if I drop my computer, it will crash to the floor. Yet, given that all laws inductively derived from experience are probabilistic, there is an infinitesimal chance that, when it is dropped, my computer will simply hover in mid-air. Does the same sort of probabilism hold true for logical laws? Does the fact that I can think "2 = 3" entail that the law of non-contradiction is only 99 percent true? What would it even mean for the law of non-contradiction to be "highly probable?" It is clearly absurd to claim that logical laws are probabilistic empirical claims—as if 2^2 *probably* equals 4. One cannot reduce logical laws to empirical laws; for, as Husserl states, "[The laws of pure logic] are established and justified, not by induction, but by apodictic inner evidence."[12]

Third, psychologism holds that logical laws have their epistemological origin in psychological matters of fact. Thus a psychologistic account of syllogisms might take the following form: "It is an empirical fact that, in circumstances X, conclusions of the form C, stamped with apodictically necessary consequence, attend upon premises of the form P. To syllogize 'correctly,' . . . one must see that the circumstances really are X and the premises P."[13] On such a reading, logical laws pertaining to syllogisms are taken as normative transformations of the empirical psychological facts involved in "correct" syllogistic reasoning. Yet this is patently false. Consider the syllogistic form *modus ponens*—i.e., for any two propositions *P* and *Q*, if it is the case that *P* necessarily implies *Q*, and *P* is the case, then *Q* must also be the case. The syllogistic form does not imply any content at all, whether empirical, psychological, or otherwise. Although syllogistic logic can govern the activities of reason, it neither implies nor depends upon any particular facts or states of affairs. As Husserl pointedly asks, "what forms of syllogism permit us to deduce facts from a pure law?"[14]

Such absurd consequences stem from one particular error: psychologism's failure to differentiate between the ideal and the real.[15] Husserl argues that logic is purely conceptual, and in no way dependent upon empirical reality. Logical laws neither describe the psychophysical events involved in reasoning, nor are they normative transformations of such events. In fact, logic is not concerned with psychophysical events at all, but with the *content* or *meaning* of those events. That is to say, logic pertains not to the *act* of knowledge, but to the *content* of knowledge. "What 'is [logically valid]' is not the thinking but the thought, not the judging but the judgment. The locus of [logical validity], therefore, is not the act (e.g., the assertion that S is P), but the contents of the act (e.g., 'S is P')."[16] In other words, according to Husserl, logic has to do with *ideal* entities, while psychology pertains to *real* empirical circumstances. Husserl cites the Pythagorean Theorem as an example: "Regardless of how frequently one repeats the theorem of Pythagoras, regardless of whom it is that thinks it, or where and when it happens, it will remain identically the same, although the concrete act of meaning will change in each case."[17] The meaning of Pythagoras's Theorem is *ideal*—it remains the same despite any differences in the psychological/empirical circumstances surrounding its use.[18]

By collapsing the distinction between ideality and reality, psychologism becomes self-defeating. If, contrary to fact, the ideal were based on the real, psychology would be impossible, for the distinction between the ideal and real pertains not only to logic but to all understanding (scientific or otherwise) and every act of meaning. As Zahavi notes,

> If ideality were really reducible to or susceptible to the influence of the temporal, real, and subjective nature of the physical act, it would be impossible to repeat or share meaning, just as it is impossible to repeat a concrete physical act the moment it has occurred. . . . (We can of course perform a similar act, but similarity is not identity.) But if this were really the case, scientific knowledge as well as ordinary communication and understanding would be impossible.[19]

Ultimately, Husserl's attempt to ground logic and mathematics has implications for all scientific knowledge and every act of communication. In criticizing psychologism, Husserl finds that naturalistic analyses of consciousness treat the mind's relationship to the world as a relationship between two empirical entities *in the world*. The cognitive relationship between the subject and object-world is largely neglected. In other words, psychology deals with objects; it cannot account for the way any object—whether logical, empirical, or linguistic—is imbued with an ideal meaning vis-à-vis the knowing subject. A larger problem thus confronts Husserl: "the relationship, in particular, between the subjectivity of knowing and the objectivity of the content of known."[20] If we assume that science and language are possible, as Husserl does, then we must also assume a distinction between ideality and reality. The question of the origin of logic thus becomes a question about the relation between the ideality, or objectivity, of logic and the reality of the knowing subject: "How are we to understand the fact that the intrinsic being of objectivity becomes 'presented,' 'apprehended' in knowledge, and so ends up by becoming subjective? . . . How can the ideality of the universal *qua* concept or law enter the flux of real mental states and become an epistemic possession of the thinking person?"[21] Accordingly, the main problem of the *Logical Investigations*—indeed, the main problem of all Husserl's early work—is the "constitution" of objectivity by the knowing subject.

Husserl's investigations of psychology and logic ultimately lead to a broader investigation of language, for logic is necessarily concerned with propositional content:

> I assume accordingly that no one will think it enough to develop pure logic merely in the manner of our mathematical disciplines . . . without also striving to be philosophically clear in regard to these same propositions, without, that is, gaining insight into the essence of the modes of cognition which come into play in their utterance and in the ideal possibility of applying such propositions, together with all such conferments of sense and objective validities as are essentially constituted therein.[22]

Accordingly, inasmuch as logic has to do with the content (or meaning) of propositions, Husserl focuses on the constitutive processes involved in the meaningful use of words.

In the *Logical Investigations*, signs have two tightly intertwined functions, which may be separated *de jure* into "indication" and "expression."

The indicative function of signs is defined as follows: "In [this] we discover as a common circumstance the fact that certain objects or states of affairs of whose reality someone has actual knowledge indicate to him the reality of certain other objects or states of affairs, in the sense that his belief in the being of the one is experienced (though not at all as evidently) as motivating a belief or surmise in the being of the other."[23] Signs, as indications, point to a non-present state of affairs. So, for example, footprints in the snow outside my house *indicate* a non-present reality: someone has recently walked by my home. Those footprints are signs, but they do not communicate a linguistic meaning; one cannot "read" footprints in the same way that one can read a meaningful sentence. Expressions, on the other hand, are *meaningful*. Thus, e.g., the sentence, "the grass is green," does not serve *primarily* to indicate a non-present reality, but to communicate a meaning symbolically.[24]

Focusing on the expressive aspects of language, Husserl notes that expressions are composed of three strata: First, there are physical phe-nomena—i.e., physical realities associated with various signs. So when one utters the word "cat," there is a physical movement of the tongue, air in the throat, and so forth, which produces the sound of the word. Second, there are *acts* by which physical phenomena are assigned meaning. So the sound "cat" comes to have the meaning of the word "cat." It is by virtue of acts of meaning (meaning-conferring acts and meaning-fulfilling acts) that, "the expression is more than a merely sounded word."[25] Third, there is an ideal meaning that is distinct from any concrete act of meaning. Thus, when ten individuals utter the Pythagorean Theorem, there are ten distinct physical utterances, ten (or more) acts of meaning, but only one meaning. The central problem of the *Logical Investigations*—namely, how is objectivity constituted by the subject?—can now be reformulated in linguistic terms: How do objective meanings relate to the acts of meaning by which they become attached to signs?

In analyzing acts of meaning, Husserl employs a revised version of Franz Brentano's idea of intentionality. "Every expression," according to Husserl, "not merely says something, but says it *of* something: it not only has a meaning, but refers to certain objects."[26] Acts of meaning therefore involve both meaning, as an ideal entity, and objects of reference.[27] This distinction becomes clear when we consider cases in which "several expres-sions may have the same meaning but different objects, and again that they may have different meanings but the same object."[28] So, for example, the sentence "this is a good computer" means the same thing no matter which computer we are talking about. Alternately, sentences with completely different meanings may be applied to the same object: "this computer is lightweight" and "this computer is blue" may both refer to my computer.

Though conceptually separable, meaning and objective reference are tightly connected in expressions through *intentional* acts of meaning: "an expression only refers to an objective correlate *because* it means something, it can be rightly said to signify or name the object *through* its meaning. An act of meaning is the determinate manner in which we refer to our object of the moment."[29] This is just to say that consciousness is not a world unto itself; it is always directed toward an object of reference. Consciousness is, by definition, consciousness *of* something. Every act of meaning necessarily *intends* an objective referent. Moreover, the intuitional content of the objective referent exists in a reciprocal relationship with the intentional act: "Expressions and their meaning-intentions do not take their measure, in contexts of thought and knowledge, from mere intuition . . . but from the varying intellectual forms through which intuited objects first become intelligibly determined, mutually related objects. And so expressions . . . as symbolic intentions, point to categorially formed unities."[30] Meaning-intention and meaning-fulfillment are essentially two sides of the same coin. A given expression has an ideal meaning, which, in the context of the expression, intends a particular object of reference. And that object of reference, which may or may not fulfill the meaning of the expression, always already exists in a particular relation to consciousness.

While the *Logical Investigations* focuses primarily on linguistic meaning and objectivity, it also introduces another important phenomenological theme: *Evidenz*. Although the English compound "self-evidence" serves as fine translation, it fails to capture the verbal sense of the German noun. One might be more inclined to translate *Evidenz* as "making self-evident," indicating the ongoing process of bringing something into self-evidence. For Husserl, *Evidenz* pertains to the justification of knowledge: How do we have certainty about what we know? How can science be certain that its results are absolute? How do we know that *ultimate* knowledge—the kind of knowledge that serves to ground science—is actually ultimate? Husserl argues that ultimate knowledge not only knows things as they are but also *knows that it knows* things as they are:

> *Ultimate* knowledge is knowledge that is so certain of the things known that what it establishes about those things can no longer be doubtful to it in any respect. It is the knowledge of an absolutely good conscience, knowledge that not only *de facto* knows things as they actually are, but also is certain beyond a doubt that it does, that is therefore in direct, actual possession of the noetic value of that attainment.[31]

The second mode of knowing—knowing that one knows, or being in possession of the noetic value of the attainment of knowledge—does not have to do with the thing given (or known), but the "quality of givenness" (or the *knowing*). *Evidenz*, for Husserl, is the criterion by which the "quality of givenness" is assessed. At its apex, which proves elusive in practical situations, *Evidenz* yields apodictic or self-evident knowledge, where the "quality of givenness" is of such a high order that "states of affairs . . . [are] given in conformity with their true being."[32] As Husserl puts it, "*Evidenz is a word for the fact that, as noeticians affirm and prove, there is a real difference between acts that not only think that something is thus and thus, but are fully certain and aware, in the manner of perspicacious seeing, of this being and being thus.*"[33] The "difference" to which Husserl refers is the difference between perception (in the broadest sense of that word) and justification: it is one thing to perceive something, and quite another to be certain that one perceives the thing as it is.[34] It should be noted, however, that *Evidenz* is not an all-or-nothing proposition, as if a perception is either fully certified or not certified at all. There can be varying degrees of *Evidenz*, varying degrees of certainty. It is the goal of phenomenology to bracket all partial certainties in pursuit of pure self-evidence (i.e., apodictic certainty): "the *epistemologically pregnant sense* of self-evidence is exclusively concerned with this last unsurpassable goal, *the act of this most perfect synthesis of fulfillment*, which gives to an intention . . . the absolute fullness of content, the fullness of the object itself. The object is not merely meant, but in the strictest sense *given*."[35] To put it another way, phenomenology seeks to "nudge" phenomena through various degrees of *Evidenz* until they gives themselves in pure self-evidence.

It is also important to point out that *Evidenz* pertains not only to the phenomenal object but also to the subject. Pure self-evidence can only be achieved through the "perspicacious seeing" of an "absolutely good conscience." In *Logical Investigations*, Husserl speaks of pure self-evidence as an adequation of intention and intuition: "there is a perfect adaptation to intuition, since the thought means nothing that the fulfilling intuition does not completely present as belonging to the thought."[36] Moreover, in pure self-evidence, intuition fulfills intention in such a way that it is *recognized* as a completely fulfilling intuition: "The intuition fulfills the intention which terminates in it as not itself again being an intention which has need of further fulfillment, but as offering us the *last* fulfillment of our intention."[37] The idea that pure self-evidence involves the *recognition* of a particular intuition as the "*last* fulfillment of our intention" suggests that self-evidence has a subjective component. Perfect self-evidence is the goal of a noetic process in which the intentions of the subject are brought in-line with the intuitive content of the phenomenal object: *adaequatio rei et intellectus*. Additionally, the *recognition* inherent to pure self-evidence involves the subject's judgment: "from the standpoint of the intention, the notion of the relationship of self-evidence yields us truth as the *rightness of our intention* (and especially that of our judgment) . . ."[38] Phenomenology, whose *telos* is self-evidence, therefore constitutes a sort of intellectual *askesis*, through which the subject's intentionality and judgment is reformed and brought in-line with intuition, so that what is finally perceived is nothing other than the "thing itself."

Phenomenological self-evidence raises an interesting possibility with regard to a phenomenology of scripture. If the goal of phenomenology is self-evidence, wherein the subject's intentions are reformed so as to be perfectly conformed to the intuitive content of the thing itself, then a phenomenology of scripture (inasmuch as it attempts to bring scripture into self-evidence) involves a scriptural transformation of subjectivity. (This idea will be explored in more detail in chapter 3.)

B. *Ideas I*

In *Ideas I* (1913), Husserl analyzes intentional consciousness itself. Following Kant, Husserl argues that a proper examination of the relationship between consciousness and objectivity requires us to analyze consciousness not as an object—for such an approach would beg questions about the origin of objectivity—but as that which is the transcendental source of objectivity. In other words, Husserl wants to examine those aspects of consciousness that make it possible to constitute any meaning or object at all.

In some sense, *Ideas I* epitomizes the two main themes of Husserl's early work: First, in accordance with a desire to ground science, a region of experience is sought on which presuppositionless or absolute science might be grounded. Physical things, which natural science takes to be foundational, cannot function as absolute ground because they are never adequately present: "the perception of a physical thing involves a certain inadequacy. Of necessity a physical thing can be given only 'one-sidedly'; and that signifies, not just incompletely or imperfectly in some sense or other, but precisely what presentation by adumbrations prescribes. A physical thing is necessarily given in mere 'modes of appearance' . . . which is not givenness proper."[39] In other words, physical things can never provide the sort of apodictic certainty necessary to ground absolute science because the possibility of error always exists. Absolute science will require a ground in absolute being, not the vague, indeterminate being of physical things. Much like Descartes, Husserl is looking for a realm of experience that is free from doubt and error, and locates such a realm in the mental processes of the Ego: "No mental process, we said, is presented. That means that the perception of a mental process is a simple seeing of something which is (or can become) perceptually given as something absolute, and not as something identical in modes of appearance by adumbration."[40] Husserl gives the example of a feeling. There are no "sides" to a feeling like joy. "If I look at it, I have something absolute; it has no sides that could be presented sometimes in one mode and sometimes in another."[41]

Husserl's Cartesian tendencies are counterbalanced by the second main theme of *Ideas I*: the constitution of the object-world by intentional consciousness. To that end, Husserl proposes a method of "neutralizing" the objective world in order to lay bare the constituting activity of intentional consciousness. Unlike Descartes, Husserl does not doubt the existence of the world; rather, he argues that one should simply *ignore* the world while doing "transcendental phenomenology." Husserl refers to the process of *ignoring* the world as *"epochē,"* from the Greek meaning "cessation" or "pause." *Epochē* involves a suspension of what Husserl calls the "natural attitude," which is a sort of commonsense realism about objects in the world. Take a statement like, "The car is red." In the natural attitude, we determine that this is true by noting that there is in fact a car "out there" that is red. The claim is true because its referent exists in the object-world. This referential notion of truth reflects our natural tendency to assume that the object-world is simply there; knowledge is simply, "a recording of 'facts' or 'objects' which we assume exist 'in the world,' complete with meanings, ready to be recorded indifferently by a knower or a camera."[42] Nowhere is this truer than in the natural sciences, whose investigations confirm or disconfirm hypotheses by verifying them in the natural world. The natural attitude, according to Husserl, "begins with experience and remains within experience . . . the collective horizon of possible investigations is therefore designated with one word: it is the 'world.' "[43]

The problem with the natural attitude is not that it is useless or false but that it is naïve; it straightforwardly and uncritically assumes that objects in the world are simply "there."[44] Because the natural attitude blindly accepts of the object-world, it does not recognize the role consciousness plays in constituting objects. There is, therefore, a tendency for the natural attitude to degenerate into a restrictive form of naturalism, which posits the object-world (or nature) as the *only* domain of knowledge, truth, and value. It is not difficult to give the lie to the natural attitude. Kohák offers an instructive example:

> Take, for instance, the experience of lighting a cigarette in a non-smoker's house. After a few puffs, the subject looks anxiously for a place to deposit his ashes. There are no ashtrays. The subject casts about, settles on a seashell or a nut dish, and, with a mixture of anxiety and relief, knocks off the ash. He did not "find" an ashtray "in the objective world"; there was none there to be found. Rather, he constituted an ashtray in his act.[45]

This example shows how objects, which are taken in the natural attitude to be constitutive of reality, are themselves constituted by consciousness. If we want to investigate the smoker's experience of the ashtray, we cannot restrict ourselves to questions concerning the objective existence of an ashtray. It is certainly true that something must have been there—a shell, a candy bowl, or something—but there are no empirical facts about the object that would *necessitate* its identity as ashtray. The object is not an ashtray in any simple factual sense; it was constituted as such by an experiencing subject. To investigate a phenomenon like the ashtray, as it functions in lived experience, the natural attitude must be bracketed, or put out-of-play, so that the constituting work of consciousness might become apparent. This is not to say that the object-world is nonexistent; rather, in *epochē*, one suspends "the common-sense thesis that a transcendent [i.e., objective] reality 'explains' experience" in order to focus on experience itself.[46]

Husserl explores the relationship between the world and intentional consciousness in a famous passage about the annihilation of the world. The individual consciousness, according to Husserl, encounters various patterns in its experience; and as these patterns become more and more regular, consciousness formalizes them into "eidetic structures" which, in turn, affect how consciousness comports itself toward objects in the world: "The existence of a world is the correlate of certain multiplicities of experience distinguished by certain essential formations."[47] Yet suppose that experience did not conform to patterns—after all, "it *cannot* be seen that actual experiences can flow *only* in such concatenated forms."[48] Suppose that the sun did not rise regularly, or that causes did not always lead to effects, or that what went up only sometimes came down. In short, suppose that the world was senseless and irregular. What would this mean for the individual consciousness? Husserl replies:

[It is] evident that while the Being of consciousness . . . would indeed be necessarily modified by an annihilation of the world of physical things its own existence would not be touched. Modified, to be sure. For an annihilation of the world means, correlatively, nothing else but that in each stream of mental processes . . . certain ordered concatenations of experience and therefore certain complexes of theorizing reason oriented according to those concatenations of experience, would be excluded.[49]

Consciousness would be modified but not destroyed by the annihilation of the world. Husserl concludes that, "no real being, no being which is presented and legitimated in consciousness by appearances, is necessary to the being of consciousness itself."[50] Thus consciousness is a "self-contained system of being" upon which the object-world depends: "The whole spatiotemporal world, which includes human being and the human ego as subordinate single realities is, according to its sense, a merely intentional being, thus one has the merely secondary sense of a being *for* consciousness. It is a being posited by consciousness in its experiences. . . ."[51] The world thus exists *for* consciousness, but it is consciousness that must do the work of constituting the objects that comprise the world—i.e., it is consciousness, through its own experience, that *intentionally* endows the outer world with meaningful reality. In the end, the transcendental reduction essentially reverses a naturalistic conception of the world: the individual is not a passive recipient of sense data. As John Caputo notes, "the outcome of this thought-experiment is to show the extent to which 'objects' are the product of the synthetic, concatenating life of consciousness which, moved by the regularity of their appearance, 'constitutes' them in a synthetic unity."[52]

The "annihilation of the world" reveals that the object-world is *contingent* upon consciousness and cannot yield apodictic certainty. Absolute science must, therefore, be a science of transcendental subjectivity. Husserl is worth quoting at length on this point:

Reality is not in itself something absolute which becomes tied secondarily to something else; rather, in the absolute sense, it is nothing at all; it has no "absolute essence" whatever . . . It now becomes clear that, in contrast to the natural theoretical attitude, the correlate of which is the world, a new attitude must in fact be possible which, in spite of the "exclusion" of this psychophysical universe of Nature, leaves us something: the whole field of absolute consciousness . . . That then, is what is left as the sought-for *"phenomenological residuum,"* though we have "excluded" the whole world with all physical things, living beings, and humans ourselves included.[53]

Husserl's critique of the natural attitude reveals that worldly reality is not an absolute origin, but a constituted result. In *epochē*, the object-world is suspended or "excluded" in order to reveal the constituting source of objectivity—namely, transcendental subjectivity, which, as the source of all objectivity, is the proper subject matter of absolute science. For any science that concerns itself primarily with the natural world can never yield apodictic certainty: "it is immediately understandable that, with the exclusion of the natural world, the physical and psychophysical world, all individual objectivities which become constituted by axiological and practical functionings of consciousness are excluded."[54] This exclusion of the natural world also includes all sciences based on the natural world: *"all natural science and cultural sciences,* with their total stock of cognition, *undergo exclusion* precisely as sciences which require the natural attitude."[55]

It is important to note that "exclusion" is not negation; rather, Husserl excludes the natural and cultural sciences only as sources of absolute science. The tools, methods, and results of natural science are certainly valid, but the sciences have no means of self-critique, no means of ensuring that dogmatic assumptions about the natural world do not become universalized in a positivistic manner. Husserl is, of course, well aware that positivism is rarely problematic in the day-to-day workings of natural science—after all, one never hears a physicist worrying about whether his scientific conclusions are positivistic! Rather, the problem with the "natural and cultural sciences," which require the natural attitude, is meta-theoretical. As Kohák puts it, "Modern science, with its positivistic bias, largely dismissed meta-theoretical considerations as meaningless, or at best irrelevant, while tacitly accepting a materialistic meta-theory."[56] On the one hand, the decision to ignore meta-theoretical concerns yields positive results: "The decision freed [science] from the interminable debates over the ultimate nature of reality . . . The incredible technological advances of the last century seemed to justify that decision."[57] On the other hand, the abandonment of meta-theory leaves science at a loss when it comes to questions about the methodological boundaries of science, the meaning of scientific progress, and the proper use of scientific procedure: "That decision [to ignore meta-theoretical considerations] becomes problematic when we begin to deal with human beings—metaphorically, when we raise not only the question of how to build a hydrogen bomb but whether to build one and on whom to drop it."[58] The sciences therefore *need* phenomenology inasmuch as phenomenology is uniquely able to situate the method and meaning of scientific inquiry in the context of the absolute source of all objectivity and meaning: transcendental subjectivity.

Additionally, by tracing various modes of objectivity back to their absolute origin in transcendental subjectivity, phenomenology distinguishes between different regions of being, and situates the sciences according to their proper regional ontology: "To each region there corresponds a regional ontology which comprises a number of regional sciences either self-sufficiently closed or perhaps based one upon another, corresponding precisely to the highest genera which are united in making up that region."[59] So, for example, the physical sciences have to do with the ontological region of material being, which has a particular eidetic (i.e., formal) structure. The physical scientist may draw upon the eidetic structure of material being to improve the "cognitive-practical performance" of exploring empirical facts. When one broaches the question of the proper regional ontology of a given science, it becomes clear that the sciences themselves are of little use. Biology, for example, cannot investigate the formal structures of natural being, since formal structures are not empirical matters-of-fact. A meta-critique of biology is therefore necessary. Phenomenology is uniquely able to investigate the constitution of objectivity in any region of being along with its formal structures. Husserl thus assigns to phenomenology a privileged place among the sciences: "As applied phenomenology, of essential necessity it produces the ultimately evaluative criticism of each specifically peculiar science; and thus, in particular, it determines the ultimate sense of the 'being' of its objects and the fundamental clarification of its methods."[60]

It is tempting to read Husserl's critique of the natural attitude as an idealistic rejection of empiricism—a sort of Cartesian retreat into inner subjectivity. For our purposes, such a reading could be quite salient. One can well imagine a critique of contemporary biblical scholarship based on parallels between the Husserlian "natural attitude" and empiricist modes of biblical scholarship (e.g., historical criticism, philology, archaeology, and so forth). Such an argument would run like this: The natural attitude naïvely locates truth and value in empirical reality without recognizing the role of transcendental subjectivity in constituting that reality. By remaining within the natural attitude, scientific approaches procrusteanly impose the empirical logic of the object-world onto the life-world. Similarly, those biblical sciences that privilege empirical insight procrusteanly impose the logic of empirical science onto the biblical text. Yet such an argument constitutes a rather shallow critique of biblical science. It is perfectly reasonable for biblical science to include insights from empirical sciences like history, philology and archaeology, for the simple reason that biblical texts were written long ago in a language not our own by a culture that is far removed from our own. That is to say, the Bible gives itself *as* a historical document (among other modes of givenness, perhaps); thus biblical science should avail itself of all the modern tools that apply to historical documents.

Not only does the preceding argument fail as a critique of biblical scholarship but it also fails as a reading of Husserl, who is quite clear that phenomenology, as absolute science, does not oppose empirical science:

> [The natural scientist] recognizes that experience has its indu- bitable right and that, on the basis of experience, undoubtedly valuable findings of endless abundance are attainable. The indubitable right of the knowledge of experience does not mean that it is absolute knowledge. Even the natural scientist himself does not think that. He knows very well that each of his assertions, regardless of how methodologically exact each is, can be considerably modified through future experience.[61]

Natural science, when rigorously applied, has to do with empirical *probability* and has no pretension of being an absolute science. Phenomenol- ogy, for its part, deals with that which is given absolutely: the immanent constituting work of transcendental subjectivity. Phenomenology does not directly call into question the tools and methods of natural science, but seeks a "phenomenological reduction" of the sciences, so that their methods, aims, and conclusions may be evaluated with respect to the constitution of objectivity within their proper regional ontologies.

So far, I have made the case that phenomenology serves an important role in grounding the "natural and cultural sciences." This provides a partial answer to the question of why phenomenology is necessary. It will also be important to understand what phenomenology *does*, or how it proceeds in the task of grounding the sciences. To put it as a question: What exactly does a phenomenologically reduced science look like?

Husserl argues that ordinary experience posits the existence of things "out there" in the world. Although the thing's existence is bracketed in the *epochē*, the positing "serves as an *index* of certain pure contexts of consciousness, which become manifest in these experiential positings by way of the phenomenological reduction, in particular, in the form of acts of phenomenological reduction."[62] So even when existence is bracketed, natural experiences indicate certain activities on the part of consciousness. Thus the everyday experience of my dog, for instance, presents itself in this particular way, with this particular color, this particular shape, in this particular place, at this particular time, and so forth. If the existence of my dog is bracketed, it becomes clear that my everyday experience of her involves a manifold of other real and possible experiences—feelings of affection, memories of my dog as a puppy, formal knowledge of dogs, expectations about the future, and so on. As Husserl puts it, "each natural experience, taken as immanent being [i.e., bracketing the existence of the thing that is experienced], motivates a manifold of other natural experiences and a manifold of real possibilities of natural experiences, and . . . we can explicate these motivational contexts . . . and direct our gaze at them."[63] This phenomenological gaze, as Husserl calls it, focuses not on the experienced thing but on the experience of the thing in the "pure immanence," or absolute givenness, of consciousness, thereby opening for investigation all actual and possible experiences of the thing (including the most basic experience of "thingness"). Phenomenologically reduced experience pertains to "the pure stream of consciousness which, of course, contains nothing of nature [i.e., the experienced thing] but only the experience of nature plus all the other acts of presenting, feeling, desiring, and willing, which are interwoven with it."[64]

As with any natural experience, objects of scientific inquiry serve as indices for phenomenological experience. Thus a physicist's experience of a quark, when phenomenologically reduced, focuses not on the existent quark, but on the manifold contexts that make up the experience of the quark, including, for example, the physicist's personal investment in the science of physics, the theoretical matrix that postulates the existence of quarks, the scientific procedure employed in physics, the goals and aims of physics, the ontological status of quarks, and so on. Similarly, a phenomenologically reduced biblical science would focus not on the objective reality of biblical texts (whether that reality is conceptualized as historical, literary, social, or what have you), but on the *experience* of scripture.

A phenomenological analysis of scripture would no doubt include experiences of scripture as a historical text, but it would also include a whole range of real and possible contexts and experiences—e.g., religious tradition(s), secular tradition(s), contemporary religious communities, the methods and aims of biblical science, the experience of individual readers, liturgical contexts, academic contexts, etc. In short, all of the many experiences and contexts that go into making scripture what it is, has been, and can be, fall under the phenomenological gaze. Consequently, if there is a phenomenological critique to be levied against current modes of biblical scholarship, it would not be that the latter are *too scientific*, but that they are *not scientific enough*. (This criticism will be explored in greater detail in the concluding chapter.) To the extent that biblical scholarship focuses on the experienced thing, rather than the experience of the thing, its field of inquiry is limited by dogmatic assumptions about the epistemological and ontological priority of the experienced thing. Moreover, the proscription of meta-theoretical concerns renders such modes of scholarship incapable of recognizing the dogmatism inherent in their assumptions. A phenomenology of scripture, by contrast, places no dogmatic restrictions on the experiences and contexts of scripture; every mode of scriptural givenness is, in principle, open for phenomenological investigation.

2

The Genetic Transformation of Absolute Science

The preceding analysis of Husserl's early work raises a number of questions (and possible objections) that will guide our treatment of his later work. First, I claimed that phenomenology is *unique* in its ability to provide an absolute ground for the sciences. Yet why should phenomenology be *unique* in that regard? There are plenty of other philosophies of science that address meta-theoretical concerns. Why do the sciences need phenomenology *uniquely*? Second, the conception of consciousness in Husserl's early work is highly Cartesian, with apodictic certainty relegated to the inner subjective realm of individual consciousness. Should Cartesian assumptions not be excluded along with the natural attitude? Third, why should phenomenology, as a science, be immune to its critique of the natural sciences? What would prevent phenomenology from implicitly substituting its own methodological dogma for that of the natural sciences, thereby reproducing the natural attitude at a higher level? This chapter will focus on the first two questions. I will argue that the concept of genesis in Husserl's later work both mitigates the Cartesian problem and points toward a genetic conception of absolute science, which can only be achieved through the "phenomenological gaze." Phenomenology's self-critique will be examined in the next chapter.

A. *Cartesian Meditations* and *Formal and Transcendental Logic*

In his later works, Husserl explicitly acknowledges his earlier Cartesian tendencies. Although he considers the "Cartesian way" valid, its shortcomings are apparent:

[W]hile [the Cartesian way] leads to the transcendental ego in one leap, as it were, it brings this ego into view as apparently empty of content, since there can be no preparatory explication; so one is at a loss, at first, to know what has been gained by it, much less how, starting with this, a completely new sort of fundamental science, decisive for philosophy, has been attained.[1]

The Cartesian way leads to the transcendental ego, but it gets there too fast; the ego is analyzed only as a philosophical correlate of the phenomenologically reduced object-world. As Eugen Fink puts it,

What is won by the first step of the reduction is a life-experience [*Erfahrungsleben*] of the world as noematic correlate, namely, as the *objective* world. This defines the concept of egology: the world as world-phenomenon is the world for me. The world-phenomenon is the phenomenon of the *objective (universally holding [allgemeingültigen]) world*. The analytic of egology does not take into account the internal structural reference [*Strukturverweisung*] of the world-phenomenon.[2]

In other words, the preliminary phase of Husserlian phenomenology reveals that the object-world is constituted by subjectivity. Yet subjectivity itself is considered only inasmuch as it contributes to the constitution of the object-world; it has no content outside of its constituting functions. So, although the Cartesian way opens up the field of transcendental subjectivity, it does not suffice as an investigation of subjectivity. The Cartesian way proves to be pedagogically valuable in communicating the phenomenological reduction, but ultimately problematic. Bruzina makes this point well:

What is particularly dangerous is that this first presentation of the epochē allows one to interpret it as applying mainly—or even exclusively!—to the 'object-side' of the correlation in question, viz., that of subject-object, of experiencer-experienced, of immanence-transcendence, so that, with the epochē not being so explicitly applied to the 'subject-side,' one can conclude too quickly that one has reached the 'pure' immanence to which constitutive action may be attributed without more ado.[3]

Absolute subjectivity, on which a truly absolute science might be based, is attainable only through the reduction of both the phenomenal object *and* subject. In his later works, Husserl therefore brackets the Cartesian subject in an attempt to uncover the transcendental processes that form the subject itself.

Husserl's critique of the Cartesian way draws on the idea of "genesis." It will be helpful, at this point, to recall some key concepts from Husserl's early work. In *Ideas I*, Husserl distinguished between *noeses*, as intentional acts of consciousness, and *hylē*, as raw sense data. The intentional object, or *noema*, is constituted when consciousness applies objective meaning to sense matter. This objective or formal meaning is assumed to exist ready-made and immediately accessible to consciousness, as a component of subjectivity. In *Formal and Transcendental Logic* (1929) and *Cartesian Meditations* (1931), Husserl rejects the matter-form schema upon which his earlier works relied. He argues that it is naïve to think of objective forms (i.e., ideal objects) as ready-made objects existing in consciousness: "*products* of reason, all of which have the character of *irreality* (that of 'ideal' objects), cannot be regarded forthwith as belonging to every concrete ego as such."[4] Thus the central question of Husserl's later work: How are ideal objects constituted in the first place?

Husserl's early phenomenology, later called "static" phenomenology, begins with fully constituted objects or states of affairs, and then investigates the intentional relationship between those objects and consciousness. Fully constituted objects are simply assumed, and taken as "transcendental clues" to an underlying intentional performance. The aim of static phenomenology is to bring to light the various intentional acts implicit in one's experience of a phenomenal object. As Bernet puts it, "The intention in thus regarding [objects] is to clarify the sense and validity of these objects by means of regressing to their systems of manifestation [*Bekundung*] and authentication [*Beurkundung*] within the consciousness by which they are primordially given."[5]

"Genetic" phenomenology, on the other hand, investigates the genesis or history of the constituting processes that culminate in the constituted object. Every phenomenon, on the genetic model, is constituted through a process, in which various assumptions, judgments, and experiences are layered upon each other to produce the final object. At the heart of genetic phenomenology is the idea that intentional consciousness is not simply an empty pole opposite the object-world (as in Husserl's early work), but has its own history of experiences that shape its constituting action. The Ego, according to Husserl, is a substrate comprised of various habitualities: "But it is to be noted that this centering Ego is not an empty pole of identity, any more than any object is such. Rather, according to a law of 'transcendental generation,' with every act emanating from him and having a new objective sense, he acquires a new abiding property."[6] Each "new abiding property" then affects the future intentional action of the Ego. Suppose, for instance, that I see a red car, and make a certain judgment: "The car is red." It then becomes possible to make that judgment into a unified object—the red car—about which I can make other judgments: "The red car is fast." Similarly, this judgment can be made into an object—the fast red car—about which I can make another judgment: "The fast red car is exciting!" This process can be continued *ad infinitum*, resulting in a single object with multiple layers of sedimented meaning, each of which is built on the layers that precede it. Yet the object is never perceived as composite. That is, I do not immediately perceive all the previous judgments and experiences that go into the object. I simply perceive a unified ready-made object: the fast, red, exciting car. The goal of genetic phenomenology is to sift through the sedimented layers in order to reveal the processes of constitution that give rise to both subject and object: "The task of phenomenology is to uncover these deposits of sense and show how they work upon the encounter and judgment that follow them, how they work upon our present intentional activity."[7] In other words, genetic phenomenology aims to reactivate or de-sediment the *originary* encounter that gives rise to a particular judgment.

In order to clarify the idea of phenomenological origin, it will be necessary to distinguish two types of genesis: active and passive. Active genesis refers to constitutive acts in which, "the Ego functions as productively constitutive, by means of subjective processes that are specifically acts of the Ego."[8] In other words, active genesis includes all acts in which consciousness synthesizes and combines various elements in the "flux" of impressions in order to constitute a new object *originally*. This includes, according to Husserl, "all the works of practical reason, in a maximally broad sense."[9] So the creation of a new work of art, the discovery of a new species of animal, and the use of logical reason would all be examples of active genesis. The crucial feature of active genesis is that, "Ego-acts, pooled in sociality . . . become combined in a manifold specifically active synthesis and, on the basis of objects already given (in modes of consciousness that give beforehand), constitute new objects originally. These then present themselves to consciousness as products."[10] Active genesis thus refers to the constituting acts through which new objects are produced.

Active genesis depends upon "objects already given," which are received passively by consciousness: "when we trace anything built actively, we run into constitution by passive generation. The 'ready-made' object that confronts us in life as an existent mere physical thing . . . is given, with the originality of the 'it itself,' in the synthesis of a passive experience."[11]

"Passive genesis" refers to the passive reception of the objective environment in which the ego finds itself. To borrow a Heideggerian term, one might say that passive genesis reflects the existential reality of "thrownness"— i.e., every Ego finds itself "thrown" into a pre-given world, already full of objects, which functions as the ego's horizon. As an example of passive genesis, Husserl considers the way an infant learns to see physical things: "With good reason it is said that in infancy we had to learn to see physical things, and that such modes of consciousness of them had to precede all others genetically. In 'early infancy', then, the field of perception that gives beforehand does not as yet contain anything that, in a mere look, might be explicated as a physical thing."[12] An infant, Husserl claims, must learn to distinguish unitary physical objects in his or her perceptual field. This example demonstrates two points: First, even the most basic level of experience—perception of a physical thing—has a history, a point of origin. Second, passive genesis is *pre*-predicative. It refers to the sheer givenness of phenomena, which function in turn as the "raw material" of active predication. Passive experience, as Bernet states, "is the passive underground domain of the active production of judgments."[13]

Passive experience need not always remain passive, according to Husserl, for one can, "penetrate into the intentional constituents of experiential phenomena themselves—thing-experiencing phenomena and all others—and thus find intentional references leading back to a 'history' and accordingly making these phenomena knowable as formations subsequent to other essentially antecedent formations."[14] Through phenomenological investigation, we can reactivate passive layers of a phenomenon, thereby tracing it back to its genetic origin. In doing so, we encounter eidetic or formal laws that regulate the passive formation of "perpetually new syntheses." That is to say, we encounter the various "habitualities" of the Ego through which pre-given objects are passively generated. As Husserl states, "Everything known to us points to an original becoming acquainted; what we call unknown has, nevertheless, a known structural form: the form 'object' and, more particularly, the form 'spatial thing', 'cultural object', 'tool' and so forth."[15] The goal, then, of genetic phenomenology is to trace the lineage of any phenomenon back to its pre-predicative origin, and to understand the various "habitualities" involved in its initial mode of givenness.

B. The *Crisis*

In the *Crisis*, Husserl attempts a genetic analysis of science itself. He argues that the modern notion of universal science stems from a mathematization of the natural world, which originates with Plato, and reaches its apex in Galilean physics. According to Husserl, ancient philosophers idealized the natural world, but this idealization was finite in its ambitions: "Euclidean geometry, and ancient mathematics in general, knows only finite tasks, a finitely closed a priori."[16] To put it in Platonic terms, there is an epistemological (and ontological, on Aristotle's reading of Plato) gulf (χωρισμός) between the ideal (Being, Form) and the real (Becoming), such that philosophical or scientific reflection on the real (Becoming) does not constitute a universal systematic science of the ideal (Being), nor vice versa. In fact, the relation between the ideal and the real is not, for Plato, one of simple and complete correspondence; rather, Plato speaks of the relationship between real particulars and ideal forms as "μέθεξις," i.e., "participation."[17] According to Husserl, this methetic relationship between the ideal and real affords Platonic philosophy and ancient mathematics a "primitive application to reality," but proscribes any universal science of everything that is. Antiquity never shares the characteristically modern assumption that, "the infinite totality of what is in general is intrinsically a rational all-encompassing unity that can be mastered, without anything left over, by a corresponding universal science."[18]

With Galilean physics, "nature itself becomes—to express it in a modern way—a mathematical manifold."[19] Galileo saw the natural world as a geometrical entity. This mode of "seeing" may have been simply obvious to Galileo, but Husserl argues that it was generated out of two scientific traditions. First, geometry: "The relatively advanced geometry known to Galileo, already broadly applied not only to the earth but also in astronomy, was, for him, accordingly, already pre-given by tradition as a guide to his own thinking, which [then] related empirical matters to the mathematical ideas of limit." The second motivation for Galileo's conception of physics is the science of measurement: "Also available to him as a tradition . . . was the art of measuring, with its intention of ever-increasing exactness of measurement and the resulting *objective* determination of the shapes themselves."[20] At the nexus of these two traditions sits Galilean physics, which employs geometry as a means to perfect the science of measurement. The basic idea is this: If objects in the natural world can be measured with increasing approximation to geometrical ideals, then the natural world can be seen as a geometrical plenum. It is, then, the job of the physicist to develop more exact modes of measurement and more complex geometrical models in order to understand the natural world better. This conception of physical and mathematical science was "pre-given" to Galileo, who had no need to reflect on the origins of geometrical idealization and the ideal of apodictic mathematical self-evidence: "It did not enter the mind of a Galileo that it would ever become relevant, indeed of fundamental importance, to geometry, as a branch of universal knowledge of what is (philosophy), to make geometrical self-evidence—the "how" of its origin—into a problem."[21] Galileo, as a physicist, focused on the τέχνη of physics, not the genetic origin of scientific and mathematical objectivity.

According to Husserl, Galilean physics epitomizes modern science in two ways: First, it assumes that the natural world is an idealized "mathematical manifold." Second, it maintains a certain naïveté with regard to the origins of its mode of objectivity. This naïveté allows an important transformation to take place: the geometrical world replaces the life-world. As Husserl states, "But now we must note something of the highest importance that occurred even as early as Galileo: the surreptitious substitution of the mathematically substructured world of idealities for the only real world, the one that is actually given through perception, that is ever experienced and experienceable—our everyday life-world."[22] In essence, modern science, in the Galilean tradition, substitutes a methodological hypothesis (i.e., that the world is mathematically quantifiable and verifiable) for Being itself: the object-world replaces the life-world.

On Husserl's interpretation of Galilean physics, the entire modern scientific transformation of the life-world rests on a geometrical idealization of the natural world. Within the context of modern science, the ideality of geometry, which Galileo *passively* inherited as universal and objective science, goes unexamined. Yet Husserl argues that such idealities can be brought out of their passivity and reactivated in order to examine the original "meaning-giving achievement" that gives rise to ideality. Even geometry has a past: "We understand our geometry, available to us through tradition . . . to be a total acquisition of spiritual accomplishments which grows through the continued work of new spiritual acts into new acquisitions."[23] Like any other set of beliefs or practices, geometry has a history. It is, therefore, reasonable to assume that the tradition of geometry has an origin. Yet how would something like geometry actually originate?[24] Husserl speculates that geometry must have originated from the creative actions of an individual or community: "[the] meaning [of geometry] itself must have an origin in an accomplishment: first as a project and then in successful execution."[25] Perhaps some primordial proto-geometer needed to figure out the area of a triangular plot of land, and in the process of completing this project, realized that the area of her land equals one-half the base multiplied by the height. She thereby understood a geometrical truth about triangles in a self-evident, or apodictic, manner, as a means of achieving a particular goal in the life-world. But this brings up a problem:

> This process of projecting and successfully realizing occurs, after all, purely within the *subject* of the inventor, and thus the meaning, as present *originaliter* with its whole content, lies exclusively, so to speak, within his mental space. But geometrical existence is not psychic existence; it does not exist as something personal within the personal sphere of consciousness: it is the existence of what is objectively there for 'everyone' (for actual and possible geometers, or those who understand geometry).[26]

So how can the subjective experience of a proto-geometer become the idealized, objectified system of universal geometrical truths available to Galileo?

According to Husserl, the process of objectification begins with language. When our proto-geometer attempts to communicate her subjective experience to others that experience takes on an intersubjective validity, for language is, by its very nature, intersubjective. It communicates a subjective experience so that an *other* can somehow understand and reproduce the original experience. As Husserl states, "In the contact of reciprocal linguistic understanding, the original production and product of one subject can be *actively* understood by others."[27] Obviously the original experience is not perfectly reproduced by the other (since it was not originally his experience), but the other reanimates the experience in such a way that he shares in the original accomplishment, becoming a sort of "co-accomplisher." Moreover, in the reciprocal linguistic exchange, the communicator and the recipient of the communication recognize the likeness of their respective mental productions, imbuing the common structure of their experiences with an intersubjective validity.[28] As this linguistic process is repeated throughout the community, the structure of the experience begins to appear universal: "In the unity of the community of communication among several persons the repeatedly produced structure becomes an object of consciousness, not as likeness, but as one structure common to all."[29]

Husserl acknowledges that the objectivity of geometric truths is not entirely constituted by transferring "what has been originally produced in one to others who originally reproduce it."[30] Geometrical truths are true even when there is no community to validate them. The Pythagorean Theorem, for example, will always be true regardless of whether it is ever "originally reproduced" again. Husserl argues that this final level objectivity is accomplished through writing: "The important function of written, documented linguistic expression is that it makes communication possible without immediate or mediate personal address; it is, so to speak, communication become virtual. Through this, the communalization of man is lifted to a new level."[31] In the process of writing, the individual or community codifies its experience of geometry in a sequence of signs, making the experience universally available. These written expressions can be understood in two ways: First, they can be received *passively* (in the mode of passive genesis) by simply understanding the language without truly reproducing the intended experience. Second, they can be *actively* comprehended (in the mode of active genesis) by reactivating the original meaning-giving activity. On the one hand, written documents can become the basis of a textual tradition in which signs are passively received and then reactivated again and again in order to reproduce the original experience in different contexts. On the other hand, texts can become sedimented when the originary experience that gave rise to the text is lost or forgotten:

> The inheritance of propositions and of the method of logically constructing new propositions and idealities can continue without interruption from one period to the next, while the capacity for reactivating the primal beginnings, i.e., the sources of meaning for everything that comes later, has not been handed down with it. What is lacking is thus precisely what had given and had to give meaning to all propositions and theories, a meaning arising from the primal sources which can be made self-evident again and again.[32]

In other words, sedimentation occurs when a textual tradition loses the moorings of its original "stance" in the life-world. The sedimented text loses the self-evidence it accrued from its functions in the life-world, but what it loses in terms of evidence, it gains in terms of ideality. A fully sedimented text (or fact or method) is completely idealized, universally applicable with no connection to any specific event or experience in the life-world. Yet such ideality can be dangerous, inasmuch as it universalizes that which has a particular place in the life-world. This is precisely the danger that Husserl points out in his analysis of Galilean physics. Galileo inherited geometry as *already idealized*, as universally applicable, with no conception of geometry's place in the life-world from which it originated: "For in the case of inherited geometrical method, these functions were no longer being *vitally* practiced; much less were they reflectively brought to theoretical consciousness as methods which realize exactness from the inside." The universality of inherited geometrical ideals made their application to the world "obvious": "Thus it could appear that geometry, with its own immediately evident *a priori* 'intuition' and the thinking that operates with it, produces a self-sufficient, absolute truth which, as such—'obviously'—could be applied without further ado."[33] Yet, as Husserl has shown, the application of geometry is hardly "obvious"; it has its own complicated past in the life-world—a past that is hidden by modern science's philosophical naïveté about its origins.

The crisis of the sciences is, for Husserl, a crisis of sedimentation. Science has "forgotten" its connection to the life-world; it has substituted a "mathematical manifold" for the life-world that it was originally supposed to serve. What is lacking in modern science, and what genetic phenomenology seeks to provide, "is that actual self-evidence through which he who knows and accomplishes can give himself an account, not only of what he does that is new and what he works with, but also of the implications of meaning which are closed off through sedimentation or traditionalization."[34] That is to say, phenomenology seeks to reactivate the sciences in the context of the life-world, and in doing so, to ground the sciences in apodictic certainty, for "the life-world is a realm of original self-evidences. That which is self-evidently given is, in perception, experienced as 'the thing itself,' in immediate presence, or, in memory, remembered as the thing itself; and every other manner of intuition is a presentification of the thing itself."[35] Yet this return to the life-world, this return to the original intuition of the "thing itself," cannot take the form of a return to pre-modernity. We cannot simply undo modernity. Rather, Husserl envisions a new naïveté: "the proper return to the naïveté of life—but in a reflection which rises above this naïveté—is the only possible way to overcome the philosophical naïveté which lies in the supposedly 'scientific' character of traditional objectivistic philosophy."[36] Phenomenology does not simply reconnect the sciences with the life-world, as a return to the original naïveté of life, but seeks the "original intuition" of scientific meaning *in a scientific manner*. Phenomenology is the *science* of the life-world; it has a *theoretical* interest in the life-world. Phenomenology thus has a *unique* ability to ground the sciences in the life-world *in a scientific way*.

To be sure, the natural sciences are always implicitly connected to the life-world; they are disciplines carried out by individuals, who have particular concerns and desires within the life-world. Moreover, the natural sciences concern things that happen in the life-world: birth, death, disease, and so forth. But, as Husserl notes, "to use the life-world in this way is not to know it scientifically in its own manner of being."[37] So what, one wonders, is a science of the life-world? What is phenomenology? How does such a science not presume naturalistic modes of objectification? The first task of phenomenology, as a science of the life-world, is "the scientific opening up of the life-world." By bracketing the modes of objectification intrinsic to natural science, phenomenology demonstrates, "how all the self-evidence of objective-logical accomplishments, through which objective theory (thus mathematical and natural-scientific theory) is grounded in respect of form and content, has its hidden sources of grounding in the ultimately accomplishing life."[38] Phenomenology brings the life-world, as the source of self-evidence (scientific and otherwise), out from hiding. Once the life-world is "opened up," phenomenology has as its horizon of investigation the entire experienceable world: "We have a world-horizon as a horizon of possible thing-experience. Things: that is, stones, animals, plants, even human beings and human products."[39] Phenomenology does not, however, "have" these things in the mode of natural scientific objectivity; rather, it "has" them as they function subjectively and relatively within the life-world. Stones, animals, and plants are not simply objects ready to be apprehended by the tools of natural science; they are phenomena whose very meaning and objectivity are bound up in the genetic processes of the life-world. A stone is not simply an aggregate of earthen minerals (though it surely is that); it can be a tool, a weapon, a religious icon, something to throw away, and something worth dying for. As Husserl puts it, "Everything here [i.e., in the life-world] is subjective and relative, even though normally, in our experience and in the social group united with us in the community of life, we arrive at 'secure' facts."[40] Phenomenology, as the science of the life-world, may investigate any fact or object in the life-world. So a phenomenology of stones, for instance, might trace out the genesis of various modes of objectivity that apply to stones. Why, a phenomenologist might ask, is a diamond worth killing for while granite is not? Aside from phenomena in the life-world, phenomenology also has as its object of investigation categorial features of the life-world itself: How does anything whatsoever "appear" in the life-world? What is the structure of givenness? How does time structure our experience of the life-world? In other words, the subjectivity and relativity of the life-world has a general structure, which may be investigated phenomenologically.

In the *Crisis*, the general structure of the life-world is singular and universal: "This general structure, to which everything that exists relatively is bound, is not itself relative. We can attend to it in its generality and, with sufficient care, fix it once and for all in a way equally accessible to all."[41]

The life-world, for Husserl, is the universal ground of experience, and has certain universal categorial features intrinsic to it. So phenomenology seeks out "what remains invariant in the life-world."[42] Specifically, Husserl claims that space-time is a universal feature of the life-world, and that space-time, along with other universal features of the life-world (e.g., correlation) may be investigated by phenomenology as "universal *a priori.*" For example, Husserl speaks of grounding logic by tracing it back to, "the universal prelogical *a priori* through which everything logical, the total edifice of objective theory in all its methodological forms, demonstrates its legitimate sense and from which, then, all logic itself must receive its norms." Phenomenology's goal, then, is to produce a sort of transcendental ontology of the life-world that derives not from metaphysical or physical presuppositions, but from self-evidence: "But however [the life-world] changes and however it may be corrected, it holds to its essentially lawful set of types, to which all life, and thus all science, of which it is the 'ground,' remain bound. Thus it also has an ontology to be derived from pure self-evidence."[43] On the basis of this self-evident ontology, life-world phenomena and the sciences that investigate them may be grounded absolutely.

At this point, a corrective to Husserl's conception of the life-world is necessary—a corrective with which I shall be concerned throughout the present work, and which constitutes the main phenomenological point of this work. Throughout his corpus, Husserl claims that phenomenology has as its aim the acquisition of absolute, self evident knowledge (*Evidenz*), which might serve to ground the sciences. He also claims that, by bringing the life-world into self-evidence, phenomenology is able to investigate the *universal*, or general, structure of the life-world "once and for all." One wonders, however, how Husserl can stipulate the universality, or generality, of his phenomenological conclusions? Why would the very notions of "universality" or "generality" not be bracketed along with all other dogmatic claims about the life-world? Indeed, Husserl makes certain claims that would seem to proscribe any attribution of universality: "It is from this very ground [i.e., the ground of the pre-given life-world] that I have freed myself through the epochē; I stand *above* the world, which has now become for me, in a quite peculiar sense, a *phenomenon.*"[44] By bringing the life-world into scientific self-evidence, phenomenology no longer lives in the life-world naïvely: the life-world becomes a phenomenon. Presumably this life-world phenomenon has its own genetic past, just like any other phenomenon; thus it can never be known "once and for all."

It is difficult to account for Husserl's inconsistency on this point. I can only speculate that Husserl's notion of universality reflects the common, though mistaken, assumption that self-evidence is also *universal*. Throughout his work, Husserl aims at absolute knowledge in the form of perfect self-evidence. Yet he often conflates absolute knowledge, which is achieved through self-evidence, and universal knowledge, which establishes knowledge "once and for all." Such a conflation is extremely common. Indeed, experience seems to teach us that, if something is completely self-evident, then it is true "once and for all." When, for example, I understand the rules of addition, it is self-evidently true that $2 + 2 = 4$. No separate proof or outside corroborating evidence is necessary. It is only a short leap from there to the notion that $2 + 2 = 4$ is a universal truth. It is a leap nonetheless. Consider another example: Once I understand the rules of geometry, it is self-evidently true that the sum of the angles of a triangle is 180°. There is, of course, a proof to that effect, but I do not need the proof or any other outside evidence to see the geometric truth: it is self-evident. It is not, however, universal. In non-Euclidean space, for instance, the angles of a triangle need not add up to 180°. In other words, self-evidence does not imply universality; justification does not imply universal truth; absolute knowledge does not imply universal knowledge. Categorial features of the life-world, such as space-time, may be made self-evident through phenomenological investigation, and may also function as a ground for the sciences, without being universally applicable. To put it in a more Husserlian fashion, the categorial features of the life-world cannot be treated as static universals; time, givenness, manifestation, and so on, are all genetic—they have a history! Thus the categorial features of any phenomenon, horizon, or region of the life-world must be uncovered through genetic investigation, and cannot be stipulated as universal in an *a priori* sense.

C. The Reduction from Givenness to Pre-givenness

Husserl's concept of the life-world is notoriously problematic. In addition to the problem of Husserl's universalist treatment of the life-world, David Carr argues that the term "life-world" [*"Lebenswelt"*] functions for Husserl as an umbrella term for "disparate and sometimes incompatible concepts." In particular, Husserl uses the term "life-world" in reference to plural cultural worlds *and* the singular structure of perceptual experience.[45] Aron Gurwitsch makes a similar point.[46] Anthony Steinbock argues that the problematic nature of the life-world stems from Husserl's mode of analysis in the *Crisis*. More specifically, Husserl's ontological analysis of the life-world is structural and static, and his transcendental analysis reflects a Cartesian version of transcendence (inasmuch as the life-world is a phenomenon whose correlate is transcendental subjectivity). Husserl's static, Cartesian analysis of the life-world has, according to Steinbock, five main characteristics:

1. The world is presupposed as having the same structure as an object.

2. Phenomenologically, this means that the world becomes a mere correlate of intentional life, bearing all the accessory problems that a Cartesian analysis of the world has.

3. The world becomes an overarching unity, which as *telos* and *archē*, forms one single constitutive force.

4. Precisely as *the* futural world, it guides the development of the unitary sense for all objects, communities and cultures. This means that all conflicts are implicitly and ultimately overcome.

5. *Ultimately*, there is no possibility of a world encountering a radically different world; it signals the impossibility of an irreducible encounter of a *home*world with an *alien*world.[47]

The problem with such a static description of the life-world is that it ignores genetic questions: Where did the life-world come from? How is the life-world generated? Husserl hints at these genetic questions, though only briefly, by distinguishing between the life-world as a *given* phenomenon, and the life-world as the *pre-given* ground and horizon of experience:

> the life-world, for us who wakingly live in it, is always already there, existing in advance for us, the "ground" [*Boden*] of all praxis whether theoretical or extratheoretical. The world is pre-given to us, the waking, always somehow practically interested subjects, not occasionally but always and necessarily as the universal field of all actual and possible praxis, as horizon . . . But there exists a fundamental difference between the way we are conscious of the world and the way we are conscious of things or objects . . . Things, objects (always understood purely in the sense of the life-world) are "given" as being valid for us in each case (in some mode or other of ontic certainty) but in principle only in such a way that we are conscious of them as things or objects *within the world-horizon*.[48]

The very idea of "pre-givenness" suggests a temporalization of the life-world that is lacking in Husserl's more Cartesian moments.[49] The move from given to pre-given, with accompanying questions about how the given arises from the pre-given, points the way to a genetic analysis of the life-world. More than that, the pre-givenness of the life-world points to an entirely new dimension of phenomenology. Static and genetic phenomenology, as articulated by Husserl, deal with *given* phenomena—either by examining the role of subjectivity in constituting those phenomena or by tracing those phenomena back to their genetic origins. A phenomenological analysis of the *pre-given* life-world is, on the other hand, not concerned with *given* phenomena, but with the generation of *givenness*, or the generation of Being itself. Thus we see in Husserl a progression, or trajectory, from static phenomenology, which analyzes given phenomena as correlates of consciousness, to genetic phenomenology, which temporalizes both consciousness and the phenomenal object, to a new form of phenomenology, which inquires into the generation of givenness—or better, the generation of genesis. This final possibility is only adumbrated in Husserl's work. (Although, as I will argue in the next chapter, the turn to the *pre-given* is a direct consequence of phenomenology's quest for absolute science.) Eugen Fink, Husserl's assistant and "co-philosophizer" from 1928 to 1938, and, more recently, Anthony Steinbock treat the pre-givenness of the life-world more fully.

Steinbock takes his cue from Husserl's analysis of the life-world in the *Crisis*, arguing that there are two modalities of transcendental analysis at play. The first is a progressive Cartesian analysis, in which, "The world itself becomes the 'One' world, a *cogitatum* writ large as a correlate of experiences, or more precisely as a correlate of intersubjective accomplishments."[50] Thus, for example, Husserl explains *epochē*:

> Given in and through this liberation [i.e., the liberation of *epochē*] is the discovery of the universal, absolutely self-enclosed and absolutely self-sufficient correlation between the world itself and world-consciousness. By the latter is meant the conscious life of the subjectivity which effects the validity of the world, the subjectivity which always has the world in its enduring acquisitions and continues actively to shape it anew.[51]

In this Cartesian mode of analysis, the life-world is treated as a totalizing phenomenon whose correlate is subjectivity. Yet, as Steinbock notes, "A transcendental analysis of the life-world that portrays the world as totality is one but not the *only* possibility for a transcendental consideration of

the life-world."[52] More specifically, Steinbock argues that Husserl employs
a regressive (moving from given to pre-given), non-Cartesian transcendental method in his analysis of the life-world as pre-given "ground" (not
in the sense of a rational ground, *Grund*, but as the ground on which we
stand, *Boden*) and "horizon," concepts that are not well suited to Cartesian
modes of thought. What is distinctive about Husserl's notions of ground
and horizon is that they are not *given*, in the sense of phenomenal objects,
and thus do not fit neatly into the Cartesian dualism of phenomenal object
and constituting subject. As Steinbock puts it, "Things or objects, Husserl
specifies, are '*given*' [*gegeben*], but not the '*world-horizon*.' World-horizon
is the condition for the appearance of things. Some-thing is always given
from the world-horizon, while the world-horizon itself is in principle never
given."[53] Similarly the idea of "ground" suggests a non-Cartesian analysis
of the life-world: "The earth-ground [*Erdboden*], like the world-horizon,
is transcendentally understood insofar as it is not merely a correlate, but
a modality in which the life-world is *constitutive* of our experience."[54]

Steinbock takes Husserl's notions of world-horizon and earth-ground
as "leading clues" to a mode of regressive transcendental analysis that he
calls "generative phenomenology"—"generative" in the sense that this mode
of phenomenology focuses on the *generation of givenness*. World-horizon
and earth-ground suggest, for Steinbock, a concept of the life-world as
"territory," which is defined as, "the most general sense of geological and
historical delimitation for a community as *ground* and *horizon*. That is,
for Husserl a territory is a *geo-historical* formation as the inscription of
'symbolic' historical limits, as it were, on the global earth."[55] In other
words, a territory consists of the concrete space(s) and history(s) that
delimit a community. Thus, as Steinbock notes, "A territory can take on
many forms: a yard, a village, a house, a ship, a nation, a province and
the flexible borders belonging to nomadic people."[56] It is important to
note that "territory" is a descriptive term that applies to the life-world; it
adds content to the concept of the life-world, but does not tell us *how* the
life-world, as territory, might ground the sciences or generate givenness.
For "territory" to do the work that Husserl envisions of the life-world, it
must have some degree of normativity.

Steinbock argues that the normative functions of "territory" become
clear when read against the backdrop of Husserl's unpublished work on
normality and abnormality. In explaining normality, Steinbock draws on two
Husserlian concepts: concordance and optimality. Husserl develops ideas
of normality and abnormality as degrees of concordance and discordance
in the lived-body's relation to its environment. Consider, for example, my

experience of my coffee mug: I look at it. It is white with a picture of the Grand Canyon on the exterior and a blue interior—just as I expect, given my past experiences of this mug. I touch it. It is warm, heated by the coffee within. I have a normal perception of the coffee mug inasmuch as the various impressions and appearances hold together and confirm one another in the context of my experience. It is the relative *concordance* of impressions and appearances that constitutes the normality of my experience of the mug. This concordance can become discordant by a rupture in the relationship between the lived-body and its environment. Suppose, for instance, that I have been sleeping on my hand. I wake up and reach for my steaming coffee mug, without realizing that my hand has gone numb, and am surprised that I cannot feel the mug's warmth. In this case there is a small degree of discord, an anomaly that breaks the *normal* coherence of my experience. My various impressions (of the steam rising from the mug, for instance, and the surprising lack of warmth) do not hang together; the experience is abnormal. Normality and abnormality thus have to do with the concordance or discordance, as degrees of internal coherence, of an experience.

The account of normality as concordance is not entirely satisfactory to Husserl. As Steinbock notes,

> Missing in the account of normality as concordance is a deeper analysis of how the lived-body is involved with the world from a certain perspective. If the lived-body is intermeshed in a network of phenomena, as Husserl's analyses point out, then there will be a perspective or situation that will be *preferred* as *better* or *best* for experiencing.[57]

Consider, once again, my coffee mug. We might say that there is a preferred way to experience it, involving the full function of all my senses (no hand numbness). We might also say that one has to be a coffee lover to truly appreciate a good mug of coffee. In other words, there are more and less *optimal* ways of experiencing something; there are more and less optimal modes of givenness. A coffee mug sitting ten feet away on the counter is not given in the same way that it is when I am holding it. There is a teleology inherent in perception that revolves around an optimal, normative perceptual situation. Merleau-Ponty gives an instructive example:

> For each object, as for each picture in an art gallery, there is an optimum distance from which it requires to be seen,

a direction viewed from which it vouchsafes most of itself:
at a shorter or greater distance we have merely a perception
blurred through excess or deficiency. We therefore tend toward
the maximum of visibility, and seek a better focus as with a
microscope . . . The distance from me to the object is not a
size which increases or decreases, but a tension which fluctu-
ates round a norm . . . There is one culminating point in my
perception which simultaneously satisfies these . . . norms, and
toward which the whole perceptual process tends.[58]

On this view, the normality of one's perception has to do with the degree
of its optimality. Thus my numb-handed experience of the coffee mug is
abnormal, not only because it is discordant but also because it is a less-
than-optimal way of experiencing the coffee mug.

In Husserl's thought, the axes of concordance and optimality do
not line up completely. My visual experience of the coffee cup might
hang together concordantly even if my vision were bad. Moreover, it
is entirely possible that a discordant experience might produce a "finer
organization of sense"—imagine a scientist seeing an image from an
electron microscope for the first time—which might then produce a new,
more optimal perceptual situation. Steinbock argues that concordance
and optimality are two modes of normality, which together suggest a
conception of normality as familiarity. The optimal, for its part, "emerges
in an affective prominence as a solicitation for taking-up and integration
into that particular life experience."[59] That is to say that the optimal, as
normative, entices the subject to adopt a certain perceptual "perspective"
as the best perspective; the optimal thereby becomes "the normal (*qua*
optimal) interrelation between the 'subject' and its environing-world as
what is best for it."[60] When the optimal is taken up, and repeated to the
extent that it is fully integrated into lived-experience, then it also attains
a high degree of concordance, such that the optimal experience is also the
one that seems to "hang together" best. Concordance, then, relates to the
optimal as a capacity to repeat the optimal until it gains a high degree of
internal coherence.[61] When the concordantly optimal is repeated over time,
it attains what Steinbock calls "genetic density," becoming integrated into
life-experience to such an extent that there is a natural *predisposition* for
the optimal. The relation between the subject and its world-environment
is not arbitrary; it is *predisposed* to certain normal (*qua* optimal) forms of
experience. As Steinbock states, "If solicitation and continued affirmation
build up a genetic density of and predisposition for what is optimal, the

interaction that is generated becomes a *privileged* basis and context for those forms of life living in this way."[62] Once it attains sufficient genetic density, a certain optimal relation between the "subject" and its environing world becomes privileged as a "typical" or "familiar" context of life-experience: "Through the stylized repetition and responsive comportment to the norm *qua* optimum, a structure of normal comportment emerges that becomes typically familiar of the experience."[63] This suggests another configuration of normality: the normal as that which is familiar.

By applying the notion of normality, as familiarity, to his analysis of "territory," Steinbock arrives at a normative conception of the life-world as homeworld/alienworld: "This entails viewing a normatively significant life-world as an intersubjectively typically familiar territory in which we are 'at home.' Accordingly, alienness will not be in the first instance an alien subject, but an intersubjective geo-historical world that is normatively alien, that is, an *alienworld*."[64] The homeworld is constituted by appropriating a normal experience of the environing-world as home; alienworld is co-constituted as that which is abnormal or transgressive with respect to normal experience. It is important to note that the alienworld does not derive from the homeworld, nor vice-versa; rather, homeworld and alienworld are co-constituted in the process of normalization, and co-generative with respect to givenness and being. As Steinbock puts it, "This constitutive duet unfolds as the *co-constitution of the alien through appropriative experience of the home, and as the co-constitution of the home through the transgressive experience of the alien*."[65] It is the co-constitutive, co-generative relation between homeworld and alienworld that gives the life-world its normativity, and determines the normative significance of that which is given in the life-world.

Consider, once again, Husserl's critique of the natural attitude in the *Crisis*. Husserl argues that the natural attitude stems from a Galilean mathematization of the life-world. The solution to the problem of the universal mathematization of nature is to situate Galilean science in the life-world, evaluating its progress in light of the life-world situation from which it originated. This solution only works if the life-world is somehow normative, if the life-world provides us with some sort of normative evidence that would allow us to say, "Galilean science has overstepped its original bounds, and I know this because. . . ." The life-world can only provide this sort of evidence if it is structured as homeworld/ alienworld. In analyzing the life-world situation of Galilean science, we (as genetic phenomenologists) must be able to recognize the world where such a science is "at home," the life-world in which such a science is "normal." Moreover, we must be able to recognize the precise point where Galilean science becomes "abnormal," where it overreaches the limits of its homeworld (delimited as it is by an alienworld). In other words phenomenology is only successful if the life-world is normative, and the life-world can only be normative if it *does not* have a universal structure, but is instead defined as a world in which we are "at home," delimited by worlds in which we are "not at home."

Steinbock's extended version of Husserl's life-world is significant for our purposes in two regards. First, the idea of the life-world, as a home-world delimited by an alienworld, provides an elegant way of thinking about the life-world that avoids postulating any sort of universal structure. At most, structural elements of the life-world apply to a homeworld, whose universality is proscribed by an alienworld. Steinbock's analysis confirms what we already suspected: The success of phenomenology depends on *not* postulating a universal structure for the life-world. So universality must be bracketed along with all other dogmatic approaches to the life-world. Second, the idea of "generative phenomenology"—as a turn from given phenomena to the pre-given homeworld/alienworld—raises interesting issues with regard to phenomenology itself. (These issues will be explored more fully in the next chapter.) Namely, if the life-world is *pre-given* as homeworld/alienworld, then phenomenology, as a scientific analysis of the life-world from within the life-world, also reflects the structure of a home-world delimited by an alienworld. Consequently, phenomenology is not a *universal* science even if it is an *absolute* science. As a scientific practice on the part of transcendental subjectivity, phenomenology is *within* the process of genesis even as it evaluates the generation of givenness. Phenomenology cannot completely escape the genetic processes of its emergence, which are related to a specific homeworld. It can provide self-evidence, but that self-evidence is always circumscribed genetically; thus phenomenology can never provide the universal *a priori* of *all* genesis. Phenomenology has no right to the phrase "once and for all."

Steinbock's turn to pre-givenness was anticipated by Eugen Fink, whose work will be the focus of the next chapter. It will be sufficient, at this point, to note a few similarities. Fink, who was a student of both Husserl and Heidegger, reformulates Husserl's natural attitude not simply as an "attitude" toward objects in the world but as the basic existential and ontological mode of existing in the world—an amalgam of Husserl's "natural attitude" and Heidegger's "being-in-the-world." For Fink, as Kevin Hart puts it, "the natural attitude is not something human beings *have* but something human beings *are*."[66] This shift in the role of the natural attitude—a shift that Fink saw as outgrowth of Husserl's own thought—produces a new understanding of the task and goals of the phenomenological reduction. In *epochē*, which precedes the reduction proper, one not only suspends scientific approaches to the world but also extends transcendental subjectivity beyond everyday worldly being. As Fink puts it, "man *un-humanizes [entmenscht]* himself in performing the *epochē*, that is, he lays bare the transcendental onlooker in himself, he passes into him. This onlooker, however, does not first come to be by the *epochē*, but is only *freed* from the shrouding cover of human being [*Menschein*]."[67] The transcendental onlooker is freed not from an "attitude" toward the world, but from a naïve worldly existence that takes the object-world to be the entirety of existence: "*What we lose* [by the *epochē*] *is not the world,* but our *captivation by the world,* the restrictedness of the natural attitude which looks upon the world as the universe of all that is existent, which is 'blind' and closed off to the true universe of that which is existent (in which the world lies only as an *abstract stratum*)."[68] By freeing transcendental subjectivity from its "captivation by the world," *epochē* sets the stage for the phenomenological reduction, in which the world and subjectivity are revealed to be genetic counterparts, both of which are constituted genetically: "subjectivity is nothing other than the *wherefrom of this genesis,* it is not there *before* the process, simply and solely *in the process.* And the world (the natural attitude) is likewise not the 'substantival' opposite member of the constitutive correlation, but the *whither of constitutive termination.*"[69] Both transcendental subjectivity and the world are constituted *within* the process of genesis.

By reframing subjectivity and the given world as constituted results, arising within genetic processes, Fink approaches the subject of pre-givenness in much the same way as Steinbock. For Fink, pre-givenness points to a depth in transcendental subjectivity heretofore unrealized by Husserl. Transcendental subjectivity, as the constitutive source of Being (and therefore not itself a being), cannot be properly conceptualized in terms that apply to beings (or Being). Phenomenological investigation of the pre-given aspects of subjectivity therefore requires a new sort of phenomenology, "constructive phenomenology," which is analogous to Steinbock's "generative phenomenology," and which is likewise not circumscribed by Being or any *given* phenomena. Fink, like Steinbock, is also acutely aware that radical phenomenology, in its generative or constructive modes, includes as an object of investigation the methods and goals of phenomenology itself. For Steinbock, this realization comes from the idea that the pre-given homeworld/alienworld structures the activity of phenomenology. For Fink, the necessity of a phenomenological investigation of phenomenology stems from the nature of the transcendental subject that does phenomenology.

In both cases, phenomenology is not a universal science sitting apart from its object of study; rather, phenomenology is bound up in the genetic and generative processes that give rise to any phenomena whatsoever.

The sorts of critiques made by Steinbock and Fink have far-reaching consequences for the phenomenology of scripture (the full elaboration of which will take place in succeeding chapters). In short, if givenness is subject to *pre-given* generative processes, then a scriptural modification of *givenness* is possible, inasmuch as scripture is itself *generative*. Yet this possibility is not particularly damaging to Husserlian phenomenology; it is more of a corrective. The goal of phenomenology, in this extended brand of Husserlian phenomenology, is not to discern the universal structure of the life-world, for doing so would constitute yet another mode of dogmatic abstraction from the life-world; rather, phenomenology seeks to ground the sciences (scriptural science included) in the self-evidence of the life-world, as a homeworld delimited by an alienworld, and then to investigate self-evidence itself, without presuming any particular categorial features of the life-world. Phenomenology thus discloses the essential unity of transcendental subjectivity and the life-world, where subject and world function as two moments in a generative process encompassing the very categories of existence.

With respect to physics, for example, phenomenology would attempt to reconnect physical science to the life-world: What life-world problems was physics meant to solve? How did physics originate, or attain self-evidence, in the conscious life of subjectivity? How does contemporary physics relate to its original purposes? And in a more categorial vein: What mode of time and givenness does physical objectivity presume? How are physical modes of time and givenness constituted? Similarly, a phenomenology of scripture would ground biblical science by situating it in the life-world context of scripture (as a pre-given, generative life-world) without assuming any particular mode of objectivity, or particular categorial feature at the outset—for it is precisely the modes of givenness of scripture, as well as the categories that arise from scripture, that are in question. Contemporary biblical science would not be negated, but grounded in the self-evidence of the hidden source of all scientific objectivity—namely, the generative life-world. Thus, historical criticism, for example, would be treated not as the source of validity and meaning of biblical texts, but as a science grounded (absolutely!) in a life-world experience of scripture.

To speak of the phenomenology of scripture as an absolute science is to speak of a science of the life-world experience of scripture. Yet, even such a non-universal, non-metaphysical notion of "absolute science" puts us on shaky ethical and philosophical ground. What exactly do we mean by the "life-world experience of scripture"? Which "life-world" are we talking about? The Protestant life-world? The Roman Catholic life-world? The life-world of first-century messianic Jews? In short, who gets to specify the life-world context of scripture? In some sense, such questions seem sensible. After all, it stands to reason that a phenomenology of New Testament texts might justifiably assume various elements of Christian dogma—e.g., the Resurrection. Yet such assumptions are phenomenologically problematic. Christian dogma is generated out of the Church's continuing engagement *with* scripture. The relationship between dogma and scripture is genetic, and subject to genetic phenomenological investigation. The scriptural life-world, including all its various categorial and dogmatic features, cannot be specified theoretically prior to phenomenological investigation. Of course, the life-world is always a *practical a priori*—all human activities take place within the life-world—but the scientific investigation of the life-world, which is phenomenology's task, cannot assume any particular theoretical features of the life-world, for such assumptions would constitute yet another dogmatic approach to the life-world—the very type of approach that Husserlian phenomenology criticizes. Likewise, the phenomenology of scripture cannot assume any particular piece of religious dogma, for the genesis of dogma is itself a facet of the phenomenology of scripture. Dogma, like scripture, has a history.

3

Phenomenology as a
Self-Referential Science

Husserl argues that sciences derived from the natural attitude can never be *absolute* because they make dogmatic assumptions about the nature and validity of knowledge and truth, thereby limiting the scope of scientific inquiry. By contrast, phenomenology, as absolute science, is supposed to eschew dogmatic assumptions, letting phenomena give themselves freely and completely. Yet how can we be sure that phenomenology is not dogmatic? How can we be sure that phenomenology is not repeating the mistakes of the natural attitude at a higher theoretical level (in the form of a "philosophical attitude," perhaps)? After all, the previous chapter showed that Husserl has a tendency to make universal dogmatic claims about ontological features of the life-world. To put the question differently, how can phenomenology guarantee that it is an absolute science? This is an important question generally, but more so for the phenomenology of scripture. For, if the phenomenology of scripture involves the application of yet another dogmatic interpretive science to scripture, then what is the point? If a phenomenology of scripture is to be worthwhile, it should be something more than simply another interpretive model; it should be an absolute science.

This chapter seeks to characterize phenomenology as an absolute science over-and-against mundane science and mundane notions of the Absolute. The first section deals with Eugen Fink's idea of a "phenomenological countertendency" in absolute subjectivity. The second section compares phenomenology and mundane science. The final section sketches a positive concept of absolute science. I will argue that phenomenology guarantees its absoluteness only to the extent that it is self-referential. Accordingly, phenomenological self-reference is an integral and necessary component of absolute science.

A. The Fracturing of Transcendental Subjectivity

In the *Sixth Cartesian Meditation*, Eugen Fink addresses the problem of phenomenology's "absoluteness." He notes that the phenomenological reduction, which leads to an apperception of the Absolute, is, "for the most part under the spell of mundane prejudices."[1] Chief among these mundane prejudices is the idea that phenomenological investigations pertain to Being *as such*; and that the Absolute is therefore restricted to ontic categories—e.g., the infinite whole, the greatest being, the most encompassing, and so forth. This ontic prejudice prevents us from grasping the Absolute *as absolute* precisely because the Absolute is not a being, but the constitutive source of Being; it cannot be restricted dogmatically to ontic categories. As Fink puts it, "In all this *ontic apperception* there lies a *dogmatism* which fundamentally prevents grasping the concept of Absolute with phenomenological *suitability*."[2] In some sense, the ontic prejudice is inescapable, for phenomenology is done by *beings*; philosophical terms necessarily reflect the ontic situations of those who philosophize. Phenomenology is therefore caught in a paradox: the act of phenomenologizing consists in *a being* trying to uncover the constitutive source of all *Being* using an ontic philosophical language. The philosophical temptation is to forestall this paradox by restricting the absolute to the ontic—a temptation that perhaps proved too alluring to both Husserl and Heidegger—but this solution does not yield an absolute science, for, as Fink notes, " 'being as such' makes up but one moment of the Absolute."[3] Consequently the phenomenologist must think in ontic terms, while understanding that those terms apply to the Absolute in an analogous sense: "The explication of the Absolute cannot do without [ontic categories], since they are needed in that explication as the *medium for transcendental analogizing*."[4] What the phenomenologist must *not* do, however, is mistake the philosophical "medium for transcendental analogizing" for the Absolute itself.

Fink argues that phenomenology has a built-in safeguard against the dogmatic application of ontic categories (or any other categories, for that matter). Namely, the dogmatic temptation is proscribed by the self-referential structure of phenomenology. In other words, phenomenology guarantees its own "absoluteness" to the extent that it is self-referential. In order to understand the force of Fink's claim, it will be necessary to unpack the idea of phenomenology as a self-referential science.

Phenomenology's self-reference derives from the phenomenological reduction itself. Fink argues that the reduction reveals a division in transcendental subjectivity: "performing the phenomenological reduction breaks open a *cleft* in the field of transcendental subjectivity and sets up a separation of transcendental being into two heterogeneous zones."[5] The first "zone" of transcendental subjectivity involves the *activity* of world constitution, which consists in "the formation of world and being."[6] This constituting work of transcendental subjectivity is directly disclosed by the phenomenological reduction. In *epochē*, naïve assumptions about the objectivity, or mode of being, of the object-world are suspended, revealing (through the reduction) the constituting work of consciousness in producing objectivity. The constituting "zone" of transcendental subjectivity is the theme, or object of investigation, of what Fink calls the "transcendental theory of elements." Husserl's work, in exploring the constituting activity of consciousness, is more or less restricted to the transcendental theory of elements.

There is also a second zone of subjectivity at play in the phenomenological reduction: the "phenomenologizing I" or "transcendental onlooker." This zone of subjectivity does not participate in the activity of world-constitution, but observes and reflects upon that activity. Put differently, if the *object* of the transcendental theory of elements is world-constitution (including both the constituting subject and constituted object), then the *subject*, the one doing the phenomenological investigating, is the transcendental onlooker, or phenomenologizing I.[7] This phenomenologizing I is different, in principle, from the constituting I. It does not participate in constituting acts. Fink therefore claims that the reduction introduces a cleft, or dualism, into transcendental life: on the one side is the constituting I, which is the theme of the "transcendental theory of elements"; on the other side is the phenomenologizing I, which is the theme of "the transcendental theory of method." The latter, as an investigation into the act of phenomenologizing, is tantamount to a phenomenology of phenomenology—a phenomenological investigation of the methods of phenomenology itself.

It is the transcendental theory of method that is lacking in Husserl's work. Even in his later period, Husserl focuses exclusively on the constituting action of transcendental subjectivity, while phenomenologizing subjectivity is completely neglected, remaining "an uncomprehended residue in the self-clarification of transcendental subjectivity."[8] If Husserl's phenomenological project of transcendental self-clarification is to be completed, if phenomenology is to serve as an absolute ground for the sciences, then "the uncomprehended residue" of phenomenologizing subjectivity must be subject to phenomenological investigation.

It is important to recognize that the transcendental theory of method is an entirely new direction for phenomenology. While the transcendental theory of elements thematizes the constituting I and its relation to the phenomenal world, the transcendental theory of method thematizes phenomenological reflection on world-constitution. Unlike the theory of elements, the transcendental theory of method does not start with the *given* phenomenal world, working backwards from there; rather, the theory of method is more speculative, starting with the "question of the transcendental meaning of *being-given*."⁹ Fink contrasts his "constructive" approach with Husserl's "regressive" approach: "If regressive phenomenology is the whole of the primordial and intersubjective explication of reductively opened up transcendental subjectivity, then there is not alongside it still another new region of *reductively given* transcendental life now to be offered as the theme for a constructive phenomenology."¹⁰ Regressive phenomenology opens up, through the reduction, the entire realm of givenness; there is, therefore, no remnant or new region of *reductively given* transcendental life available to serve as a theme for constructive phenomenology. Yet the reduction also reveals a hidden depth of transcendental subjectivity, the phenomenologizing I, which is *not* itself *given*, but which is able to investigate, or phenomenologize about that which is given. Thus constructive phenomenology, which is primarily concerned with the phenomenologizing I, is not homogenous with the regressive approach; the "transcendental cognitions" of constructive phenomenology are "heterogeneous in content," and cannot therefore be disclosed by regressive phenomenology:

> The "object"—or better, *the objects*—of constructive phenomenology are *not* "given." The theorizing directed to them is not an "intuitive having given" ["*anschauliches Gegebenhaben*"], is not "intuitive" ["*intuitiv*"]; but as referral to something that precisely by its transcendental mode of being is *in principle* deprived of "givenness," is "non-given," this theorizing is *constructive*.¹¹

In other words, constructive phenomenology is not concerned with the *given* but the *pre-given*.

The relationship between the phenomenologizing I and constituting I is of critical importance in determining the nature of phenomenology's self-reference and the status of phenomenology's claim to absoluteness. Since the phenomenological reduction is the original site of this "cleft" in transcendental subjectivity, it is appropriate to start there. Fink points to two "moves" in phenomenological reduction: *epochē* and reduction. *Epochē*, which Husserl defined in *Ideas I* as a bracketing of the natural attitude, takes on a slightly different inflection for Fink: "the disconnection of all belief-positings," including human being-in the world and the "being of the world as a whole."¹² Whereas Husserl (at least in the early works) described *epochē* as a way of bracketing theoretical assumptions about the world, Fink sees *epochē* as applying to both the object-world and the self: "The main weight of the phenomenological *epochē* lies in the disconnection of ourselves as subjects existing in the world, in the conversion of ourselves into the transcendental subject, more precisely, in self-recognition as this subject."[13] In other words, *epochē* involves bracketing *both* the object-world *and* subjective being-in-the-world. This "self-disconnection" is tantamount to removing, "the worldly shape of the interiority sphere of our life as an apperceptive meaning-structure, [separating] it as a covering and concealment from a subjectivity that is only brought into the open by this removal . . . only then does self-bracketing have a putative sense."[14] Thus for Fink, the "natural-attitude," which is bracketed in *epochē*, refers not simply to a set of assumptions about objectivity but to the native situation of human being-in-the-world. As Fink puts it, the natural attitude is "the set-up belonging essentially to human nature, making up human being itself, the setting up of man [*das Eingestelltsein des Menschen*] as a being in the whole of the world, or . . . the set-up of mundanized subjectivity: the natural being of man in and to the world in all his modes."[15]

One consequence of Fink's radical notion of the natural attitude is that phenomenological *epochē* cannot be motivated from within the horizon of the world: "Man cannot *as man* phenomenologize, that is, his human mode of being [*Menschsein*] cannot perdure through the actualization of phenomenological cognition. Performing the reduction means for man to *rise beyond* (to transcend) *himself*, it means to *rise beyond himself in all his human possibilities*."[16] Fink's point, expressed somewhat hyperbolically in this passage, is that performing *epochē* requires a dimension of transcendental subjectivity far beyond that of being-in-the-world. *Epochē* is possible only because of a "transcendental tendency," which is concealed in natural subjectivity, and which only comes to light through the performance of *epochē*. That is to say, performing *epochē* unearths a new layer of transcendental subjectivity: "the phenomenological onlooker." As Fink states, "The transcendental tendency that awakens in man and drives him to inhibit all acceptednesses nullifies man himself; man *un-humanizes* [*entmenscht*] himself in performing the *epochē*, that is, he lays bare the transcendental onlooker in himself, he passes into him."[17] By performing *epochē*, transcendental subjectivity becomes *aware* of its previously concealed constituting action. A division is thus effected within transcendental subjectivity between the "phenomenological onlooker," which becomes aware of the constituting activity of subjectivity, and the "constituting I," which does the actual work of constitution.

Phenomenological *epochē* is the precursor to reduction proper. Fink distinguishes the two in the following manner:

> If by the *epochē* we understand *abstention from belief*, then under the concept of "action of reduction proper" we can understand all the *transcendental insights* in which we *blast open captivation-in-acceptedness* and first recognize the acceptedness *as* anacceptedness in the first place. Abstention from belief can only be radical and universal when that which falls under disconnection by the epochē comes to be seen precisely *as a belief-construct, as an acceptedness.*[18]

Put differently, if *epochē* calls into question the being of the world and human being-in-the-world as belief-constructs, then reduction reveals an absolute subjectivity that is, "not itself subject to the conditions of world-inherence."[19] Through this radicalized reduction, the horizon of the world (and Being, which necessarily appears within the horizon of the world) is recognized as a constituted result, a *telos*, whose source is transcendental subjectivity.

In the act of reduction, the phenomenological onlooker, "*inquires back* from *experience* of the world to *constitution* of the world, inquires back from *finished and ready* ways-of-taking-things-as-holding-in-being [*Seinsgeltungen*] to the *processes of the formation* of those ways of accepting things in being and thus also to the *deep constitutive strata of acts of reflection.*"[20] What is discovered in this inquiry is a "teleological tendency" that structures all constituting life: namely, a tendency toward being. The *telos* of constituting activity is Being, or worldly existence: "*the existent is only the result of a constitution,* and that *constitution* is *always constitution of the existent.*"[21] Fink thus refers to the constituting activity of transcendental subjectivity as "enworlding." It is important to note that the enworlding tendency of transcendental subjectivity applies to both phenomenal objects and subjects: "The world-aiming tendency of transcendental constitutive process terminates not only in mundane '*Objects*,' as the end-products of constituting performances, but just as much in the mundane *subject*: in man, who likewise represents a *result* of a constitutive sense-bestowal."[22] Both the world and mankind, as beings-in-the-world, are the *results* of constituting acts on the part of transcendental subjectivity.

Where does this leave the phenomenologizing I? Can its activity be characterized as enworlding? As Fink asks, "is this *uncovering* of the being-tendency of all constituting life itself caught up *in* the being-tendency?"[23] The answer to Fink's rhetorical question is clearly, "No." The act of phenomenologizing—i.e., the act of reflecting on the constituting work of subjectivity—does not itself constitute anything; the phenomenologizing I is not involved in the work of constitution. With the advent of the phenomenologizing I (in and through the phenomenological reduction) a countertendency is introduced into transcendental subjectivity: "Now, in the reductive epochē a *countertendency* is formed in transcendental life, a countercurrent to itself, a noncompliance and nonassociation with the direction that life takes in performing the action of constitution; and there is instead a movement back *against* this direction of life, a *breaking up of the tendency of life toward the world as its finality.*"[24] The teleological tendency that structures the phenomenological I is not a being-tendency, but a tendency *against* the enworlding activity of constitution. The phenomenological I, produced in the reduction, uncovers a transcendental subjectivity that is the source of the constituting action that terminates in worldly existence. The horizon of the world (and Being, which necessarily appears within the horizon of the world) is recognized as a constituted result, a *telos*, whose source is transcendental subjectivity. In other words, "the onlooker discloses, by reduction action, the transcendental source and dimension of origin for belief in the world, he 'discovers' transcendental subjectivity as constituting."[25] This division in transcendental subjectivity is intrinsic to the phenomenological project; in order to investigate the constituting activity of consciousness, transcendental subjectivity must be "stretched" beyond its constituting functions so that those functions might be evaluated and investigated. Yet it is important to note that it is transcendental subjectivity itself that is doing the "stretching"; subjectivity divides itself against itself. In the phenomenological reduction, transcendental subjectivity investigates its own constituting activity. Consequently, if phenomenology is going to be complete, if it is going to investigate all aspects of transcendental subjectivity, then it must investigate its own investigation, in the form of a transcendental theory of method.

The relationship between the phenomenologizing I and the constituting I, as inherently different aspects of a unified transcendental subject, results in a self-reference peculiar to phenomenology based on two factors: "a) on the *self-sameness* of phenomenologically thematized and thematizing life, inasmuch as both are enclosed within the comprehensive unity of 'transcendental being,' and, on the other hand, b) on their *difference*, in that one is world constituting and the other is not."[26] Consider, by way of contrast, a few other self-referential and non-self-referential sciences. Botany, for instance, takes flora as its object, and in no way includes the botanist as an object of investigation; this is clearly a non-self-referential science. Contrast that with psychology, in which the investigator examines something that he himself *is*, namely, human consciousness; this is a self-referential science. Phenomenology is similarly self-referential. The ultimate "object" of phenomenology is the transcendental subject. As Fink puts it, "The *theme* of the transcendental theory of method is the phenomenological onlooker. At the same time the onlooker is also the *subject*, i.e., the one doing the cognizing and theorizing in the theory of method."[27] There is, however, an important distinction between psychology's self-reference and phenomenology's self-reference. The former is self-referential because of a unity in being: the psychological investigator, as human consciousness, shares a mode of being with the object of his investigation. Alternately, the phenomenological subject (i.e., the phenomenologizing I) shares no unity of being with what is disclosed in the phenomenological reduction (i.e., the constituting I). As we have seen, the subjective performance of phenomenologizing is distinct from the constituting activity of transcendental subjectivity.

The transcendental self-reference peculiar to phenomenology is a wholly new form of self-reference. Fink even speculates that worldly logic may not be sufficient to characterize the "unity in difference" of transcendental life. Yet whether or not logical specificity is possible, it is clear that the whole phenomenological project turns on the nature of the division that is introduced into transcendental life through the reduction. If that division were too great (in which case the phenomenologizing I and constituting I would be two separate subjects) or too small (in which case there would be no difference between the phenomenologizing I and constituting I), then phenomenological reflection would be impossible. Suppose, for the sake of argument, that the phenomenological reduction introduces nothing new into transcendental life—no phenomenologizing I, no countertendency to being, no "cleft," no extension of transcendental subjectivity. In that case, transcendental subjectivity would remain forever hidden. Subjectivity would be restricted to its constituting functions. Moreover, without the possibility of a non-constituting reflection on its constituting activity, subjectivity would not even be able to recognize its own constituting activity. It could never escape the natural attitude.

Alternately, suppose that the phenomenological reduction introduced a complete break between the phenomenologizing I and constituting I, such that two separate subjectivities were produced. Putting aside, for the moment, the idea that this possibility is *prima facie* absurd—as if transcendental subjectivity had some sort of dissociative identity disorder—such a situation would render phenomenology impossible. For, if the act of phenomenologizing produced a wholly different form of subjectivity, then phenomenology would not be self-referential at all. It would be analogous to botany, where the object of investigation shares no common being with the subject who is doing the investigating. This poses no particular problem in the case of botany, but phenomenology is a science of subjectivity conducted by *human subjects in the world.* If the act of phenomenologizing produced a wholly new form of subjectivity, completely separate from worldly human subjectivity, then the phenomenologist must somehow become completely nonhuman or extra-worldly; this would, of course, be absurd. These two extreme possibilities serve to show that the "cleft" introduced into transcendental subjectivity is a delicate one: transcendental subjectivity must "stretch" beyond its everyday constituting functions without being cleaved entirely in two. Fink characterizes phenomenology's effect on subjectivity as follows:

> [I]n the actualization of the reduction a self-reflection occurs that has a wholly new kind of structure: it is not that man reflectively thinks about himself, but rather that transcendental subjectivity, concealed in self-objectivation as man, reflectively thinks about itself, and taking itself down as man all the way to the ground, namely, down to the innermost ground of its life.[28]

In other words, in the phenomenological reduction, the subject rises above its being-in-the-world in order to analyze the constitutive source of that being in the "innermost ground of its life." The transcendental subject is thus both a being-in-the-world and a non-being—a "μηον."[29]

B. Mundane Science and Phenomenology

Transcendental self-reference is not only necessary for the phenomenological reduction to "get off the ground" but it is also necessary for phenomenology to achieve its goal of absolute science.[30] Fink develops the notion of phenomenology, as an absolute science, by taking worldly science as, "a clue for a corresponding inquiry into the 'scientificity' of transcendental phenomenologizing."[31] The reason that worldly science functions as a "clue" is that phenomenology is also, at least in part, a worldly science; it is performed within the horizon of world. There is, as Fink notes, "a kinship in structure [that] holds between the *mundane appearance* of phenomenologizing and *mundane science*."[32] One notices immediately that the "kinship" is not between phenomenology itself and mundane science, but between the "mundane appearance" of phenomenology and mundane science. There is a kinship between the *form* of phenomenology, as it is practiced in the world, and mundane sciences, but there is no kinship between mundane sciences and the "concept of science that is actualized *in phenomenologizing* itself."[33] The formal similarities between phenomenology and mundane science mask crucial differences: "The Idea of phenomenological science altogether *transcends* all known notions of science or any that are ever possible in the natural attitude. Mundane sciences are one and all *sciences of that which is existent*; phenomenological science refers to the constitutive *becoming of the existent*."[34] Mundane sciences are concerned with that which is given in the world; phenomenology is concerned with *how* the given becomes given.

To better understand Fink's argument, it will behoove us to explore the relation between phenomenology and worldly science. Fink notes three significant characteristics of mundane science. First, all science is done by humankind, and applies to objects that appear within the horizon of the world: "It is a fundamental characteristic of every *worldly* science that the 'subject' of the action of doing science . . . is *man*; and thus that every science is *human* science. The doing of science and the result of this action are together in the unity of the world."[35] Second, all worldly science (as science done by humans) lies within the realm of human possibility, and in no case transcends human possibility: "in the case of no science does man go beyond himself."[36] Third, all sciences, both real and possible, are communicative in the sense that they aim at intersubjective objectivity and refer to objects that exist for everyone. Sciences are also communicative in the sense that they seek objective findings that can be communicated genetically in historical communities, objectivized through time as so many spiritual acquisitions: "The 'infinity horizon' of mundane science relates to the *historico-generative communication* of individual finite life, which is only capable of handing down its scientific acquisitions thanks to the 'objectivation' of those acquisitions."[37]

By characterizing science in terms of *who* does it, its potential scope, and its intersubjective communicability, Fink sets up three points of comparison with phenomenology. First, we may ask, who is it that phenomenologizes? Is it "man," as in the case of mundane science? If not man, then who? On the one hand, it is clearly humans who phenomenologize; on the other hand, Fink claims that, "Man cannot *as man* phenomenologize."[38] As a solution to this paradox, one might think that phenomenology simply teaches that all human actions are, in the end, transcendental. Accordingly, human phenomenologizing is also a transcendental act; it is man, as a transcendental actor, who phenomenologizes. Yet this solution is problematic because, as Fink notes, "Phenomenologizing is not an activity that can or does lie on one and the same level, so to speak, with other human activities."[39] It is not as if phenomenologizing is an activity that is done first in the natural attitude, then later accorded transcendental significance. Rather, getting the phenomenological reduction "off the ground" requires a deepening of transcendental subjectivity (producing the phenomenologizing I), so that the natural attitude can be viewed from the proper transcendental perspective. Phenomenologizing within the context of the world, within the natural attitude, does not occur before the reduction, but after it. As Fink puts it, "the construal of phenomenologizing as a human action . . . does not arise from a *naïve captivation* in the natural attitude that would be got rid of and could be annulled by performing the phenomenological reduction. It is not a *dogmatism before the reduction*, but *a dogmatism after the reduction*."[40] The idea that all human acts, including phenomenologizing, are transcendental is itself a human theory, a piece of phenomenological dogma that does not precede the reduction, but grows out of it. One cannot answer the question of who phenomenologizes by pointing to man as a transcendental actor without stumbling into a vicious methodological circle, for the conception of man as a transcendental actor is a philosophical theory that arises out of the act of phenomenologizing.

More broadly, Fink argues against the possibility that it is "man and man alone" (in any capacity transcendental or otherwise) who phenomenologizes. For the sake of argument, let us suppose the contrary: phenomenologizing is done by man. If that were true, then the phenomenologist would have to claim something like the following: "by the fundamental reflection of the 'phenomenological reduction' [the phenomenologist] has in a quite definite sense gone beyond a restrictedness and captivation which is otherwise common to all men, that in some ultimate depth within his 'self' he has discovered 'world-constituting' (world-creative) subjectivity."[41] Fink rightly regards this possibility as pure hubris, as if an individual somehow possessed the power of world-constitution, which is tantamount to, "the usurping of creation by putting oneself in the place of God."[42] One can also imagine an existential critique of such a position: "Is this bold 'titanism,' documented in the construction of the transcendental subject, ultimately but mental sloth, a frivolous intellectual contrivance by a life that is alienated from the truly menacing and terrifying realities of human existence (death, fate, guilt, and other 'Last Things')?"[43] If phenomenologizing were *simply* a human act, then the resulting adequation of the individual (or any group of individuals) and transcendental subjectivity would render phenomenology nothing more than a "flight from finitude."

Yet if phenomenologizing is not *simply* a human act, what kind of act is it, and *who* is the actor? Fink argues that the mundane "look" of phenomenology, as a human act, does not exhaust its significance or meaning; for the mundane "look" occurs within the horizon of the natural attitude. In order to understand phenomenology *phenomenologically*, the natural attitude—including the mundane "look" of phenomenology—must be bracketed. Accordingly, as Fink states, "sentences in which the one phenomenologizing makes statements about the phenomenological reduction are not understandable at all if one does not *oneself* perform the phenomenological reduction."[44] The reduction introduces into transcendental life a cleft wherein subjectivity, "passes from the stage of sheer *'being-in-itself'* to *'being-for-itself.'*"[45] It is the transcendental onlooker, i.e., phenomenologizing I, that awakens in the reduction to view the previously hidden world-constituting activity of transcendental subjectivity. Consequently, it is not man, as a being-in-the-world, who ultimately performs the reduction, but the transcendental onlooker: "Performing the reduction produces the unambiguous, secure, and unforgettable certainty that the proper (ultimately actual) subject of phenomenologizing is the *transcendental* onlooker."[46] In other words, phenomenologizing is not an act that is possible so long as the world-constituting activity of subjectivity goes unrecognized in the natural attitude; rather, by phenomenologizing, transcendental subjectivity awakens to itself. Phenomenologizing is thus a *transcendental act*—"the transcendental *self-movement of constituting life.*" There is, therefore, a crucial difference between mundane science and phenomenology: The one who phenomenologizes is not the same one who performs mundane scientific acts. The subject (i.e., the *who*) of mundane science is man; the phenomenologizing subject is not man *qua man*, but transcendental subjectivity self-objectivated *as man*. As Fink puts it,

> The *full-sided* subject of phenomenologizing is neither the transcendental I (sticking to its transcendentality), nor "man" closed off against the transcendental, this closure being what constitutes the naïveté of the natural attitude; the full-sided subject is rather *transcendental subjectivity "appearing" ["erscheinende"] in the world* . . . the "who" under inquiry is a theorizing subject that must be characterized *both as transcendental and mundane.*[47]

The transcendental onlooker, the phenomenologizing I, is *meontic*—a transcendental subject (and thus a non-being) that exists *enworlded*, as a being-in-the-world. Yet the "enworlding" of the *meontic* phenomenologizing subject is not in the mode of forgetfulness with respect to its transcendental origins, "but is precisely the worldly objectivation of *knowing about transcendental origin*."[48]

The second point of comparison between phenomenology and science is "potential scope." Mundane science, for its part, is conducted by humans, and has as its objects of investigation those things that exist in the world. Thus the potential scope of worldly science "lies *from the very first in the horizon* of man's possible ways of behaving in relation to the existent."[49] Of course the "possibility" of a science does not imply its actuality. Modern astronomy was not an actual mode of relation between man and the cosmos before Galileo; astronomy was nonetheless within the horizon of human possibility. As Fink puts it, "in the opening of a new science *man* recognizes . . . that he has thereby *not transgressed the horizon of his possibilities* but only fulfilled them."[50]

Phenomenology is, as we have seen, a very different sort of science, whose objects of investigation include that which is *given* in existence as well as that which is *pre-given* as the constituting source of existence. Moreover the phenomenologizing subject is not man *as man*, but transcendental subjectivity self-objectivated *as man*. In the reduction, man rises above himself, *un-humanizes* himself, "passing . . . into the transcendental subject."[51] Phenomenology is not primarily a human act; it is a *transcendental* act. In other words, phenomenology is not a preexisting human possibility. Phenomenology becomes possible through transcendental subjectivity's self-awakening in the act of phenomenological reduction; it is not there beforehand as a human possibility in the way that, say, modern astronomy was a *possibility* for those living before Galileo. That is to say, the *possibility* of phenomenology is not preexistent in the realm of human possibility. When phenomenology appears as a human science, through the self-awakening of transcendental subjectivity, it constitutes an enlargement of man's possibilities. Fink puts it well:

> If then, *before* phenomenologizing *becomes actual*, its appearance as a human potentiality is not given in the natural attitude, if the self-satisfied naïveté of that attitude consists precisely in *blindness* to the transcendental interiority of life and thus in a restricted and biased openness for *possibilities that are only human*, then there occurs with the fact of the (non-proper) *enworlding* of phenomenologizing an *apparent enlargement* of the realm of man's possibilities.[52]

After the reduction, the transcendental source of existence becomes a theme for human investigation; the "appearance" of the existing world (and beings-in-the-word) becomes transparent with respect to its transcendental significance. Thus the potential scope of phenomenology is *transcendental truth*, which includes the realm of *given* existence along with its *pre-given* transcendental context.

The third point of comparison between mundane science and phenomenology is intersubjectivity. On Husserl's interpretation of the genesis of objectivity, scientific objectivity has to do with intersubjective communicability. The claims generated by science gain objectivity in direct proportion to the ability of such claims to, "make possible an institutional habituality in knowledge ('science') that persists throughout all the change intrinsic to human transitoriness."[53] So, for example, a claim like, "the Earth orbits around the Sun," attains scientific objectivity because it can be communicated and verified by any number of different individuals at different places and times; it is true no matter who says it or where they say it.

Clearly, the mundane appearance of phenomenology can be intersubjective in the sense of a worldly science; we can all read Husserl and discuss phenomenological theory across cultures and times. Yet the mundane appearance is the *result* of a transcendental phenomenological performance. There must, therefore, be some difference between the intersubjectivity of worldly science—an intersubjectivity based in the realm of human possibilities—and the intersubjectivity of phenomenology, as a *"transcendental cognitive process."*[54] The question is whether phenomenology, as a *transcendental* science, is intersubjective. And, if so, what is transcendental intersubjectivity?

Fink argues that phenomenological intersubjectivity has two senses. First, there is an intersubjective relation between co-phenomenologizers: "Transcendental intersubjectivity, then, is the community relationship, played out purely in the transcendental theater, on the part of the *many who perform the reduction* and achieve phenomenological knowing and which now 'appears' in the world as the intersubjectivity of those philosophizing."[55] Transcendental intersubjectivity, in this sense, is constituted through an "intentionality of empathy" toward other subjects, who also have a constitutive relation to the world, and who form a transcendental community of monads. When phenomenology appears in the world, there is the possibility of conveying phenomenological knowledge to others, thereby creating an intersubjective community of phenomenologizing subjects.

The second sense of transcendental intersubjectivity is much broader, including not only co-phenomenologizing subjects but also the entire sweep of the "history of world-constitution." With regard to its mundane appearance, phenomenology occupies a particular point in world-history. It began at a certain time (arguably with Husserl's work in the early 1900s) in a certain place (Germany), and has a particular role in the progression of Western thought. Yet phenomenology's place in world history has everything to do with its mundane appearance (and mundane history), not its transcendental content. Just as the object-world is constituted, so also mundane history is, "*constituted* in a transcendental, intermonadic sense-bestowal, just as is the world as a whole; that mundane history is nothing other than the universal *constituted time-form* for constituted beings; that it is fundamentally *something constituted in end-constitution,* just as they are."[56] By establishing that world-time, and hence world history, are *constituted,* the phenomenological reduction brings into view a transcendental idea of history, in which all constituting processes that affect worldly "destinies of the spirit" are open for phenomenological investigation. According to Fink, the reduction opens up the possibility of a "*transcendental-concrete history of world constitution.*"[57] World history becomes "constituting intermonadic historicity."[58] Phenomenology is thus temporally intersubjective, in the sense that it brings to light (and investigates) the entire history of co-constituting (intermonadic) acts of world constitution, despite its particular historical situation in Western culture.

In sum, it is clear that phenomenology differs vastly from mundane science. Whereas the latter is fundamentally human, phenomenologizing is an act performed not by man *as man,* but by transcendental subjectivity self-objectivated as man. Where worldly science is restricted to the horizon of human possibility, phenomenology enlarges the realm of human possibility by making the world, and everything contained in it, transparent with respect to its transcendental origin. Additionally, the intersubjective constitution of objectivity in mundane science bears only a slight resemblance to the intersubjective community of co-philosophizers. The temporal intersubjectivity of science, based as it is in world-time, is a constituted result, whose source(s) may be investigated by phenomenology in a "transcendental-concrete history of world constitution." In short, the relation between mundane science and phenomenology is little more than analogical, though the analogy itself is quite instructive, if only in a negative sense. As Fink states, "the scientificity of phenomenological knowledge, organized as it is into the unity of a science, is *toto caelo different* from that of the mundane sciences as a whole."[59]

C. Absolute Science as Self-Referential Science

Having defined phenomenology negatively, as that which is *not* a mundane science, it behooves us to advance a positive concept of phenomenology as an absolute science. This section will attempt to adumbrate the basic structures of absolute science.

The whole question of absolute science turns on one's notion of the Absolute. Given that phenomenologizing is a transcendental act, its "absoluteness" must be assessed in transcendental terms—i.e., one cannot uncritically adopt worldly meanings of the term "absolute." Particularly problematic is the common idea of the Absolute as that which stands in opposition to relative truths. For instance, Fink notes a mundane-ontological concept of the Absolute arising from Platonic and Aristotelian philosophy: "the mundane concept of 'absolute' is a *counterconcept to 'relative'* and means *a mode of being*, namely, being as non-relative, self-sufficient substance (οὐσία)."[60] Such non-relative substances are linked in the "commercium" of the "universal being complex of the world."[61] Thus it is the existence of the world that is absolute, and the world itself becomes "the Absolute."

Mundane conceptions of the Absolute will not suffice for phenomenology, for the phenomenological reduction shows that the world is not, in fact, an absolute self-sufficient totality. The world is, "only a *relative 'universe'* which in itself refers back to transcendental subjectivity."[62] The world, as the horizon of the existent, does not constitute an absolute totality unto itself, but it is the constituted counterpart of transcendental subjectivity. It is important to note that the "relativity" of the world does not indicate a separation between the world and transcendental subjectivity, as between two substances. As Fink puts it, the relativity of the world should be construed as, "a relation in play *within* transcendental life itself."[63] Transcendental life includes both the world, as *telos*, and constituting subjectivity.

Given the transcendental "thrust" of phenomenology, we might suspect that the Absolute is tantamount to the constituting life of transcendental subjectivity. Yet this is problematic too. On the one hand, before the reduction (when transcendental subjectivity has not "awakened" to its own activities), world-constitution is the Absolute; it is a totality unto itself. After the reduction, however, the constituting life of subjectivity is no longer an absolute totality, for the reduction introduces a non-constituting countertendency into transcendental life in the form of the phenomenologizing I. Hence the Absolute, after the reduction, encompases both transcendental constitution and transcendental phenomenologizing. As Fink states, "the Absolute is the overarching total unity of transcendental life as a whole, which in itself is articulated into opposites. The division between constituting and phenomenologizing life determines now the concept of the Absolute: the Absolute is the synthetic unity of antithetic moments."[64] Consequently, phenomenology, as absolute science, involves reflection on the constituting life of subjectivity (including its *telos*: the world) and the transcendental process of phenomenologizing. In others words, phenomenology is necessarily self-referential, integrating reflection on constitution with reflection on its own procedure.

Granting this concept of the Absolute, what would an absolute science "look like" in practice? Fink characterizes absolute science in three ways: "1) with regard to the *object*, 2) with regard to its '*subject*,' 3) in the *mode* of its knowing."[65] First, the object of absolute science is the Absolute itself, as the synthetic unity of world-constitution and phenomenologizing life. When absolute science is actualized, the Absolute moves from being-in-itself, in the unconcsious unity of world-constitution, to being-for-itself, aware of its own constituting and phenomenologizing activities. The Absolute is thus a synthetic dualism of two antithetic transcendental tendencies: the tendency toward world-constitution and the countertendency toward self-reflection. The science of the Absolute must have as its *object* the synthetic unity of both tendencies: "Both the constitutive and the countermoving 'transcendental' tendencies . . . compose in their *play 'together' against each other* precisely the *synthetic unity of the Absolute*."[66] Thus the being-in-itself of the Absolute together with the being-for-itself, which occurs through the transcendental performance of the phenomenological reduction, makes up the "object" of absolute science. This implies that phenomenology, as absolute science, has as its purview the constituting acts of subjectivity, which terminate in the world, as well as the phenomenologizing acts through which the Absolute becomes "for-itself."

The being-in-itself and being-for-itself of the Absolute are reflected in Fink's division of phenomenology into the "theory of elements" and "theory of method": "It is as the transcendental *theory of elements* that absolute science is thematically directed to the mere *being-in-itself* of the Absolute, i.e., to the synthetic unity of world-constitution and world . . . But as transcendental *theory of method* it refers to itself, it is the *thematization of the absolute tendency of becoming-for-itself*."[67] Having characterized the Absolute as the "object" of absolute science, the crucial question, which determines the phenomenological sense of the Absolute, is: How are the theory of elements and the theory of method related in regard to the subject and method of absolute science?

If the Absolute is the object of absolute science, it is also the "subject" of such a science. When comparing phenomenology and mundane science, it was shown that the one who phenomenologizes is not man, but transcendental subjectivity self-objectivated as man. In the previous treatment of the "subject," we sought to resolve the worldly appearance of phenomenology—i.e., that it is man who phenomenologizes—by subsuming it in transcendental truth: it is not man, but transcedental subjectivity who phenomenologizes. It is now no longer necessary to resolve the antithesis between human philosopher and the transcendental phenomenologizing I; rather, given that the Absolute is a synthetic unity of antithetical tendencies—namely, world-constitution and phenomenologizing—the antithesis between enworlded man and the transcendental, phenomenologizing I may be rightly seen as, "a necessary antithesis *in* the synthetic unity of the Absolute."[68] The human philosopher is as much a part of the Absolute as the phenomenologizing I is; phenomenology is *both* an enworlded human activity *and* a transcendental activity on the part of the phenomenological onlooker. Phenomenology is, as Fink claims, "just as much something *mundanely existent* [*mundan seiend*], i.e., human philosophizing, as it is something '*transcendentally existent*' ['*transzendental-seiend*'], i.e., the cognitive action of the phenomenological onlooker."[69]

Yet even as phenomenology is *both* enworlded *and* transcendental, it is important to recognize that the enworlding tendency remains antithetic to the transcendental tendency within the synthetic life of the Absolute. Recall from our comparison of phenomenology and mundane science that the following hypothesis was considered and rejected: it is man who phenomenologizes because all human actions are transcendentally significant. We are now in a better position to see why that hypothesis was fundamentally misguided. Enworlded activity is not transcendentally significant by virtue of being enworlded, but precisely because the enworlding tendency is *diametrically opposed* to the transcendental tendency (though both tendencies exist in the synthetic unity of the Absolute). Enworlded activity *becomes* transcendentally significant by virtue of the Absolute becoming for-itself through the transcendental *countertendency* of self-elucidation, which arises in and through the phenomenological reduction. In other words, that which is enworlded *is* transcendentally significant, but only inasmuch as it coexists in synthetic unity with the transcendental countertendency of self-reflection. The Absolute, as the subject of absolute science, contains both of these antithetic tendencies—i.e., the enworlding tendency and the tendency toward phenomenological self-elucidation. Moreover, that which it elucidates is its own constituting and phenomenologizing activity. That is to say, the Absolute is both the object and the subject of absolute science—not in the sense that it projects itself outside itself as an object (*à la* Hegel), but in the sense that its being-in-itself exists in a synthetic unity with its being-for-itself.

Having clarified the subject and object of absolute science, we may now speculate about the mode of cognition appropriate to absolute science. In mundane science, the goal is *certainty*, or at least a very high degree of certainty. Phenomenology, on the other hand, aims at *evidence*, which Husserl defined as an adequation of intention and intuition.[70] Yet, as a transcendental performance, the *evidence* to which phenomenology aspires cannot be restricted to worldly notions of apodicticity. In the reduction, even Husserl's early definitions of *Evidenz*, relying on concepts of intentionality and intuition, must be bracketed.

Fink rightly recognizes that what is at stake in a transcendental notion of evidence is, "a *reduction* of the *Idea of the 'thematic domain,'* an Idea which belongs to every worldly science."[71] Mundane science, according to Fink, "is science by man about that which is existent . . . The totality of the existents which man is not is the *external* world for him. Originating in the natural attitutde, science is first of all a particular theoretical behavior on the part of man *toward his external world*."[72] In bracketing the natural attitude, phenomenology also brackets those concepts of evidence that rely upon a relation between man and the outer world: subject and object, interior and exterior, transcendence and immanence, intention and intuition. For absolute science, the object of cognition is not something outer-worldly, in the mundane sense of "objective," nor is it something inner, in the mundane sense of "subjective." As Fink notes, "the *self-cognition of the Absolute is not 'relative'*; there is no external world for the Absolute, and therefore also no *self separated off* from some such world."[73] Hence the mode of cognition, or mode of evidence of absolute science cannot be reckoned in terms of transcendence and immanence; in fact, the very idea of self-elucidation, inasmuch as it presumes a sort of transcendental self-objectification, functions only as an analogy for Absolute being-for-itself.

In the final analysis, even the distinction between the theory of elements, as a thematic approach to world-constitution, and the theory of method, as a thematic approach to the phenomenologizing subject, is only an analogy (via worldly conceptions of phenomenal objects and phenomenologizing subjects) for Absolute being-for-itself: "the transcendental theory of method . . . now *sublates itself* in the concept of absolute science, insofar as the *antithetic distinction* of the transcendental theory of elements and the transcendental theory of method disappears in the final synthesis of absolute knowing."[74] The thematization of world-constitution is interwwoven with the thematization of phenomenologizing; both constitute "moments" in the Absolute's becoming-for-itself. In absolute science, the Absolute comes to know itself *absolutely* in all its myriad functions. As Fink puts it, "*Absolute science*, toward which phenomenologizing is organized, is, as the *actuality of the being-for-itself of the Absolute, the system of living truth* in which *it knows itself absolutely.*[75] This "truth" is not a truth in the mundane universal, "once-and-for-all" sense, but a *living* truth that encompasses in a single unity both the constituting performance, whose *telos* is the world, and the phenomological performance, whose telos is being-for-itself.

How, one wonders, would such absolute cognition work "on the ground"? How does one phenomenologize absolutely? Fink, rather unfortunately, has little to say on this point, though he does make two very suggestive claims in his characterization of absolute science. First, he claims that the antithetic divide between the theory of elements and the theory of method disappears in absolute science. He does not say that the antithesis between enworlding and phenomenologizing disappears (rather, it remains in the synthetic unity of the absolute), but the distinction in *thematic domain* disappears. The *theory* of elements and the *theory* of method become one interrelated theoretical enterprise—i.e., reflection on the world, including phenomenal objects appearing in the world and constitutive acts that terminate in the world, is bound up with theoretical reflection on the act of phenomenologizing. One leads to the other. The *theory* of elements, which first becomes possible through the phenomenologizing acts of transcendental subjectivity, also produces the thematic field of the theory of method—namely, the phenomenologizing I. In the synthetic unity of the absolute, the two theoretical approaches are revealed as one continuous theoretical enterprise, through which the Absolute becomes for-itself. In other words, phenomenology, as an absolute science, is a continuous hermeneutical circle: phenomenological investigation of phenomena in the world (theory of elements) leads to a phenomenological investigation of phenomenology itself (theory of method), which then results in a transcendentally clarified theory of elements.

A phenomenology of biology, for instance, might start by examining a biological phenomenon like human life, asking questions like: What is the region of being thematized in biology? Does biological science exhaust the phenomenological significance of human life?[76] If not, what is the proper regional ontology of human life, and how would it be formulated phenomenologically? In asking about the *proper* regional ontology, phenomenology turns from a theory of elements to a theory of method, for what the phenomenologist really asks is: How might the theoretical and methodological assumptions of phenomenology be adjusted in order to reveal the true transcendental significance of human life? Once that is accomplished, the biological approach to human life can be situated—better, *grounded*—in the Absolute's becoming for-itself. Similarly, a phenomenology of scripture would examine scripture as a phenomenal "element," which would then have implications for the method of phenomenology itself, which would, in turn, have implications for a phenomenology of scripture. One might wonder where the hermeneutical circle stops. When does phenomenology stop and say, "*this* is absolute knowledge" or "*this* is the absolute science of scripture?" Fink is suggestive on this point as well. The Absolute, for Fink, is "meontic." It is neither a being nor a non-being, but a synthetic unity of both *given* being and the *pre-given* constitutive source of being. For this reason, the Absolute cannot be completely conceptualized in wordly terms or any other terms that properly apply only to *given* being. Similarly, the *telos* of absolute science does not derive from the aims of worldly science. It is not as if the Absolute is an object "out there" in the world, whose final truth, meaning and significance might be revealed by the correct scientific practice. Rather, absolute science is, "a system of living truth"—the science of the ever-evolving *life* of the meontic Absolute. The becoming-for-itself of the Absolute is not an inquiry that reaches a final conclusion. Absolute science, i.e., phenomenological science, is part and parcel of the *life* of the meontic Absolute; phenomenology cannot transcend the Absolute in order to offer a final objective account of the Absolute. Bruzina puts it well:

> [W]hen the ultimate level of [phenomenological] interpretation is *meontic*, the effect is to cancel utterly the possibility of final positive interpretive sense; the heart of phenomenology is the opening in which the ultimate source of the very movement of constitution in temporalization turns out to be an Absolute structured by radical methodological negation.[77]

Thus phenomenology, as a science of the meontic Absolute, is an infinite hermeneutic.

One might imagine that phenomenology's lack of finality is a cause for despair, a nihilistic admission of scientific failure. Yet the *desire* for interpretive finality does not properly belong to absolute science; it belongs to those sciences whose goals and methods derive from the natural attitude. To put it in terms of Husserl's argument in the *Crisis*, it is only through a Galilean mathematization of nature (which gives rise to the natural attitude) that the desire for complete and final mathematical knowledge of nature arises. Such a desire is rightly suspended in the phenomenological reduction. More importantly, phenomenology does not need interpretive finality in order to ground the sciences, for the ground [*Boden*] on which the sciences rest is precisely the "living truth" of the meontic Absolute.

The scientific crises that phenomenology hopes to solve are not universal; they are particular crises that have arisen at a particular time in the history of the West. Phenomenology's solution to these crises need not be universal and final, but practical, addressing concrete problems in the evolving life (the becoming-for-itself) of the Absolute. Additionally, phenomenology's lack of interpretive finality is in no way nihilistic. As Fink states, "Meontic philosophy is not a flight into Nothing, but rather fidelity to the world [*Welt-treue*] in the deepest sense: the finite, being, time will not be abandoned (left aside) for the sake of a mystical sinking into the Nothing, but instead will be *drawn out of the Nothing*, 'created.' "[78] Phenomenology is not a retreat into interpretive nihilism, but an "opening-up" of the entire panoply of the Absolute. Far from despair, the phenomenologist shares the Psalmist's joy at the infinite wonders of creator and creation: "marvelous are thy works; and that my soul knoweth right well" (Ps. 139:14).

Conclusion to Part I

Phenomenology *Ex Vivo*

The previous chapters introduced the major tools and methods of phenomenology, while also pointing out a trajectory of radicalization beginning with static phenomenology, proceeding through genetic phenomenology, and culminating in generative or constructive phenomenology. Husserl's early work, while profound, was limited by Cartesian assumptions about subjectivity. Genetic phenomenology avoided the "Cartesian way" by historicizing both subjectivity and objectivity as genetic counterparts originating in the life-world, though Husserl's reflections on the life-world were complex and problematic. On the one hand, Husserl retained his early regressive mode of analysis, seeking to conceptualize, or "ontologize," the life-world by reasoning "backwards" from phenomena appearing in the world. On the other hand, Husserl hinted at a progressive mode of analysis that takes the life-world as *pre-given* ground and horizon. The full implications of this turn to *pre-givenness* were, perhaps, not grasped by Husserl, but were later explored by Anthony Steinbock and, more saliently for our purposes, Eugen Fink, whose phenomenological notion of the Absolute includes both *given* world-constitution and the *pre-given* constitutive and phenomenological performances of absolute subjectivity. The Absolute, for Fink, is the synthetic unity of given and pregiven, of constituting life and phenomenologizing life. Thus absolute science, as the self reflection of the Absolute, is, *"the system of living truth* in which [the Absolute] *knows itself absolutely."*[1]

In all of this, one of the fundamental structures of phenomenology becomes apparent: phenomenology involves a hermeneutical return to its founding goals and methods, re-interpreting them in light of new philosophical problems and practical concerns. In Fink's work, phenomenological self-reference is lifted to a new level. No longer is self-elucidation simply a *tendency* of phenomenology, but a *necessity*. Phenomenology,

73

as a unified theoretical enterprise, including both thematic reflection on world-constution and thematic reflection on the act of phenomenologizing, is *necessarily* self-referential and proceeds in a hermeneutical circle. Phenomenological reflection on "elements" leads ineluctably to phenomenological reflection on the transcendental method of phenomenology, which leads, in turn, to a transcendentally clarified reflection on the "elements." Moreover, the hermeneutical circle of phenomenological investigation is ceaseless. The meontic Absolute profers no final interpretive sense.

In the end, the radicalized, meontic idea of absolute science developed in part I stands as a reproach to the text of the first three chapters. Inasmuch as I have specified in advance the theoretical concerns relevant to a phenomenology of scripture, I have vivisected the Absolute, excising theoretical speculation from the the phenomenological hermeneutic that should properly begin with scripture; I have theorized *about* absolute science outside of the "living truth" of the absolute science of scripture. If one takes the transcendental hermeneutic of absolute science seriously, then the theory and method of a phenomenology of scripture cannot be properly specified apart from a phenomenological engagement with scripture. The *ex vivo* treatment of absolute science, while certainly useful in establishing the philosophical "landscape" of phenomenology, will prove valuable only to the extent that it can be situated *in vivo*—in the "living truth" of the absolute science of scripture.

Part II

Absolute Science in Practice

The Kenotic Reduction

Introduction to Part II

In part I, I argued that theoretical reflection on the phenomenological method exists in a "synthetic unity" with phenomenological analysis of elements within the circular hermeneutic of absolute science. That is to say, phenomenology, as an absolute science, has as its theme both phenomenal objects and the performance of phenomenology. My original focus on the phenomenological method was necessary to clarify the idea of absolute science, but the theory of method remains incomplete as long as it is detached from concrete life-world phenomena. Accordingly, part II completes the hermeneutical circle by tying reflection on the phenomenological method to a particular phenomenon: the kenōsis hymn (Phil. 2:5–11). The resulting phenomenology of scripture has the structure of absolute science: a phenomenological reading of the kenōsis hymn leads to clarification of the phenomenological method, which leads to a more intricate reading of scripture and a kenotically radicalized notion of the phenomenological method. The upshot is an absolute science of scripture whose categories and methods are defined in the process of reading scripture.

To that end, chapter 4 recounts the history of interpretation of the kenōsis hymn, focusing on interpretive disputes arising from particular theological, philosophical, and historical assumptions. Chapter 5 offers a phenomenological reading of the kenōsis hymn, with two practical goals: First, by drawing an analogy between kenōsis and the phenomenological reduction, I offer a phenomenologically reduced reading of the hymn that neutralizes the problematic assumptions explored in chapter 4. Second, by expanding the analogy between kenōsis and reduction, I develop a phenomenologically radicalized notion of the "kenotic reduction" as a reduction from *cosmos* to *new creation*. Chapters 6 and 7 explore the spatiotemporal character of the *new creation* disclosed in the kenotic reduction.

4

The Life and Times of Philippians 2:5–11

^{2:5}τοῦτο φρονεῖτε ἐν ὑμῖν ὃ καὶ ἐν Χριστῷ Ἰησοῦ, ⁶ὃς ἐν μορφῇ θεοῦ ὑπάρχων οὐχ ἁρπαγμὸν ἡγήσατο τὸ εἶναι ἴσα θεῷ, ⁷ἀλλὰ ἑαυτὸν ἐκένωσεν μορφὴν δούλου λαβών, ἐν ὁμοιώματι ἀνθρώπων γενόμενος· καὶ σχήματι εὑρεθεὶς ὡς ἄνθρωπος ⁸ἐταπείνωσεν ἑαυτὸν γενόμενος ὑπήκοος μέχρι θανάτου, θανάτου δὲ σταυροῦ. ⁹διὸ καὶ ὁ θεὸς αὐτὸν ὑπερύψωσεν καὶ ἐχαρίσατο αὐτῷ τὸ ὄνομα τὸ ὑπὲρ πᾶν ὄνομα, ¹⁰ἵνα ἐν τῷ ὀνόματι Ἰησοῦ πᾶν γόνυ κάμψῃ ἐπουρανίων καὶ ἐπιγείων καὶ καταχθονίων ¹¹καὶ πᾶσα γλῶσσα ἐξομολογήσηται ὅτι κύριος Ἰησοῦς Χριστὸς εἰς δόξαν θεοῦ πατρός.

^{2:5 NRSV}Let the same mind be in you that was in Christ Jesus, ⁶who, though he was in the form of God, did not regard equality with God as something to be exploited, ⁷but emptied himself, taking the form of a slave, being born in human likeness. And being found in human form, ⁸he humbled himself and became obedient to the point of death—even death on a cross. ⁹Therefore God also highly exalted him and gave him the name that is above every name, ¹⁰so that at the name of Jesus every knee should bend, in heaven and on earth and under the earth, ¹¹and every tongue should confess that Jesus Christ is Lord, To the glory of God the Father.

For first- and twenty-first-century Christians alike, Philippians 2:5–11 stands as one of the most alluring and theologically significant parts of the New Testament. The "kenōsis hymn" has been read as a Christological statement, an ethical example, a soteriological story, and a dogmatic summary of the incarnation and cross.[1] The goal of this chapter is to take stock of three important exegetical issues that will inform a phenomenological interpretation of the hymn: first, the overall purpose of the hymn as stated in 2:5; second, the nature of Christ's "equality" with God in 2:6; and third, the relation between the hymn's two parts—namely, 2:6–8, which narrates Christ's "self-emptying," and 2:9–11, which recounts Christ's exaltation.[2] In each case, I will argue that recent interpretations of the hymn involve hermeneutical and theological tensions that may be resolved by a phenomenological approach.

A. The Hymn's Purpose

The purpose of the kenōsis hymn has been debated since antiquity. Generally speaking, readers regard it in one of three ways: (1) as a statement of Christology; (2) as an ethical example of self-sacrifice; and (3) as a summary of God's salvific activity. Ancient readers often saw these three modes of interpretation as complementary. Cyril of Alexandria, for instance, links the Christological, soteriological, and social/ethical functions of the hymn to the differing functions of the Father, Son, and Spirit in the οἰκονομία (economy) of the Trinity:

> Let us reflect, then, that being by nature God, since he even appeared from God, shining forth ineffably and incomprehensibly from God the Father's very substance, he is for this reason quite reasonably regarded as completely in his form and in equality with him, as is in fact true; and yet "he humbled himself," as Scripture says, "taking the form of a slave," becoming, that is, as we are, that we might become as he is, refashioned by the activity of the Spirit into his likeness by grace. Since, then, he is one of us, he is a human being like us because of us; but he is God because of himself and the One who begot him, both before the Incarnation and when he became a human being.[3]

For Cyril, the various functions of the hymn converge in the unity of the economic Trinity: The Son, though equal with the Father (Christological), humbly became man so that "we might become as he is" (soteriological), and so that the body of Christ (social/ethical) might be conformed to his likeness by the grace of the Spirit. Paul's readers, then, are meant to conform to Christ's example of obedience and humility through the action of the Holy Spirit, as befits membership in the body of Christ. Cyril's Trinitarian theological commitments serve to unify various interpretations of the hymn. Modern biblical criticism, by contrast, lacks a theological grounding. (After all, a modern Bible scholar might claim that the Trinity is never explicitly mentioned in scripture. Patristic Trinitarian readings of the hymn are therefore anachronistic.) Accordingly, modern readers tend to view the Christological, soteriological, and ethical interpretations of the hymn as mutually exclusive—the hymn is either Christological *or* ethical *or* soteriological.

Modern debates about the hymn's purpose and function revolve around the exegesis of 2:5, which exhorts readers to be like Christ in some way: "τοῦτο φρονεῖτε ἐν ὑμῖν ὃ καὶ ἐν Χριστῷ Ἰησοῦ"—"Let the same mind be in you that *was* in Christ Jesus." Much of the dispute centers on a missing word in the Greek text. The relative clause in the second part of the verse is elliptical; there is no verb. English translations often supply the verb "was," and while that may seem like an insignificant addition, the choice of verb potentially alters the meaning and function of the hymn. To illustrate this point, let us consider a few different ethical and soteriological interpretations of the hymn.

Ralph P. Martin notes three types of ethical interpretation of the hymn, which differ based on the verb supplied in 2:5: (1) the imitative interpretation, (2) the paradigmatic interpretation, and (3) the mystical interpretation.[4] The imitative interpretation, which is perhaps the most well known, supplies a form of the verb "to be," usually "ἦν," the third person singular imperfect form of "εἰμί"—"I am." The NRSV thus renders the verse: "Let the same mind be in you that *was* in Christ Jesus." Paul exhorts his readers to *imitate* the "mind that *was* in Christ Jesus," which is now exemplified in the hymn. O'Brien summarizes the force of this reading: "The Philippians are to have among themselves the same disposition and manner of life as Christ Jesus in his freely willed renunciation of the heavenly power and glory that he possessed before the incarnation."[5] On this interpretation, the phrase "ἐν Χριστῷ Ἰησοῦ"—"in Christ Jesus" refers to the individual person, Jesus Christ, whose conduct the Philippians are meant to imitate.

The paradigmatic interpretation is a variation on the imitative interpretation. Recall that the NRSV translates the first part of 2:5 as, "Let the same mind be in you . . ." This translation relies upon an inferior text (i.e., a version that is not well-attested in the manuscript tradition), which uses the passive imperative, "φρονείσθω" in place of the active imperative "φρονεῖτε," which has far better attestation in the manuscript tradition.[6]

The NRSV's translation treats "τοῦτο" ("this") as the subject of the passive imperative ("let *this* mind be . . ."), and the preposition "ἐν" ("in") is used in the locative sense of "in" or "within" ("in you (ὑμῖν)"). Yet if one uses the active imperative, "φρονεῖτε," the meaning of the verse changes dramatically. C. F. D. Moule reconstructs 2:5 using the superior text and filling in the ellipses as follows: "τοῦτο [τὸ φρόνημα] φρονεῖτε ἐν ὑμῖν ὃ καὶ ἐν Χριστῷ Ἰησοῦ"—"adopt towards one another, in your mutual relations, the same attitude which was found in Christ Jesus."[7] In this case "τοῦτο [τὸ φρόνημα]"—"the same attitude" is the *object* of the active imperative "φρονεῖτε," and "ἐν ὑμῖν" has the locative sense of "among you" or "toward one another." Additionally, "ἐν Χριστῷ Ἰησοῦ"—"in Christ Jesus" refers to the person of Jesus Christ, in whom the attitude of humble obedience is found. Moule also accepts the addition of "ἦν" ("was") in the second part of 2:5, so long as it is understood as, "which (mind or attitude) was also found in (the case of) Christ Jesus."[8] On this reading, the humble obedience of Christ serves as a *paradigm* for personal interaction within the body of Christ.

A mystical interpretation of the hymn's function is also possible if one supplies the verb "to have" or "to regard" in the second part of 2:5. C. H. Dodd argues for such an interpretation. Supplying the verb "to have," and reading the phrase "ἐν Χριστῷ Ἰησοῦ" as referring to a mystical communion with Christ, Dodd translates 2:5 as follows: "In a word, have the same thoughts among yourselves as you have in your communion with Christ Jesus."[9] Interpreted in this way, the mystical communion with Christ gives rise to a communal ethic that is exemplified by Christ's humble obedience in the hymn. As Dodd puts it, "Here we have ethics developing directly out of Christ-mysticism."[10] Similarly, Adolf Deissmann reads the hymn as a "cultic confession" that reinforces the community's mystical connection to Christ: "[The kenōsis hymn is] a confession of the primitive apostolic cult, made by Paul the prisoner in order to rally his fellow-worshippers of Jesus Christ round the object of their cult, round a form at once divine, human, and divine again. The confession can be understood only by the pious simplicity of silent devotion."[11] On the mystical reading, the hymn is an expression (or confession) of the mystical union with Christ, which has vast moral implications for the body of Christ.

On the imitative, paradigmatic, and mystical interpretations, the hymn functions as a moral exemplar: "Christ is presented as a model to be followed."[12] Although such ethical interpretations are widespread, there are notable detractors. Ernst Käsemann, in particular, rejects the idea that the hymn presents Christ as an ethical example, and suggests a soteriological reading of the hymn instead. His argument centers on the meaning of the phrase "ἐν Χριστῷ Ἰησοῦ" (2:5), which, on the "moral exemplar" interpretation of 2:5, refers to the individual Jesus Christ, whose humble obedience we are meant to imitate. There is, however, considerable evidence that "ἐν Χριστῷ Ἰησοῦ" refers not to a particular person, but to the corporate body of Christ. On this point, Käsemann echoes Rudolf Bultmann, who argues that the phrase "ἐν Χριστῷ Ἰησοῦ" is an ecclesiological or eschatological formula denoting not the individual, Jesus Christ, but membership in the body of Christ:

> "In Christ," far from being a formula for mystic union, is pri-marily an *ecclesiological formula*. It means the state of having been articulated into the "body of Christ" by baptism, although baptism need not be implied in every instance . . . Since the Church, into which baptism incorporates the member, is the *eschatological* Congregation, the formula "in Christ" has not only ecclesiological but at the same time eschatological meaning.[13]

As an example, Bultmann cites II Corinthians 5:17, "ὥστε εἴ τις ἐν Χριστῷ, καινὴ κτίσις· τὰ ἀρχαῖα παρῆλθεν, ἰδοὺ γέγονεν καινά"—"So if anyone is in Christ, there is a new creation: everything old has passed away; see, everything has become new!" In this case, "ἐν Χριστῷ"—"in Christ" clearly does not refer to the individual person of Jesus Christ but the ecclesiologi-cal body of Christ; the reference to "new creation" (καινὴ κτίσις) in Christ is patently eschatological. The ecclesiological use of "ἐν Χριστῷ Ἰησοῦ" is also clear in Galatians 3:28: "οὐκ ἔνι Ἰουδαῖος οὐδὲ Ἕλλην, οὐκ ἔνι δοῦλος οὐδὲ ἐλεύθερος, οὐκ ἔνι ἄρσεν καὶ θῆλυ· πάντες γὰρ ὑμεῖς εἷς ἐστε ἐν Χριστῷ Ἰησοῦ"—"There is no longer Jew or Greek, there is no longer slave or free, there is no longer male or female; for all of you are one in Christ Jesus." Here, being "one" in Christ Jesus refers to the *ecclesia* rather than Jesus Christ the individual. One could also argue that the unity of the body of Christ ("you are one in Christ"), which transcends the distinc-tions between Jew and Greek, slave and free, and male and female, is an eschatological unity.[14]

Based on Bultmann's insight into the ecclesiological formula, Käse-mann argues that "ἐν Χριστῷ Ἰησοῦ" is a technical formula meaning "in the realm of Christ."[15] Such formulae were common in the Hellenistic world, deriving from, "an understanding of being, according to which man conceives his existence on the basis of the world that determines him."[16] By proclaiming themselves to be "in the realm of Christ" ("ἐν Χριστῷ Ἰησοῦ"),

Paul's readers proclaim Christ as "Lord of all" ("κοσμοκράτωρ," over and against the current "powers and principalities"), the basis of a new world that is already inaugurated in the body of Christ. In doing this, "the new world is already manifest in the community itself, and it becomes evident that the obedient one is himself the author of the obedient ones."[17] Taking "ἐν Χριστῷ ᾽Ιησοῦ" in this way, Käsemann adds "φρονεῖν δεῖ" to 2:5b, rendering the verse: "τοῦτο φρονεῖτε ἐν ὑμῖν ὃ καὶ φρονεῖν δεῖ ἐν Χριστῷ ᾽Ιησοῦ," the sense of which is, "Behave in the same way toward each other as it is fitting to behave within the realm of Christ Jesus."[18] The force of the hymn, then, is to remind Paul's readers that they are "in Christ" and, as such, occupy a particular place in the soteriological drama of salvation-history. Ralph P. Martin nicely summarizes Käsemann's interpretation of the hymn:

> The Philippians had been guilty of quarrelsomeness and arrogance (2:1–4). They have set before them in this passage of 2:6–11 not a lesson to imitate or an ethical ideal to follow, but a solemn reminder that they are "in Christ" and as such brought into the sphere of redemptive history, i.e. into the Church by the One who was obedient and wrought salvation by placing them in a new world. Let them confess with all creation the lordship of Christ and take upon themselves the true obedience in submission to his authority.[19]

On Käsemann's reading the hymn does not provide an ethical example but a soteriological story, which vividly illustrates how Paul's readers came to be "in Christ." As Käsemann states, "Paul did not understand the hymn as though Christ were held up to the community as an ethical example. The technical formula 'in Christ' . . . unquestionably points to the salvation-event; it has soteriological character, just as, according to Paul, one comes to be 'in Christ' only through the sacrament."[20] For Käsemann, the soteriological reading and the ethical reading are mutually exclusive. The soteriological reading makes better exegetical sense of "ἐν Χριστῷ ᾽Ιησοῦ." It also allows for a comprehensive reading of the hymn. The ethical interpretation, on the other hand, fits verses 2:6–8, where Christ empties himself—such behavior is surely worth emulating!—but it makes little sense when applied 2:9–11, where Christ is exalted by the Father, for how can Christ's exaltation be *imitated*? If, however, one reads the hymn as presenting the drama of salvation history, 2:6–11 may be read as one cohesive unit. Käsemann argues, therefore, that the soteriological reading of the hymn is preferable on exegetical and theological grounds.

To summarize: the Church Fathers often read the hymn as a dogmatic Christological statement, a moral exemplar, and a summary of salvation-history. These interpretations were knit together by Trinitarian theology. Specifically, in the case of Cyril of Alexandria, the different "layers" of interpretation reflect the actions of the Father, Son, and Holy Spirit within the economy of the Trinity. Modern interpreters, who do not share Patristic theological commitments (at least as far as historical methodology is concerned), tend to see the Christological, ethical, and soteriological functions of the hymn as mutually exclusive: the verb in 2:5a is either φρονεῖτε or it is not; "ἐν Χριστῷ Ἰησοῦ" is either an ecclesiological formula or it is not. It is, however, important to note that such dyadic thinking is not in the text itself; 2:5 does not explicitly tell us that it is *either* ethical *or* soteriological. Modern divisions between Christological, ethical, and soteriological readings are not products of the text, but products of the modern mind imposed onto a text that is not specific about such things. Yet how can this situation be remedied? It is naïve to think that biblical scholarship can return to pre-modern modes of interpretation. Modernity happened, after all! As will be argued in the next chapter, a phenomenological reading of the hymn allows for the integration of the ethical, Christological, and soteriological functions of the hymn without presupposing Patristic theological commitments.

B. Christ's Equality with God

It will be helpful to examine briefly the nature of Christ's relationship to God in the context of the hymn. Verse 2:6 states that Christ was "in the form of God" ("ἐν μορφῇ θεοῦ") and did not regard equality with God as "something to be exploited" ("ἁρπαγμὸν . . . τὸ εἶναι"). Both phrases influence the sense of the verb "ἐκένωσεν"—"he emptied himself" in 2:7. Consequently, interpretation of 2:6 plays a large role in debates about Christology and the nature of kenosis, which will inform the phenomenological interpretation of the hymn in the next chapter.

Readings of "ἐν μορφῇ θεοῦ"—"in the form of God" fall into roughly two camps. First, it is possible to read μορφή (form) as a synonym for οὐσία (being, essence).[21] On this reading, 2:6 reveals something about the nature or essence of the preexistent Christ. As Hawthorne puts it, "Thus when this word is applied to God, his μορφή must refer to his deepest being, to what he is in himself, to that 'which cannot be reached by our understanding or sight, precisely because God is ἀόρατος [invisible]: in fact the word has meaning here only as referring to the reality of God's being.'"[22]

Interpreted in this way, the hymn relates the process through which the divine, preexistent Christ "emptied himself" to become human. On this view, the hymn's theological significance has to do with the metaphysics of incarnation. As Sarah Coakley asks, "What *is* being 'emptied' in this hymn? On one reading, which is the more obvious one if one assumes that the hymn is talking about Christ's person pre-existence . . . the 'emptying' refers to the moment of incarnation and the humility of the divine act in becoming human."[23]

Second, it is also possible to interpret "ἐν μορφῇ θεοῦ" as a "functional" reference to Christ's stature with respect to the Father, rather than a metaphysical statement of Christ's preexistent essence or being. James D. G. Dunn, for example, claims that "μορφὴ θεοῦ" (form of God) is lexically equivalent to "εἰκὼν θεοῦ" (image of God), as both μορφή and εἰκών are used in the Septuagint (and elsewhere) to translate the Hebrew "צלם."[24] By reading "μορφή" as "εἰκών," Dunn sets up a parallel between Christ, who is "in the image of God" (2:7) and Adam, who was created "in the image of God" (Gen. 1:26–27). The kenōsis hymn therefore presents Christ as a new Adam, who fulfills God's plan for creation where the old Adam failed. So Dunn:

> *The Christ of Phil. 2.6–11 therefore is the man who undid Adam's wrong*: confronted with the same choice, he rejected Adam's sin, but nevertheless freely followed Adam's course as fallen man to the bitter end of death; wherefore God bestowed on him the status not simply that Adam lost, but the status which Adam was intended to come to, God's final prototype, the last Adam.[25]

On Dunn's reading, "ἐν μορφῇ θεοῦ" has nothing to do with the metaphysical elements of Christ's preexistence; rather, it has to do with Christ's status as the last Adam. The kenōsis hymn turns not on the incarnation, but on the cross, which is the "bitter end" of Adam's path, and the resurrection, which accomplishes God's original design for humanity.

Similarly, interpretations of "ἁρπαγμός" in 2:6 can be grouped into two camps, reflecting grammatical and semantic ambiguity in the hymn's use of the word.[26] It may refer to a thing *already having been* seized (*res rapta*) or a thing *to be* seized (*res rapienda*).[27] The first sense, *res rapta*, implies a "prize which, already in the possession of the owner, is held on to."[28] Karl Barth has something like this in mind in his interpretation of 2:6: "The thing that is '[Christ's] own' is in fact his equality with God. He could lay hold on that and assert and defend his property as a robber does his spoil. That is the meaning of *harpagmon hēgeisthai*: to cling tooth and nail to something."[29] On this reading, equality with God was something that Christ possessed as part of his preexistent nature. He did not "cling tooth and nail" to that equality, as a robber might his spoils, but renounced it (or at least renounced the "μορφή" of equality) in the incarnation: "Christ, *being* equal with God, has no need to assert himself in that or cling to it, but can renounce the outward appearance and credit that correspond to such being."[30] 2:6 therefore has to do with Christ's preexistence and the decision to become incarnate. Indeed, Barth is very clear that Christ's "self-emptying" in the hymn has to do with the incarnation: "He comes to 'exist in the image of man' (we recall by way of explanation the *sarx egeneto*, 'and the Word became flesh,' of John 1:14, and the still sharper Pauline parallel in Rom. 8:3: *en homoiōmati sarkos hamartias*, 'in the form of *sin-dominated* flesh'!)."[31] Martin nicely summarizes the implications of reading "ἁρπαγμός" as *res rapta*: "The chief point that Paul is making—on this understanding of the text—is the assertion that He already possessed this equality and, being tempted to hold on to it, He chose rather to let it go in His decision to become incarnate."[32] The interpretation of "ἁρπαγμός" as *res rapta* supports a reading of the hymn wherein Christ's preexistence and the metaphysics of incarnation are the central issues.

The "ἁρπαγμός" phrase may also be interpreted as *res rapienda*—that is, a thing to be seized. On this view, equality with God is something *to be* seized, something *not* in Christ's possession during the time period represented by the participle "ὑπάρχων" in 2:6. The idea is that Christ does not usurp or steal equality with God in the way that Adam tried to become like God; rather, equality is freely given to Christ by God: "In the Pauline context, it expresses the truth that He was tempted to seize what He did not actually possess, namely, the equality with God."[33] Accordingly, the *res rapienda* interpretation has to do with Christ's soteriological status, not his nature: although he was in the form of God, Christ did not try to seize equality by force (like Adam), but received it through humble obedience. Jean Héring argues for this view, claiming that Christ received a greater dignity at the exaltation than he had in his preexistence ("*une dignité supérieure à celle don't il avait joui dans se preexistence*").[34] Martin summarizes Héring's interpretation:

> This greater dignity is understood in the context to follow from the fact that, in his eternal status, Christ was in the *image* of God, but not then King of the universe. The choice which faced

Him was whether He would aspire to the dignity in His own right by snatching at it, or receive it from the Father by treading the path of lowly submission and obedience. He chose the latter course; and is rewarded by being exalted above the rank which he enjoyed as the eternal image of God.[35]

As Martin's summary makes clear, the res rapienda view comports well with the idea that "μορφή" is synonymous with "εἰκών": Christ is eternally "in the image of God," but receives the status of "κύριος" ("Lord") at the exaltation recounted in 2:9–11. The res rapienda view also characteristically involves a parallel between Christ and Adam. A. M. Hunter is explicit about this:

But if μορφή here has the sense "image," at once we get a clue to what follows . . . There is a clear reference to the Genesis story of the First Adam's fall . . . The Second Adam might have conceived the senseless project of seizing by force (ἁρπαγμός = res rapienda) the equality with God he did not as yet possess, but conquering this temptation to which the First Adam fell, he chose the way of obedience unto death.[36]

Thus, on the reading of ἁρπαγμός as res rapienda, the hymn is concerned not with metaphysical truths about the incarnation, but Christ's soteriological status as the Second Adam.

Having delineated two ways of reading "μορφή" and "ἁρπαγμός"—one that focuses on Christ's preexistent essence and another that focuses on Christ's soteriological status vis-à-vis the Father—we might wonder what, if anything, is at stake in the distinction. Sarah Coakley points out that each interpretation has theological consequences:

If Philippians 2 is *not* talking about Christ's divine pre-existence, then the whole matter of kenōsis is, from the start, not a matter of speculating about divine characteristics and the effect on them of the incarnation, but rather a *moral* matter of Jesus' 'self-sacrifice' *en route* to the cross . . . If, on the other hand—as has been the more normal reading from early in the church's exegesis—pre-existence and incarnation are assumed to be at stake in the passage, then sooner or later the metaphysical question necessarily presses: What, exactly, has been 'emptied' at the incarnation? Is this merely a figure of speech, or does it connote an actual loss of divine power—temporary or otherwise?[37]

As Coakley notes, the kenōsis hymn is source material for metaphysical speculation about the incarnation *if and only if* one takes Christ's pre-existence to be the main subject of the hymn. If, on the other hand, one takes the hymn to be a soteriological drama about Christ's status in salvation-history, then the metaphysical Christological questions never come up. What is important to notice, for our purposes, is that modern biblical criticism once again takes a dyadic view of the hymn: either it is about Christ's preexistence or it is not; either it recounts Christ's status in salvation-history (as a new Adam) or it does not. A phenomenological reading, as will be shown in the next chapter, is able to hold these two readings of the hymn together. Ultimately, the hymn has to do with both the metaphysics of incarnation and the "moral matter" of Jesus' sacrifice on the cross.

C. Kenōsis and Exaltation: Feminist Readings

The kenōsis hymn includes a rather stark division between Christ's self-empyting (2:6–8) and exaltation (2:9–11). In the first section of the hymn, which recounts Christ's humble obedience "unto death—even death on a cross," Christ is the subject of every verb. In the latter part of the hymn, which tells of Christ's exaltation, God is the actor. The shift from 2:8 to 2:9 functions as an instance of *peripeteia*—namely, "a change of fortunes into the opposite . . . where such a change is, as we say, likely or necessary."[38] Indeed, this "shift of fortunes" is marked in the Greek by the double conjunction "διὸ καί," where "διό" is an inferential conjunction, suggesting that the succeeding verses should be inferred as the natural outcome of those preceding: Christ's exaltation is to be inferred from his humble obedience.

The inferential connection between 2:6–8 and 2:9–11 is nearly universally accepted (though its theological significance is often contested). As Martin puts it, "There is no quarrel with the general understanding of the verse as depicting the reversal of Christ's fortune and His elevation from the depth of humiliation to the glory of His Father's acknowledgement in Resurrection and exaltation."[39,40] In contrast to this general trend, however, feminist theologians have noted theological and exegetical problems stemming from the idea that Christ's exaltation results from his humiliation. Such readings run the risk of mischaracterizing kenōsis by reinforcing cultural and religious paradigms that idealize feminine self-abasement. The dispute between Daphne Hampson, Rosemary Radford Reuther, and Sarah Coakley (among other feminist thinkers) about the nature of kenōsis is particularly important for our purposes.

In *Theology and Feminism*, Hampson argues that the Christian myth (particularly the Christian conception of God) idealizes masculinity: "Thus God is seen as all-powerful. He does not need to consult. His will is what is right—by definition. He may appear to humans to be arbitrary, but the fact that He is God is justification enough for what He chooses to do. Perhaps even more significant, He is said to be self-sufficient . . . He is *a se*, entire unto himself."[41] God's aseity is an inherently non-relational, masculine ideal: "He is the eternal King, the Chairman of the board, the President of the institution, the Guru of the youth, the Husband of the wife, the General of the army, the Judge of the court, the Master of the universe . . . He is a rapist, never a lover, of women and of anyone else beneath Him."[42]

Hampson recognizes that she is presenting "God at his worst," but argues that masculine notions of God are inherent in the "Christian myth." Moreover, Hampson claims, "Such a conceptualization of God affects also the way in which human beings are understood."[43] God is strong; humans are weak. This pattern repeats itself in the relation between man and woman: "man is held to be superior to and the opposite of woman. Indeed 'man' may be held to represent God in relation to humanity, while 'woman' is conceived to represent humankind in relation to God."[44] The Christian notion of God thus exemplifies a hierarchical structure at odds with ethical trends of the post-Enlightenment period, such as, "self-actualization, equality and empowerment of others."[45] The Christian myth must, therefore, be abandoned: "we need to reconceive the notion of God in such a way that it will become tenable in this day and age (as I do not believe the Christian notion to be)."[46]

In contrast, Rosemary Radford Reuther argues that Christology rooted in the Jesus of the synoptic Gospels can be feminist:

> Once the mythology about Jesus as Messiah or divine *Logos*, with its traditional masculine imagery, is stripped off, the Jesus of the synoptic Gospels can be recognized as a figure remarkable compatible with feminism. This is not to say, in an anachronistic sense, that 'Jesus was a feminist,' but rather that the criticism of religious and social hierarchy characteristic of the early portrait of Jesus is remarkable parallel to feminist criticism.[47]

By focusing on Jesus's ethical teachings and ministry in the synoptics, Reuther emphasizes Jesus's prophetic opposition to unjust social practices and hierarchies: "the Word of God does not validate the existing social and religious hierarchies but speaks on behalf of the marginalized and despised groups of society . . . This reversal of social order doesn't just turn hierarchy upside down, it aims at a new reality in which hierarchy and dominance are overcome as principles of social relations."[48] Jesus's ministry, far from supporting masculinist social hierarchies, calls such hierarchies into question. Nowhere is this truer than in the kenōsis hymn, which Reuther reads as a "kenōsis of patriarchy":

> In this sense Jesus as the Christ . . . manifests the *kenōsis of patriarchy*, the announcement of the new humanity through a lifestyle that discards hierarchical caste privilege and speaks on behalf of the lowly. In a similar way, the femaleness of the social and religiously outcast who respond to him has social symbolic significance as a witness against the same idolatrous system of patriarchal privilege . . . Jesus, the homeless Jewish prophet, and the marginalized women and men who respond to him represent the overthrow of the present world system and the sign of a dawning new age in which God's will is done one earth.[49]

Thus the kenōsis hymn represents the "emptying" of unjust earthly social hierarchies, and the dawning of a new age where such hierarchies no longer form the basis of social interaction. Accordingly, Reuther argues that the Christ represented in the kenōsis hymn and synoptics is in keeping with feminist critiques of social hierarchies.

Hampson ultimately rejects Reuther's interpretation of the kenōsis hymn as insufficiently feminist. The "kenōsis of patriarchy" is a male answer to a male problem. The construction of patriarchal hierarchies in which men are superior to women is a particularly male activity; criticism of those hierarchies is, then, a solution to a largely male problem. Hampson is worth quoting at length here:

> Clearly *kenōsis* is indeed a critique of patriarchy. That it should have featured prominently in Christian thought is perhaps an indication of the fact that men have understood what the male problem, in thinking in terms of hierarchy and domination, has been. It may well be a model which men need to appropriate and which may helpfully be built into the male understanding of God. But . . . for women, the theme of self-emptying and self-abnegation is far from helpful as a paradigm. *Kenōsis*

is a counter-theme within male thought. It does not build what might be said to be specifically feminist values into our understanding of God.[50]

Self-abnegation is surely a valuable message for men who think in terms of their superior place in social hierarchies. Yet for women, the valorization of "self-emptying" or "self-abnegation" is far from useful in the context of hierarchies where women already occupy a lower status than men. The valorization of self-sacrifice, as a prerequisite to eternal salvation, can be particularly damaging to women in abusive relationships, for example. More helpful, according to Hampson, would be an example of "the mutual empowerment of persons," but that example seems to be lacking in "the symbolism of Christian theology."[51]

Sarah Coakley criticizes Hampson's reading for relying on a particularly modern notion of kenōsis, "where the 'emptying' is regarded as compensating for an existing set of gender presumptions that might be called 'masculinist.'"[52] In its original context, the kenōsis hymn probably meant nothing of the sort. Coakley sketches out four possible "Christological blueprints" of the hymn:

> Philippians 2 [is] a matter of Christ: (1) temporarily *relinquishing* divine powers which are Christ's by right (as cosmic redeemer); or (2) *pretending* to relinquish divine powers whilst actually retaining them (as gnostic redeemer); or (3) choosing *never to have* certain (false and worldly) forms of power—forms sometimes wrongly construed as "divine"; or (4) *revealing* "divine power" to be intrinsically 'humble' rather than "grasping."[53]

Of these four options, Hampson's critique would potentially apply to (1) or possibly (2), though Hampson presumably does not intend her critique to apply to (2), since a gnostic reading of the hymn is largely irrelevant to orthodox Christianity, which is the subject of Hampson's broader critique. Yet even restricting our consideration to (1), it is not entirely clear that Hampson's critique hits the mark. Referring particularly to the "history of religions" approach to the hymn, Coakley argues that,

> even though 'pre-existence' of a 'mythical' form was presumed in the interpretation of Philippians 2, the 'emptying' here was not seen to imply the *divesting* of some clearly defined set of divine characteristics . . . Rather, if anything, the Docetism

of the gnostic redeemer mythology still hung over its Pauline reworking: the Christ figure appeared only 'in the *form* of man,' feigning human weakness for the purposes of salvific activity.[54]

On this reading, the sort of "compensatory emptying" that Hampson criticizes is never in play. If anything, Christ only *pretends* to divest himself of divine powers, or only does so *temporarily*. The "emptying" is not therefore a simple act of self-abnegation, but an artful salvific act.[55]

As far as New Testament scholarship goes, Coakley considers Hampson's critique of kenōsis misguided. Yet we might argue on Hampson's behalf that her criticism does not presume the technical machinations of New Testament scholarship, but instead aims at a more general notion of kenōsis.[56] Moreover, it could be argued that Hampson's criticism is germane to the hymn itself: so long as kenōsis is a necessary precursor to exaltation, and so long as 2:6–8 is the inferential foundation of 2:9–11, then there is reason to read the hymn as valorizing self-abnegation, in which case the hymn certainly falls under Hampson's criticism of kenōsis.

New Testament interpretation aside, Coakley argues that Hampson relies upon the very gender stereotypes that she means to question. In particular, Hampson aligns masculinity with worldly power and femininity with a lack of power. The solution to this power imbalance involves women seizing power, simply replacing male with female at the top of a masculinist gender hierarchy. As Coakley puts it, "[Hampson's argument] appears to presume the very questions it is begging about gender stereotypes: the alignment of 'males' with achieved, worldly power, and women with lack of it. The presumption is that women *need* 'power'—but of what sort? How are they to avoid the 'masculinism' they criticize?"[57] Hampson presumes a masculine notion of power to which women should aspire. Her brand of feminism thus exists as the opposite of "masculinism," and as Aquinas tells us, "*eadem est scientia oppositorum*—one and the same is the science of opposites." Hampson's analysis ultimately has no room for notions of power that are not construed on worldly, masculine terms.

For Coakley, the answer to the problem of masculinist hierarchies does not consist in simply replacing male with female in the context of existing power structures. Rather, Coakley argues that "power" must be reconceptualized: "For what . . . if true divine 'empowerment' occurs most unimpededly in the context of a *special* form of human 'vulnerability'?"[58] Such divine power is paradigmatically and paradoxically expressed in the kenōsis hymn, which invites not just dispassionate Christological speculation, but entry into the body of Christ. Kenōsis thus involves a sort of *askēsis*, "a regular and willed *practice* of ceding and responding to the divine," which also consists in refraining from "grasping" abusive human power.[59] Kenōsis allows divine power to manifest itself because, "we can only be properly 'empowered' here if we cease to set the agenda, if we 'make space' for God to be God."[60] Coakley refers to the kenotic convergence of vulnerability (primarily toward God) and power as the "paradox of power and vulnerability," where "vulnerability" is a form of *contemplatio*, "not an invitation to be battered."[61] Given this analysis of kenōsis, Coakley argues that Hampson's view is problematic insofar as it consists in, "the *repression* of all forms of 'vulnerability,' and in a concomitant failure to confront issues of fragility, suffering, or 'self-emptying' except in terms of victimology. And that is ultimately the failure to embrace a feminist reconceptualization of the power of the cross and resurrection."[62] Because of her underlying commitment to masculine notions of power, Hampson is unable to entertain the possibility that true divine power *is* kenotic.

In the end, one sees the specter of Nietzsche in the background of Hampson's critique of kenōsis, Reuther's defense, and Coakley's response. Hampson claims that the kenōsis hymn valorizes self-emptying or self-sacrifice as a precursor to exaltation. If that were true, then Paul might well be accused of promoting a gospel that is ultimately life-denying, a gospel of "bad conscience," in which exaltation is the reward for a lifetime of denying one's natural will-to-power. Indeed, we hear clear resonances of kenōsis in Nietzsche's description of Christianity's divinization of self-hatred: "God sacrificing himself for the guilt of man, God himself exacting payment of himself, God as the only one who can redeem from man what has become irredeemable for man himself—the creditor sacrificing himself for his debtor, out of *love* (is that credible?), out of love for his debtor!"[63] Underneath this kenotic drama, Nietzsche argues, lies a will to self-torment, *ressentiment* turned inward. The Christian's debt to God, which is infinitely compounded by God's self-sacrifice (how could such self-sacrifice ever be paid back?), becomes the ultimate instrument of self-torture: "this man of bad conscience has taken over the religious presupposition in order to drive his self-torture to its most gruesome severity and sharpness. Guilt before *God*: this thought becomes an instrument of torture for him."[64] The parallels with Hampson's argument are clear: by valorizing self-sacrifice, the kenōsis hymn encourages women to accept on the basis of divine authority (and what could be more authoritative than that?) a social hierarchy in which their own will-to-power is inherently thwarted; this amounts to little more than religiously sanctioned self-torture. Far from empowering his readers, Paul's message encourages them to empty themselves of their own will-to-power.

This Nietzschean critique is exactly what Coakley hopes to avoid by redefining power to include vulnerability: "the paradox of power and vulnerability."[65] Coakley contends that kenōsis does not thwart the will-to-power, but fulfills it. In becoming vulnerable toward God, one achieves divine power through membership in the body of Christ, where "power" has been redefined kenotically. Coakley's answer to Hampson—and by extension, Nietzsche—is promising, though the appeal to paradox is somewhat unsatisfying. How, one wonders, is kenotic power ultimately "empowering" in a way that would escape a Nietzschean critique? More to the point, how can one be sure that Paul's message is life-affirming rather than life-denying? These important questions will guide our phenomenological reading of the hymn in the next chapter.

D. Conclusion

The history of interpretation of Philippians 2:5–11 raises a number of thorny exegetical, theological, and philosophical issues that will guide our phenomenological reading of the hymn. Specifically, recent interpreters tend to view the hymn's hermeneutical possibilities in terms of mutually opposed dyads: either the hymn is Christological, or it is not; either it serves as an ethical example, or it does not; either it is soteriological, or it is not. Such dyadic thought is hermeneutically problematic, as the text does not *authorize* one mode of interpretation over another. On the basis of the text, it is entirely possible that the hymn is simultaneously Christological, ethical, and soteriological. It remains for us to explain *how* such a reading is possible. Additionally, recent feminist critiques of kenōsis raise an important question about whether the kenōsis hymn, and by extension Paul's gospel, is ultimately life-denying. If self-emptying is a necessary a precursor to exaltation, it is difficult to see how kenōsis would not be subject to a Nietzschean critique of religion. While Coakley's reading of the kenōsis hymn is promising, it remains for us to show exactly *how* kenōsis can be empowering.

5

Kenōsis and
Phenomenological Reduction

The previous chapter explored a number of problems related to the history of interpretation of Philippians 2:5–11. This chapter lays out a phenomenological reading of the hymn that avoids those pitfalls by holding together the Christological, ethical, and soteriological functions of the hymn. Moreover, a phenomenological reading subverts the Nietzchean critique of self-sacrifice by refiguring divine power. By drawing an analogy between kenōsis and *epochē*, on the one hand, and *exaltation* and *reduction*, on the other, it will be argued that the kenōsis hymn operates as a type of phenomenological reduction—a *kenotic reduction* that is, in the end, far more radical than Husserl's reduction. Moreover, since the absolute science of phenomenology is inherently circular (see chapter 3), the kenotic reduction has implications for both our reading of the hymn and our conception of the phenomenological method.

A. A Brief Aside: What Does it Mean to Read
Phenomenologically?

If a phenomenological reading of the kenōsis hymn is possible, we need to know what it means to *read* phenomenologically.[1] On the one hand, the application of a philosophical methodology to scripture is a familiar tactic. A sort of "knight's move" has become fashionable in contemporary biblical studies: instead of moving straight ahead in prescribed patterns of interpretation, one situates scripture in the context of a tangential philosophical discussion.[2] So, for instance, the Tower of Babel becomes the subject of Derridean deconstruction;[3] the Apostle Paul undergoes Marxist analysis at the hand of Žižek;[4] and the Book of Job is read in terms of Bahktinian

97

polyphony.[5] In one sense, a phenomenological reading of scripture is no different: phenomenology functions as an external hermeneutical strategy applied to scripture.

Yet in another, deeper sense, a phenomenological reading of scripture is not akin to the "knight's move." Phenomenology, as absolute science, is not simply one more in a long list of philosophical hermeneutical strategies. The goal is not to import phenomenology as a tangential philosophical language, but to articulate an absolute science of scripture. That is to say, phenomeno-logical reading is a circular hermeneutical process with implications for both scripture and phenomenology. Phenomenology elucidates scripture, which in turn elucidates the phenomenological method. The *telos* of this process is a phenomenological method that perfectly matches the phenomenon at hand—scripture—so that it gives itself unrestrictedly or *self-evidently*. In the process of reading phenomenologically, the phenomenological method and scriptural phenomena approach each other asymptotically, resulting in an adequation of the phenomenological method and intuitive textual content. The kenōsis hymn is a particularly salient text because it describes a type of reduction and therefore directly implicates phenomenology's most important methodological procedure: the phenomenological reduction. Phenomenology is not a tangential philosophical discipline applied to the kenōsis hymn; rather, phenomenology is *essential*, for it allows one to grasp the transcendental significance of scripture, which in turn aids the transcendental processes of phenomenology. In other words, the affinity is mutual: the kenōsis hymn is phenomenological and phenomenology *is*—or *becomes*, in the hermeneutical process of reading—kenotic.

B. The Evolution of the Phenomenological Reduction

In order to assess the claim that the kenotic reduction radicalizes Hus-serl's phenomenological reduction, it will be necessary to examine how the reduction developed and changed over the course of Husserl's work, for only then will the "trajectory" of the reduction, as it moves toward its kenotic *terminus*, become apparent. In *Erste Philosophie*, Husserl speci-fies six reductions: the transcendental reduction, the phenomenological reduction, the apodictic reduction, the reduction to pure subjectivity, the phenomenological-psychological, and the reduction to intersubjectivity.[6] These reductions can be grouped according to Husserl's various "ways" into phenomenology. In a now famous article, Iso Kern delineates three ways: (1) the Cartesian way, (2) the psychological way, and (3) the ontological way.[7] Sebastian Luft follows Kern's divisions, but calls the third way, "The Way via the Lifeworld."[8] This name change reflects a significant amount of "play" in Husserl's treatment of the life-world. As was shown in chapter 2, Husserl's analysis of the life-world occurs in two modes: at times, the life-world is treated as an ontological correlate of intentional life; at other times, the life-world is treated as the pre-given ground and horizon of all experience. Husserl's reflection on the life-world therefore contains two "ways" into phenomenology: the ontological way and the way via pre-givenness. Consequently, we may distinguish four ways into phenomenology: (1) the Cartesian way, (2) the psychological way, (3) the ontological way, and (4) the way via pre-givenness.

The Cartesian "way" stems from Husserl's Kantian commitment to grounding the natural sciences on an apodictically certain foundation of truths. The central question is: how does one find apodictically certain truths? Our natural inclination may be to look toward experience, but experience of objects in the world is surely not indubitable. When I perceive my coffee mug, for instance, I perceive it only from one angle; I cannot perceive the whole thing at once. Moreover, my eyes play tricks on me: what looks like my favorite coffee mug from across the room may turn out to be an entirely different mug upon closer inspection. Once doubts about external perception and cognition are introduced, it becomes clear that the only way to guarantee our cognitions is to base them epistemologically on the indubitable inner workings of the Ego:

> If we are uncertain or unclear as to how it is possible for cognition to reach its object, and if we are inclined to doubt that such a thing is possible, we must have before us indubitable examples of cognitions or possible cognitions which really reach, or would reach, their respective objects . . . Here the *Cartesian method of doubt* provides a starting point. Without doubt there is *cogitatio*, there is, namely, the mental process during the [subject's] undergoing it and in a simple reflection on it . . . The *cogitationes* are the first absolute data.[9]

Following Descartes's method of doubt, Husserl claims that the processes of thinking are the first indubitable truths. Yet, whereas Descartes focuses on the Ego, using the indubitable *cogitationes* to prove that the *cogito* exists, Husserl focuses on the *cogitationes* themselves, arguing that the existence of the I, the *cogito*, is not an absolute datum. What is given indubitably is not the "mentally active ego, the object, man in time," but the pure phenomenon of cognition.[10] According to Husserl, Descartes's guiding question was something like: "how can I, this man, contact in my mental processes something existing in itself, perhaps out there, beyond me?"[11] Yet the "I" in this question carries with it transcendental baggage: the stable Ego, the "man in time," is an *object* of cognition, and is therefore subject to doubt as much as any other object. The "pure question," for Husserl, is not "how can *I* know the world around me?" but "How can the pure phenomenon of cognition reach something which is not immanent to it? How can the absolute self-givenness of cognition reach something not self-given and how is this reaching to be understood?"[12] In other words, how do the indubitable immanent processes of cognition give rise to any sort of transcendent objectivity? Husserl's earliest configuration of the reduction is designed to answer precisely this question.

The first step of the reduction, *epochē*, opens up the field of constituting subjectivity by suspending the natural inclination to look toward the object-world as the source of objectivity and meaning. In *Ideas I*, Husserl explores *epochē* through a thought experiment about the annihilation of the world.[13] This experiment is not intended as an idealistic negation of the world out-side consciousness, as was the case with Descartes's evil demon hypothesis. Rather, the experiment demonstrates that the "natural attitude" is a naïve orientation toward the object-world—a simple acceptance of what is given there. The annihilation of the world reveals that the object-world exists not as a reality unto itself, but in relation to consciousness. Thus, if one is going to examine *how* objectivity comes to be in relation to consciousness, the *general thesis* of the natural attitude, which isolates the objects of cognition, must be "put out of play" in order to examine the cognitive, constitutive action of consciousness. What remains after the natural attitude has been suspended is the absolute data of constituting consciousness.

Epochē, then, consists in suspending the natural attitude so that one might examine *how* objectivity comes to be. In *epochē*, I do not doubt that the object-world exists, but I refrain from making assumptions about how the object-world exists. As Husserl puts it, "The modes of acceptance opera-tive in naïve experience, the naïve effecting of which is one's 'standing on the basis of experience,' I put out of operation, I deny myself this basis."[14] Prior to the *Crisis*, Husserl does not draw a strict distinction between the methodological procedures of *epochē* and reduction. What remains after the *epochē* is considered reduced: "though we have 'excluded' the whole world . . . Strictly speaking, we have not lost anything but rather have gained the whole of absolute being which, rightly understood, contains within itself, 'constitutes' within itself, all worldly transcendencies."[15] Thus, in the "Cartesian way," the reduction takes its cues from Cartesian doubt, but does not focus on the individual *Ego cogito* over-and-against the object world; rather, the reduction brings to light the constitution of objectivity in the immanent life of consciousness. Despite modifying Descartes's method, Husserl's early work maintains Descartes's search for apodictic certainty, and reproduces the Cartesian duality of immanent consciousness and transcendent object-world.

The "psychological way" has roots throughout Husserl's corpus, from his critique of psychologism in the *Logical Investigations* to his clarification of transcendental psychology in the *Crisis*. The reason for Husserl's persistent engagement with psychology is that it shares phenomenology's object of investigation: consciousness.[16] Psychology, as a science within the natural attitude, takes as its object of study the object-world, particularly one aspect of the object-world: the human ego. Yet, inasmuch as it is beholden to the natural attitude, psychology can neither recognize nor analyze the transcendental depths of consciousness. As Sebastian Luft notes, "psychology is at first the thematization of a systematic science of (worldly) consciousness, but not transcendental subjectivity, because psychology as a positive science, due to its methodological naïveté, remains blind to the transcendental dimension."[17] Because psychology let its "task and method be set according to the model of natural science," it ultimately fails to "inquire after what was essentially the only genuine sense of its task as the universal science of psychic being."[18] If psychology were purely descriptive, without the limits of the natural attitude, it could not help but notice the *intentional* relationship between consciousness and the object world, leading ineluctably to transcendental reflection: "the consistent and pure execution of [psychology's task] . . . had to lead, of itself and of necessity, to a science of transcendental subjectivity and thus to its transformation into a universal transcendental philosophy."[19] On this view, the reduction is motivated not by a desire to exclude naïve belief in the being of the world, but by a desire to advance the discipline of psychology in its original scientific task.

Within the "psychological way," *epochē* brackets not just the general thesis of the natural attitude, but psychology's particular claim that the object-world suffices to explain the whole sphere of psychic being. The reduction, then, expands the science of psychology (in accordance with its original aims) to include the whole sphere of transcendental life, where object-world and transcendental (inter)subjectivity coexist as the end and beginning, respectively, of the transcendental process of world-constitution. As Husserl puts it,

> All the new sorts of apperceptions, which are exclusively tied
> to the phenomenological reduction . . . all this, which before
> was completely hidden and inexpressible, now flows into the
> self-objectification, into my psychic life . . . I [now] know of
> this whole dimension of transcendental functions, interwoven
> with one another throughout and extending into the infinite. [20]

Like the Cartesian way, the psychological way seeks out an absolute "realm" on which to ground the sciences, but in the psychological way, that realm is the entirety of transcendental subjectivity, not the *cogitationes* of individual subjectivity. The subject/object distinction that was the crux of the Cartesian way is not central to the psychological way, for both subject and object are enfolded in intersubjective transcendental life. Husserl thus moves away from his earlier focus on individual subjectivity, though his notion of intersubjectivity is still primarily individualistic, as a collection of transcendental "monads."

The "ontological way" and the "way via pre-givenness" both stem from Husserl's conception of the life-world in the *Crisis*; the difference consists in whether the life-world is treated as the ontological correlate of constituting subjectivity or the pre-given horizon of all experience. The ontological conception of the life-world can be seen as an outgrowth of the "Cartesian way." Husserl speaks of three headings within the Cartesian schema: "*ego—cogitatio—cogitata*: the ego pole (and what is peculiar to its identity), the subjective, as appearance tied together synthetically, and the object-poles."[21] Whereas the Cartesian way focused on the subjective *cogitatio* and ego-pole, the ontological way takes its cues from the *cogitata*, the object-pole: "although these headings are inseparable from one another, one must pursue them one at a time in an order opposite to that suggested by the Cartesian approach. First comes the straightforwardly given life-world, taken initially as it is given perceptually: as 'normal,' simply there. . . ."[22] The world, as it is given in simple perception, becomes the starting point for a regressive analysis via "manners of appearing" and "intentional structures," leading to transcendental subjectivity as the source of the constitutive processes that terminate in the life-world. As in the Cartesian way, the *epochē* of the ontological way involves the suspension of the general thesis of the natural attitude—i.e., the thesis that the object-world is a reality unto itself. Yet the *epochē* does not point to subjective *cogitationes*, but to the "universe of life-world objects." The *epochē* removes the "veil" of the natural attitude, revealing the world as life-world in "pure ontic certainty."

The reduction, in the "ontological way," does not seek to clarify the subjective structures of transcendental life; rather, the reduction opens up the possibility of an apodictically certain ontology of the life-world. As Husserl puts it, "But however [the life-world] changes and however it may be corrected, it holds to its essentially lawful set of types, to which all life, and thus all science, of which it is the 'ground' remain bound. Thus it also has an ontology to be derived from pure self-evidence."[23] Accordingly, the ontological way into phenomenology still relies upon a Cartesian schema, but does not take its cues from the Cartesian subject. In the Cartesian way, subjective *cogitationes* are taken as given, and the world is "constructed" thereupon; in the ontological way, the world is taken as given and subjectivity is constructed through a phenomenological regression from the life-world.

The way into transcendental phenomenology via pre-givenness is, in some sense, a counterpart to the psychological way, but without the Cartesian schema of the ontological and Cartesian ways. The turn to pre-givenness is adumbrated in Husserl's conception of the life-world as the "pre-given ground and horizon of experience," but is presented most clearly in Eugen Fink's *Sixth Cartesian Meditation*.[24] Husserl's Cartesian articulations of phenomenology tend to privilege that which is *given*—either individual consciousness, as the site of self-evidently given *cogitationes*, or the life-world, as the *given* ontological correlate of transcendental subjectivity. In contrast, Fink argues that what is *given* within the world-horizon is, in fact, the end result of transcendental processes of constitution. In order to investigate the sources of world constitution—and, hence, the source of all worldly science—everything having to do with *given being* (including the fundamental phenomenological category of *givenness*, and subcategories like finitude, presence, and even worldly forms of *pre-givenness*) must be bracketed. It is, then, the *pre-given* (perhaps it may be better to say "ungiven," since "pre-" has worldly temporal connotations) source of constituting life that is the target of the reduction.

Epochē, for Fink, does not bracket the *general thesis* of the natural attitude, but brackets everything that appears as given within the world-horizon, including individual consciousness, the ontological life-world, and all explanatory concepts derived from worldly being (e.g., finitude, presence, and all "mundanely pre-given time-structures"). The reduction, then, "places the just established 'onlooker' before *nothingness*: the world is bracketed and thereby as well the whole *pre-givenness* of the world, all world-possibilities; there remains as the single first theme . . . actual-moment flowing transcendental life with its undisclosed horizons."[25] The *pre-given* life-world is accordingly bracketed in the *epoché*, and revealed, through the reduction, to be the product of an enworlding tendency, which exists in synthetic unity with a transcendental tendency in the life of the Absolute. As in Husserl's early work, the goal of the reduction is to open up transcendental life for investigation, but the "depth" of transcendental life is much greater for Fink than it was in Husserl's Cartesian, psychological, and ontological ways. All facets of individual and intersubjective consciousness, and the entire life-world (as pre-given ontological correlate), are bracketed as the end results of the transcendental activities of Absolute life, which can never be captured entirely in worldly concepts of cognition, psyche, and being (*ontos*).

Throughout the various modes of reduction a trajectory becomes clear: individual consciousness and other concepts related to worldly being become less and less prominent. While the Cartesian way focused on *cogitationes*, the psychological way opens up a phenomenological psychology that transcends individual cognitive structures, revealing an intersubjective dimension to transcendental life. And while the psychological way individualizes intersubjectivity, as "monadic," the ontological way focuses on the life-world as a correlate to transcendental constituting life. Finally, Fink's notion of *epoché* and reduction radicalizes the "transcendental turn" by rejecting all conceptual categories derived from worldly existence, thereby calling into question all the previous ways into phenomenology. "Consciousness," "givenness," "being," "monadic" are all worldly terms that cannot be predicated of the Absolute in a univocal sense. What is really at stake, in the end, is the reduction from the world, and everything that appears within the horizon of the world (including Being and the individual), to the *pre-given* constitutive source of the world.

C. The Initial Hypothesis: The Kenōsis Hymn as a Reduction from Cosmos to Creation

In Fink's articulation of the phenomenological reduction, the analogy between reduction and the kenōsis hymn becomes clear.[26] By bracketing the world, and all being in the world, the human "I" of the natural attitude calls into question that which it fundamentally *is*. The human "I" relinquishes its ties to the world, emptying itself of its own humanity. As Fink states, "The transcendental tendency that awakens in man and drives him to inhibit all acceptednesses nullifies man himself; man *un-humanizes* [*entmenscht*] himself in performing the epochē, that is, he lays bare the transcendental onlooker in himself, he passes into him."²⁷ In other words, *epochē* empties the world and worldly existence of the significance assigned to it in the natural attitude: "It puts into question what all 'existential' philosophies of this kind presuppose, that upon which they rest assured: human being itself. . . . [I]t makes the world *questionable* in a way in which this is never possible on the basis of the world."²⁸ The *epochē* suspends worldly modes of thought and worldly values; even reason and language come under the purview of *epochē*: "[the phenomenological onlooker] 'reduces' language by demoting the natural-meaning sense of language in the explication of transcendental constitution to a mere '*analogization*,' he makes language into a *mere means* for the explications for which he himself has at his disposal no suitable language of his own."²⁹ *Epochē* ultimately constitutes a complete abdication of worldly being, truth, value, and reason. The character and meaning of an experience, an act, or a life, cannot be defined by values and terms derived from the world.

   Epochē is the kenotic moment *par excellence*—the putting-to-death of the world—a moment paradigmatically expressed by Christ on the cross, and recounted in the first stanza of the kenōsis hymn: "Christ Jesus, though he was in the form of God, did not regard equality with God as something to be exploited, but emptied himself, taking the form of a slave, being born in human likeness. And being found in human form, he humbled himself and become obedient to the point of death—even death on a cross" (Phil. 2:6–8). What is ultimately emptied in kenotic *epochē* is not Christ's divinity, nor his status vis-à-vis God, but the status of the *cosmos* as the ultimate ground of truth and value; Christ's kenotic act—whether one emphasizes the incarnation or the cross—turns worldly hierarchies upside down. The very idea that one who is equal to God, or who has equality with God within his grasp, would choose to become human and be crucified is completely at odds with worldly notions of power and authority. From the worldly standpoint, it makes little sense to forgo divine power in favor of human existence and slavish death. One would never choose to die like a slave when given the option to be Caesar; to do so would be inhuman. Kenōsis, as *epochē*, gives the lie to worldly values and modes of thought precisely by calling into question the *primacy* of worldly values and ways of thinking; *epochē* forces us to be open to the possibility that the cosmos, and its values, are *derivative* and ultimately limited in a pernicious sense. Philippians 2:6–8, as kenotic *epochē*, sets the stage for a kenotically reduced conception of the world, not as *cosmos* but as κτίσις (creation).

The phenomenological reading of kenōsis, as a "calling into question" of worldly values, is not particularly new. One finds a very similar idea in the ascetic Syriac tradition. Specifically, the fourth-century author of the *Book of Steps* claims that kenōsis is a "hidden self-emptying of the heart," an emptying of the heart's worldly desires.[30] Accordingly, the author summarizes 2:6–8:

> Christ did not want to become an equal of God by grabbing, as did Adam, but instead he emptied himself . . . of wanting to become God amid earthly riches; instead he took the likeness of a servant while he was in the likeness of that created first Man, in his obedience, love and humility, in order to show us how someone becomes a brother, son, heir and neighbor.[31]

Christ emptied himself of the *natural* human desire for wealth and power, adopting a "hidden purity." The notion of hiddenness in the *Book of Steps* comports nicely with Fink's idea of *epochē*, as a bracketing of that which is *given* within the horizon of the world. According to the *Book of Steps*, the hidden purity of kenōsis "cannot be seen by eyes of the flesh." Similarly, on the phenomenological reading, kenotic *epochē* is a transcendental "move" which opens up spiritual or transcendental realities that are not *given* within the horizon of the *cosmos*.[32]

The kenotic *epochē* is succeeded by the reduction proper. Just as the kenōsis hymn does not end at 2:8, so the phenomenological reduction does not end with *epochē*. As Fink states, "By the production of the phenomenological onlooker [in the *epochē*] we *gain* an immense new thematic field, the sphere of *transcendental subjectivity*, which was *hidden* in the natural attitude."[33] Whereas *epochē* suspends the world, reduction brings to light all the transcendental processes involved in constituting the world. Fink distinguishes between *epochē* and reduction in the following manner:

> If by the epochē we understand *abstention from belief*, then under the concept of "action of reduction proper" we can understand all the *transcendental insights* in which we *blast open captivation-in-acceptedness* and first recognize the acceptedness *as* an acceptedness in the first place. Abstention from belief can only be radical and universal when that which falls under disconnection by the epochē comes to be seen precisely *as a belief-construct, as an acceptedness.*[34]

The reduction thus discloses both the constituted world and constituting transcendental subjectivity as two moments in the synthetic unity of Absolute life. Through the reduction, I come to stand above the world, which is no longer the pre-given source of all truth and value, and "which has now become for me, in a quite peculiar sense, a *phenomenon*."[35]

Phenomenological reduction is, for Fink, a type of exaltation. In fact, reduced philosophical cognition is explicitly likened to divine knowledge: "already in German idealism there was the recognition that the traditional antithesis between '*intellectus archetypus*' and '*intellectus ectypus*,' which constituted the metaphysical difference between human and divine knowledge, in truth signified the antithesis between human and un-humanized [*entmenscht*] philosophical cognition."[36] Through the kenotic movement of *epochē*, human and worldly possibilities are put out-of-play. In reduction, the transcendental subject achieves that which is impossible for human subjectivity, namely, un-humanized or "divine" philosophical cognition of the world: "Man cannot *as man* phenomenologize, that is, his human mode of being [*Menschsein*] cannot perdure through the actualization of phenomenological cognition. Performing the reduction means for man to *rise beyond* (to transcend) *himself*, it means to *rise beyond himself in all his human possibilities*."[37] In reduction, man rises above the world as the pre-given ground of truth and value, and therefore exceeds worldly possibilities. The world, the *cosmos*, is revealed as the end product of the constituting acts of transcendental subjectivity; or to put it theologically, the *cosmos* is revealed as *created*.

The second stanza of the kenōsis hymn vividly relates Christ's exaltation: "Therefore God also highly exalted him and gave him the name that is above every name, so that at the name of Jesus, every knee should bend, in heaven and on earth and under the earth, and every tongue should confess that Jesus Christ is Lord, to the glory of God the Father" (Phil. 2:9–11). Through Christ's "emptying," the world is re-fashioned into a "new creation." The Word is restored to its rightful place and creation is brought into a right relationship with God, such that "every tongue should confess that Jesus Christ is Lord." In the kenotic *epochē*, the *cosmos* is called into question, while in the kenotic reduction proper, the *cosmos* comes to be seen in its proper transcendental context as *creation*, as a product of divine activity—i.e., the *cosmos* gains the transcendental sense of καινὴ κτίσις (new creation), where Christ is not δοῦλος (slave) but κύριος (Lord, master). Accordingly, the basic structure of the kenotic reduction, as presented in the kenōsis hymn, is a reduction from cosmos to "new creation."

D. Love and Power: Refining the Initial Hypothesis
after the Kenotic Reduction

If the kenotic reduction is a component of the absolute science of scripture, it must ultimately effect a hermeneutical return to both scripture and
the phenomenological method, clarifying both in light of transcendental
insights afforded by the reduction. In other words, in regard to scripture,
one might ask: how does the kenotic reduction help us *read* the kenōsis
hymn? And in regard to phenomenology: what does the kenotic reduction
tell us about the phenomenological method? This section will deal with
the first question; the implications for phenomenology will be discussed
in a succeeding section.

   The analogy between the kenōsis hymn and phenomenological reduction suggests a sort of kenotic reduction, but that analogy does not tell us
how to read the kenōsis hymn *in a kenotically reduced way.* Understanding *what* the structure of the kenotic reduction *is* does not automatically
produce an understanding of the meaning of the kenōsis hymn *after* the
kenotic reduction. What, one wonders, does the reduction teach about
reading? First, the kenotic *epochē* instructs us to bracket the *cosmos* as the
source of truth, validity, and meaning. No language or mode of reasoning
derived from the *cosmos* should predetermine our reading of scripture. So,
for instance, Heidegger's *Dasein*, restricted as it is to a worldly conception
of finitude, cannot determine our phenomenological hermeneutic in the
way that it determined Rudolf Bultmann's strategy of "demythologization."[38]
More importantly, in bracketing worldly modes of reason and language,
huge swaths of Platonic and Aristotelian philosophy, which have been
immensely influential in Christian theology, are ruled out. Salient for our
purposes is the Platonic and Aristotelian conception of *eros*, which has had
an enormous impact on modern understandings of kenōsis.

   In the Socratic tradition, love always stems from privation: one loves
what one does not have. Thus, in the *Symposium*, Socrates asks Agathon,
"Has he [i.e., the one who loves] or has he not the object of his desire and
love when he desires and loves it?" To which Agathon replies, "He does
not have it, most likely." Socrates then corrects Agathon. The connection
between love and privation is not only likely but necessary: "consider if
the desiring subject must have desire for something it lacks, and again, no
desire if it has no lack. I at least, Agathon, am perfectly sure it is a necessity." Love, for Socrates, is ultimately based on imperfection: "in general all
who feel desire, feel it for what is not provided or present; for something
they have not or are not or lack."[39]

For Aristotle, the Socratic notion of love implies an *erotic* hierarchy. One who is less perfect has need of one who is more perfect, but not vice versa: "the better of the two parties, for instance, or the more useful or otherwise superior as the case may be, should receive more affection than he bestows."[40] Warren Zev Harvey notes the implication: "This rule means, for Aristotle, that children should love parents more than parents love children, subjects should love rulers more than rulers love subjects, and wives should love husbands more than husbands love wives. It also means that the Unmoved Mover is loved, not loving."[41] God, for Aristotle, is the perfect being, lacking nothing. As such, God cannot love; the Unmoved Mover can be the object of love, but never the subject.

The Aristotelian paradigm of divine love is a widespread presence in Christian theology, particularly theologies of kenōsis. Aristotle's idea of love establishes a normative relation between perfection/power and imperfection/powerlessness: the one who is more perfect or powerful (and God is the most perfect and powerful) cannot love one less perfect or powerful. One who is more perfect never desires to become less perfect. Love is economic; it is about getting what one lacks. It therefore makes little sense for one as perfect as God to sacrifice himself for an imperfect creation; God needs nothing from creation. That kind of love can only appear as a paradox on the Aristotelian paradigm.

There are two primary ways of interpreting the kenōsis hymn that maintain the normative Aristotelian pattern: first, one may argue that God somehow maintains divine perfection throughout; the imperfection of creation does not negate divine perfection. On this approach, one must either explain *how* the Incarnate Son maintains divine perfection while being both fully divine and fully human (the main question of Patristic Christology prior to the Council of Chalcedon in 451 AD), or argue that the humanity or divinity of Christ is only an appearance (the Docetist and Arian approaches). The essential thing is that God never sacrifices God's power. The Aristotelian paradigm is maintained inasmuch as that which is perfect (God) would never desire to become imperfect. But a question arises: if God is perfect and powerful, and cannot love that which is less perfect, then why would God perform the kenotic act? This suggests a second Aristotelian approach to kenōsis: Christ's obedient vulnerability is a paradoxical form of divine power. That which is perfect and powerful would never desire to become imperfect and vulnerable, so power and vulnerability can only coexist *paradoxically*. (See, for example, Sarah Coakley's idea of "the paradox of power and vulnerability.")[42] Yet the coexistence of power and vulnerability is only paradoxical if power (perfection) cannot love vulnerability (imperfection). That is to say, "the paradox of power and vulnerability" is only paradoxical on an Aristotelian paradigm of love, where kenōsis is an inscrutable demotion from perfection to imperfection. Critics of kenōsis assume the Aristotelian paradigm just as readily. Like Aristotle, it is anathema to Nietzsche that one would truly sacrifice power for love. Authentic love can only be a form of the will-to-power, by which one acquires what one lacks, or by which one revels in one's own natural power; any other sort of self-sacrificial love is symptomatic of a "bad conscience" poisoned by ressentiment. Robert C. Solomon summarizes Nietzsche's critique of Christian love:

> Nietzsche's main argument concerning erotic love does not condemn eros but celebrates it. . . . Nietzsche points out, quite plausibly but also polemically, that love . . . is an emotional strategy of all-embracing possessiveness . . . Not surprisingly, Nietzsche sometimes subsumes both kinds of love, Christian and erotic, under his general rubric "the will to power," but the former quite straightforwardly so, the latter as part and parcel of his diagnosis of the slave morality of the weak in spirit.[43]

Love, for Nietzsche, is erotic; it has to do with getting what one lacks; it is agonistic. Self-sacrificial love, a love in which one who is more powerful sacrifices power on behalf of one who is less powerful, is a product of ressentiment. Thus love reflects an Aristotelian hierarchy of desire, in which the less perfect desires the more perfect only in order to gain something. The reverse possibility, in which the more perfect desires the less perfect, is ruled out in the very concept of eros. Self-sacrificial "love" is not truly love, but a life-denying desire on the part of a bad conscience bent on self-torture. The erotic paradigm is clear: power and kenōsis cannot coexist in any authentic sense. A vindication of kenōsis is, as Daphne Hampson argues, tantamount to an inauthentic valorization of powerlessness and weakness.[44]

In sum, the erotic paradigm is routinely invoked to explain, defend, or criticize various concepts kenōsis. It is, however, clear that eros is a concept derived from worldly finitude, for only that which is finite can truly lack something. As such, eros ought to be bracketed in the kenotic epochē. Yet what would non-erotic love look like? And how would that change our reading of the kenōsis hymn? In Or Adonai (Light of the Lord), Hasdai Crescas develops a phenomenologically suggestive notion of divine love, which effectively brackets Aristotelian eros, and which will be helpful in articulating a reduced conception of kenōsis. Let us consider Crescas's argument in more detail.[45]

Aristotle argued that God, as the perfect being, and as the ultimate object of love, lacks nothing and therefore cannot love. Crescas agrees with Aristotle's notion of God as the ultimate object of love, but rejects the idea that love stems from lack. Love, for Crescas, stems not from need or imperfection, but from power and perfection: "the love is in proportion to the perfection of the *lover.*"[46] Crescas supports his anti-Aristotelian notion of love by appealing to God's perfection:

> Inasmuch as it is known that God, may He be blessed, is the source and fountain of all perfections, and in virtue of His perfection, which is His essence, He loves the good, as may be seen from His actions in bringing into existence the entire universe, sustaining it perpetually, and continuously creating it anew, and all by means of his simple will, it must necessarily be that the love of the good is an essential property of perfection. It follows from this that the greater the perfection [of the lover], the greater will be the love and the pleasure in desire.[47]

Accordingly God, for Crescas, is both the ultimate object of love and the ultimate lover. God's perfection implies an infinitely abundant love, which is ultimately manifest in creation. In opposition to Aristotle's claim that love only flows up the hierarchy of perfection (the more perfect party always receives more love than is given), Crescas argues that love, originating in God, flows down the hierarchy of perfection (the more perfect party *gives more* love than is received). As Zev Harvey puts it, "God's love for the world is greater than the world's love for Him."[48] Crescas demonstrates this by examining the love between the Patriarchs and God in scripture:

> when it mentions the love of the Patriarchs for God, it uses the term *ahabah* [love], saying "Abraham my loving friend" [Isaiah 41:8], and in the commandments it also uses *ahabah* [e.g., Deuteronomy 6:5], but when it mentions the love of God for the Patriarchs, it uses the term *hesheq* [passionate love], which indicates the strength of the love, saying "Yet the Lord did passionately love [*hashaq*] the fathers" [Deuteronomy 10:15].[49]

On the Aristotelian paradigm, one would expect the Patriarchs' love for God to be of greater intensity than God's love for the Patriarchs, but the opposite is true: "*ahabah*," the everyday word for love, describes the Patriarchs' love for God, while "*hesheq*," denoting an exceedingly great love, describes God's love for the Patriarchs. The logic of Crescas's claim is the exact opposite of Aristotle's: God is perfect, so God loves perfectly!

By linking God's power with love, Crescas develops a concept of creation as an act of "overflowing" love. God, who finds joy in his own will, rejoices in causing his goodness and love to "overflow" onto creation. Crescas is worth quoting at length here:

> [Since] it has been demonstrated true beyond doubt that God is the true Agent of all existing things intentionally and vol- untarily, and sustains their existence through the overflowing of His goodness perpetually, and thus the Rabbis fixed the benediction, "He creates in His goodness each day continuously the Work of Creation" . . . it follows that in His intention- ally and voluntarily causing His goodness and perfection to overflow, He necessarily loves the increasing of goodness and the causing of his goodness to overflow. And love is nothing other than pleasure in his will, and this is the true joy, as it is said, "Let the Lord rejoice in his works" [Psalm 104:31]. This states explicitly the joy is in His works, that is, it is in His causing His goodness to overflow unto them by His sustain- ing their existence continuously in the most perfect of ways. In this regard, our Rabbis of blessed memory said in several places that the Holy One, blessed be He, "lusts for the prayer of righteous individuals."[50]

God loves causing His goodness to "overflow" onto creation, and thus "rejoices" in *creating*, which, as a supreme act of power, is also a supreme act of love. In God's great love for creation, Crescas situates the rabbinical claim that God "lusts for the prayers of righteous individuals"—a claim that makes absolutely no sense on an Aristotelian notion of love. For Crescas, all of creation is suffused with divine love; God "lusts" for the prayers of *created* individuals: "We may now envision Crescas's infinite spatiotem- poral universe as pulsing with love. Its infinite worlds are generated in love, sustained in love, and perfected in love."[51] Creation is effected and sustained by God's overflowing love.

In *eros*, there is a divergent relationship between love and power. God, who is supremely powerful, does not love. There exists, for Aristotle, a hierarchy in which one who is more perfect cannot love one who is less perfect; love flows only up the hierarchy of perfection, *from* imperfect *to* perfect, and not the other way around. Christ's kenotic "self-emptying," paradigmatically expressed in the incarnation and crucifixion, can only be seen as a retrograde, paradoxical sort of love: a demotion from divine perfection to human imperfection. In contrast, for Crescas there is a *convergent* relationship between love and power: God is supremely powerful, so God loves supremely. This implies that creation, as an act of power, is also an act of love. Moreover, by extending Crescas's insights to the incarnation and crucifixion, it may be claimed that God's love for humanity, recounted so vividly in the kenōsis hymn, is not a diminution of God, but an "overflowing" of divine power. Kenōsis is not a demotion from perfect to imperfect, not an emptying out of God's perfection, but an "overflow" of God's power and love for creation. By bracketing *eros,* as Crescas does, a *kenotically reduced* notion of kenōsis becomes possible, not as an "emptying out" or depletion of God's perfection, but as a "pouring out" of God's love and power onto creation, in the sense of an "overflow." Just as God's overflowing power and love generate and sustain creation, so also does God's love generate and sustain the "new creation" (καινὴ κτίσις). The kenōsis hymn, as the story of the "new creation," is not a story about God becoming powerless, but a story of God's supreme power and love for creation. A kenotically reduced paraphrase of the kenōsis hymn might go something like this: Christ Jesus, sharing God's power and love for creation, did not regard power as something to be held onto selfishly, but poured divine love onto creation, inaugurating through his life, death and resurrection a "new creation" to the glory of God. After the kenotic reduction, there is nothing paradoxical about the confluence of kenōsis and divine power, for God's creative power and love for humanity go hand-in-hand.

E. Ramifications of the Kenotic Reduction for Scriptural Studies

The initial hypothesis—i.e., that the kenōsis hymn is analogous to phenomenological reduction—solves many of the problems raised in the last chapter. Specifically, interpreting 2:6–8 as kenotic *epochē* and 2:9–11 as kenotic reduction allows for the accommodation of Christological, ethical, and soteriological readings without assuming any opposition between them. Additionally, a kenotically reduced re-reading of the hymn allows for a response to Nietzschean critiques of kenōsis.

The main point of the *initial* phenomenological reading of 2:6–8 is that Christ's kenotic act brackets worldly truth. Supposing that one reads "ἐν μορφῇ θεοῦ" as a Christological statement about the son's essence (οὐσία), 2:6 indicates that Christ has the same essence as God. 2:7 then says that Christ already possessed equality with God (*res rapta*), but did not regard it as something to guard jealously, as a robber might his spoils. Accordingly, in 2:8, he humbled himself out of obedience to the Father. Such a Christological reading calls into question worldly values, and serves as a fine demonstration of kenotic *epochē*: why, from the perspective of the cosmos, would one who shares the divine essence become human and die on a cross? What is "emptied" on this reading is not necessarily Christ's divinity (though that would still exemplify the kenotic *epochē*), but the cosmic system of values wherein it makes no sense for God to become man. 2:6–8 thus bracket the cosmos, and 2:9–11 offers a kenotically reduced picture of creation, in which Christ's true pre-existent divinity is given its rightful status so that, "every tongue should confess that Jesus Christ is Lord, to the glory of the Father."

A soteriological reading also fits with the idea of kenotic reduction. Suppose, for instance, one reads "μορφὴ θεοῦ" in 2:6 with James D. G. Dunn, as a synonym for "εἰκὼν θεοῦ." In that case, 2:6 sets up a parallel between Christ who is "in the image of God" and Adam who was made "in the image of God." 2:7 then indicates that Christ, who, like Adam, is in the image of God, did not make the same mistake that Adam did: Christ did not regard equality with God as something to be seized by force (*res rapienda*), but remained obedient to God, humbling himself to the point of death on a cross. Here again, the soteriological story of 2:6–8 calls into question worldly values: why would someone choose to die like a slave when it is possible to seize divine power? What is "emptied," here, is the cosmic hierarchy, in which divine status is always something to be seized, provided the opportunity. 2:9–11 brings the Christ/Adam parallel full circle, offering a kenotically reduced vision of creation in the scope of salvation-history. By remaining obedient, by not seizing divine power, Christ undoes the damage that Adam did, thereby renewing creation in accordance with God's soteriological vision, so that "every knee should bend, in heaven and on earth and under the earth."

When read phenomenologically, the soteriological and Christological elements of the hymn also comport nicely with an ethical interpretation. Ernst Käsemann argued that a soteriological reading necessarily *excludes* any ethical reading. He claimed that any interpretation where Christ serves as an ethical example cannot make sense of the division between 2:6–8 and 2:9–11. Christ's self-emptying may well provide an example to be imitated, but Christ's exaltation in 2:9–11 is by nature inimitable. In contrast, the phenomenological reading allows for the idea that Christ's performance of the reduction (whether it is a Christological or a soteriological performance) is meant to be replicated by Paul's readers in both its phases: kenotic *epochē* and reduction. In their interactions with each other, the Philippians should not proceed according to worldly values—"Do nothing from selfish ambition or conceit, but in humility regard others as better than yourselves" (2:3). Rather, Paul exhorts the Philippians to perform the kenotic reduction—"Let the same mind be in you that was in Christ Jesus" (2:5)—so that they might exemplify a kenotically reduced "new creation" in their ethical interactions with each other and the larger community. On this reading, 2:6–8 and 2:9–11 serve as examples to be imitated, even though the division between 2:8 and 2:9 is in no way negated. If 2:6–8 is the bracketing of cosmic value, truth and meaning, then 2:9–11 is the transcendental disclosure of the new creation—two important and distinct transcendental acts unified in the kenotic reduction.

Finally, *after* the kenotic reduction, a reading of the hymn becomes possible that subverts Nietzschean critiques of kenōsis. By bracketing *eros*, in which power and love ultimately diverge, a concept of divine love *as* divine power emerges. Creation, as Crescas envisions, is the result of an "overflowing" divine love. Similarly, the "new creation" is generated and sustained by God's loving power. The kenotically reduced kenōsis hymn does not valorize weakness or vulnerability, as Daphne Hampson claims, but provides an example of God's supreme creative power in the inauguration of a "καινὴ κτίσις." Moreover, by performing the kenotic reduction, Paul's readers become part of the new creation, integrating themselves into divine life, participating in God's creative power, and mirroring divine love in their interactions with each other and the broader community. The kenōsis hymn is not an expression of the Christian "bad conscience," but a supreme expression of will-to-power. In the kenotically reduced new creation, the confluence of kenōsis and power is not paradoxical; rather, the self-seeking power valorized in the hierarchies of the cosmos is paradoxical. True loving power cannot help but "overflow" onto others.

F. Ramifications of the Kenotic Reduction for Phenomenology

In absolute science, insights obtained through phenomenological investigation effect not only a reappraisal of phenomena but also a reappraisal of phenomenology itself. What, one wonders, does the kenotic reduction teach us about phenomenology? First and foremost, it teaches that Husserlian phenomenology is beholden to the *cosmos* in its methodology. For Husserl, the reduction ultimately points to the transcendental subject as a monadic "unity of world and world consciousness," which, along with the broader transcendental community, *co*-constitutes the world: "[What] lies at hand under the title "world" is *not, so to say, a private* (primordial) constitutive construct of the individual transcendental ego, but the correlate of a transcendental *communalization* of the living constitutive processes which are realized by the *transcendental community of monads.*"[52] This monadic, or individuated, conception of the absolute is problematized by Fink, but it is left as a problem. As Fink puts it,

> we can now ask whether the phenomenologizing I, as the I of reflection, is in the last analysis projected out from the ego as standing *in* transcendental individuation, or whether the dimension of the *ultimate* determination of phenomenologizing . . . must not be sought by a regressive move to a *more original depth* of absolute life. However, we shall have to let this stand simply as a *problem.*[53]

It is here that the kenotic reduction goes beyond the phenomenological tradition. The reduction presented in the hymn resolves the monadic qualities of absolute subjectivity by transcendentally extending Husserl's notion of subjectivity. Just as Christ's sacrifice brings the world into a right relationship with God, the transcendental reduction of the kenōsis hymn reintegrates the Husserlian unity of "world and world-consciousness" into the divine life, thereby basing the world-constituting activity on "a more original depth" of divine life. The two transcendental trajectories of kenotic reduction—i.e., bracketing the cosmos and "enworlding" the new creation—are unified as two moments in divine life. The world-actualizing activity of the transcendental subject (divine life) thus takes a particular direction in the kenōsis hymn: the world (*cosmos*) becomes a new creation (καινὴ κτίσις). It is precisely this transcendentally extended reduction that Paul exhorts the Philippians to undertake when he asks them to cultivate the same "frame of mind" as Christ. By imitating the kenotic activity of Christ, the Philippians manifest the new creation, becoming, according to Paul, "children of God without blemish in the midst of a crooked and perverse generation, in which you shine [φαίνεσθε] as stars in the world, manifesting the living word [λόγον ζωῆς ἐπέχοντες]" (2:15–16).[54]

When carried to its kenotic extreme, the reduction not only discloses a unity of world and world-consciousness but also locates that unity in the divine life. The idea of monadicity is not relevant here; divine life is the source of infinitely overflowing power and love, while "monadicity" is a concept derived from worldly finitude. The kenotic reduction therefore expands Husserlian notions of transcendence and subjectivity by integrating the transcendental subject into the divine life. It also radicalizes Husserl's and Fink's attempts to free phenomenology from methodological commitments derived from the natural attitude. The implications of this transcendental "extension" are massive. By disclosing the "new creation" as a theme for phenomenological investigation, the kenotic reduction raises a host of questions about the transcendental nature of creation. Most importantly, for our purposes: What is the nature of space and time in the new creation? As Husserl recognized, notions of space and time are crucial to understanding the reduction, for experiences are always given in a temporal flow. A complete understanding of the kenotic reduction therefore requires an understanding of kenotic time *within* the new creation.

6

Kenotic Time

Husserl and Apocalyptic Eschatology

In order to understand kenotic time within a Pauline context, it is necessary to consider Paul's eschatology. To that end, in the first part of this chapter, I will explore apocalyptic eschatology both in general and with specific reference to Paul. I will argue that Paul's eschatology is largely in keeping with Jewish eschatology of the Second Temple Period, though Paul diverges from the latter in his belief that the messiah has already come. Paul's apocalyptic eschatology is thus partially realized with the *eschaton* having the temporal structure of "already—not yet." In the second section of this chapter, I will evaluate Husserl's notion of time-consciousness to determine whether it is sufficient to make sense of the Pauline conception of time. I will argue that Husserlian temporality, inasmuch as it privileges intra-worldly monadic perceptual experience, ultimately diverges from Pauline temporality, in which remembrance (the already) and expectation (the not yet) are fundamental aspects of temporal lived experience. In other words, by the standards of the kenotic reduction, Husserlian time-consciousness is not fully reduced. In the next chapter, I will explore two eschatological expansions of Husserl's work: Jean-Yves Lacoste's phenomenality of anticipation and Eugen Fink's temporality of depresencing.

A. Apocalypses and Apocalyptic Eschatology

Apocalyptic texts are, if anything, strange and impenetrable to the modern mind. The modern reader, who is unable to relate to the cosmological and spiritual commitments of apocalypses, tends to find such texts and associated social movements embarrassing or crude. Yet, in the last half-century, modernity's dismissal of apocalyptic thought has become increasingly problematic as the significance of apocalypses and apocalyptic eschatology in the early Church has become apparent. Anyone aspiring to an historical understanding of the church and its scriptures—particularly Pauline scriptures—would be remiss in simply brushing aside apocalyptic phenomena.

Recent biblical scholarship has distinguished between "apocalypse" as a literary genre, "which is one of the favored media used by apocalyptic writers to communicate their messages"; "apocalyptic eschatology," which is "neither a genre nor a socioreligious movement, nor a system of thought, but rather a religious perspective"; and "apocalypticism," which "refers to the symbolic universe in which an apocalyptic movement codifies its identity and interpretation of reality."[1] The upshot of this distinction is that "apocalyptic eschatology" or "apocalypticism" may apply to texts that do not have the literary features of apocalypses. So, for example, one may speak of Paul's apocalyptic eschatology, though none of Paul's letters are apocalypses.

Since Schweitzer's *The Mysticism of Paul the Apostle* (1931), scholars have situated Paul's apocalyptic eschatology not against the background of the Gospels or early Christianity, but against the background of Jewish apocalyptic eschatology. As Schweitzer states, "Since Paul lives in the conceptions of the dramatic worldview characteristic of the late Jewish Eschatology, he is by consequence bound to the logic of that view."[2] For Schweitzer, the "dramatic worldview" of Second Temple Judaism existed in contrast to the Stoic worldview, which equates reality with the natural world:

> In the Stoic view the world is thought of as static and unfaltering. The world is Nature, which remains constantly in the same relationship to the world-spirit pervading it and pervaded by it. For Paul, however, the world is not Nature but a supernatural historical process which has for its stages the forthgoing of the world from God, its alienation from Him, and its return to Him.[3]

Paul's eschatology and Jewish apocalyptic eschatology more broadly rest on a distinction between nature and super-nature: the Stoic worldview enfolds all reality within nature, while Paul's worldview postulates a separation between nature and super-nature. The world, for Schweitzer, is caught up in the supernatural historical process of creation, alienation, and reunification with God. Paul's eschatology is, therefore, "cosmologically conceived." The whole *cosmos* is transferred eschatologically from a "perishable" state to an "imperishable state."[4] While the details may be debatable, the general features of Schweitzer's analysis of Paul—namely the idea that Paul's apocalyptic eschatology is essentially Jewish—remain largely acceptable. The question is, what is Jewish apocalyptic eschatology and how is it present in Paul's letters?

Following Schweitzer and Vielhauer, Paul Hanson argues that the essential characteristics of Jewish apocalyptic eschatology derive from the belief in two ages separated by a great judgment:

> The essential characteristics of apocalyptic eschatology are drawn together into a coherent whole in Isaiah 65: the present era is evil; a great judgment separating the good from evil and marking the crossroads between the present world and the world to come is imminent; a newly created world of peace and blessing ordained for the faithful lies beyond that judgment. These teachings of world epochs, universal judgment and a modified dualism are basic components of later apocalyptic eschatology.[5]

As Hanson notes, the dualism of the "two ages" is at once temporal, inasmuch as it involves the present and past of the current world and the future of the world to come, and spatial, inasmuch as it concerns the earth and a new creation. Additionally, apocalyptic eschatology is *universal*; judgment is not a matter of individual belief or action, but concerns everyone, everywhere, for all times.

Martin C. de Boer argues that there are, in fact, two versions of "two age" dualism in the Jewish literature. The first is a "cosmological" pattern in which God's authority over the world, as sovereign creator, has been usurped by evil. In this pattern, "the world has come under the dominion of evil, angelic powers in some primeval time, namely in the time of Noah."[6] A day of judgment is then promised (and promised soon!) in which God will invade the dominion of evil, defeat the evil powers in a cosmic war, and reestablish God's sovereignty. This pattern is exemplified in the Book of the Watchers (1 Enoch 1–36). The second pattern is "forensic." Cosmic forces are de-emphasized while free will and human decision play a major role. Specifically, Adam's willful defiance of God ushers sin and death into the world. God then gives the law as a remedy.[7] The judgment, as de Boer notes, "[is] conceptualized not as a cosmic war but as a courtroom in which all humanity appears before the bar of the judge, [where] God will reward with eternal life those who have acknowledged his claim . . . (the righteous), while he will punish with eternal death those who have not (the wicked)."[8] On this pattern, the Adamic past is the epoch of disobedience, the present is the epoch of decision-making, where a decision to follow the law allows one to participate in the future epoch of glory. This pattern is exemplified in 4 Ezra.

Paul's eschatology blends these two patterns. His use of the Christ/Adam parallel in Romans 5 and 1 Corinthians 15 conforms to the forensic pattern, emphasizing the personal responsibility of Adam (and every individual) for his disobedience toward God: "Therefore just as one man's trespass led to condemnation for all, so one man's act of righteousness leads to justification and life for all" (Romans 5:18). Alternately, Paul's repeated references to a cosmic battle between God and Satan adhere to the cosmological pattern. Thus in the closing of his letter to the Romans, Paul reminds his readers that, "The God of peace will shortly crush Satan under your feet" (Romans 16:20).

De Boer points to Romans 1 through 3 as an example of how the two eschatological patterns come together. In this passage, Paul draws upon the forensic pattern of Jewish apocalyptic eschatology in enumerating the function and salvific power of the law: "For it is not the hearers of the law who are righteous in God's sight, but the doers of the law who will be justified" (2:13). Yet all fall short of the law: "Both Jews and Greeks are under the power of sin, as it is written: 'There is no one who is righteous, not even one'" (3:9–10, quoting Psalm 14:3). De Boer, in a rather unfortunate turn of phrase, claims that the universal power of sin derives from the "inability of the law to provide deliverance from sin's lethal clutches."[9] Paul thus seems every bit the supersessionist: the law is *unable* to break sin's hold on the world, so Christ comes to save the day! De Boer envisions a cosmological *dénouement* to the forensic pattern: "the meaning of faith is actually determined by the cosmological-apocalyptic disclosure of God's righteousness and of sin in the crucifixion of Christ. Christ's death cannot be understood in exclusively forensic terms, since it marks God's triumphant invasion of the world 'under sin.'"[10]

While one may agree with de Boer's claim that the forensic and cosmological patterns intertwine in Romans 1 through 3, his characterization of that passage is objectionable. For Paul, the universality of sin is not due to a failure or inability on the part of the law, as de Boer claims, but a failure on the part of humankind to follow the law. The law, as Paul is clear to point out, is not sin (Romans 7:7). Moreover, in Romans 1 through 3 the cosmological pattern is not simply the *dénouement* to the forensic pattern; rather, the two are thoroughly intertwined throughout Paul's letters.

So, for instance, Paul offers a cosmological explanation for humankind's "forensic" failure to follow the law: "For I delight in the law of God in my inmost self, but I see in my members another law at war with the law of my mind, making me captive to the law of sin that dwells in my members" (Romans 7:22–23). Humankind falls short of the law precisely *because* the world, from Adam's transgression onward, is captive to the law of sin. Christ, as the antitype of Adam, breaks the world's captivity to sin and ultimately fulfills the law. Christ's life, death, and resurrection therefore fit the forensic pattern (contrary to de Boer's claim), which is tightly intertwined in Paul's thought with the cosmological pattern of two "dominions" governed by two laws.

While Paul's eschatology is generally in keeping with Jewish apocalyptic eschatology, there is one particular element that Paul does not share with the Jewish texts and milieu from which his eschatology is drawn—namely, Paul believes that the messiah has already appeared. As John Collins notes, "The primary difference between Christian and Jewish apocalypticism in the first century CE was that the Christians believed that the messiah had already come and that the firstfruits [*sic*] of the resurrection had taken place."[11] Paul's eschatology is therefore apocalyptic, with the characteristic "two age" structure of Second Temple Jewish eschatology, and realized, reflecting the idea that the messiah has *already* appeared and broken sin's hold on the world. In other words, Paul's eschatology reflects the cosmological status of the *interregnum* in which Christianity exists: the dominion of evil has already been decisively defeated, though the new creation is not yet complete. There is, for Paul, an apocalyptic *anticipation* of the new creation, which has already been inaugurated in the life, death, and resurrection of Christ, and is currently manifest in the body of Christ, but which will not fully arrive until the *Parousia*, when the Son of Man returns as cosmic judge. John Collins summarizes the already-not yet character of Paul's eschatology: "The coming of the Son of Man and the day of the Lord are not yet, but they are imminent, and the readers are urged to be alert and watchful. In the interim, life [is] to be lived, but lived in the consciousness that this world [is] passing away."[12]

In sum, we may note two temporal features of Paul's eschatology that are essential to a phenomenological notion of kenotic time: First, Paul's eschatology reflects Jewish apocalyptic ideas about "two ages," which are both temporal (inasmuch as two historical epochs are envisioned) and spatial (inasmuch as the world is distinguished from the new creation). Second, Paul's eschatology reflects a belief that the messiah has already appeared in the person of Jesus Christ, who inaugurated (in the past) a new creation that will be completed (in the future) with the *Parousia*. Pauline eschatology thus enfolds the "two ages" in an "already-not yet" temporal structure.

B. Husserlian Options for Characterizing Kenotic Time

An understanding of temporality is, in some sense, the central goal of Husserlian phenomenology.[13] A phenomenology of kenōsis must, therefore, turn to the question of time: how can we understand Paul's temporality *phenomenologically*? Is Husserl's conception of time-consciousness an adequate phenomenological framework for understanding Pauline temporality?

In his 1905 lectures on internal time-consciousness, Husserl relates the problem of temporality to the broader problem with which phenomenology has always been concerned: the constitution of objectivity. Husserl hopes to "gain an understanding of how temporal Objectivity—therefore, individual Objectivity in general—can be constituted in subjective time-consciousness."[14] This implies that an understanding of temporality is not a tangential philosophical project, but an integral part of phenomenology. All experience—the experience of objectivity, for instance, and the experience of subjectivity—is temporal; and not only does experience occur within time but it is also structured by time. The fundamental categories of experience (causality, for instance) are temporal. Thus, as Robert Sokolowski notes, "it is in the domain of temporality that phenomenology approaches what could be called the first principles . . . Time pervades all things, both noematic and noetic, that are discussed in phenomenology, and the description of the phenomenological 'origin' of time gets to a kind of philosophical center."[15] A phenomenological understanding of temporality is therefore essential for understanding the methodological tools and goals of phenomenology. The phenomenological reduction, the kenotic reduction, and that which is disclosed in them, are temporal.

Husserl notes three modes of temporality: Objective time, immanent time, and time-consciousness. The first, "Objective time," refers to "transcendent" temporal presuppositions about that which exists.[16] By "transcendent" Husserl does not refer to Kantian transcendence but that which transcends consciousness—namely, objective reality. Objective time, then, is the temporality of the objective world; it is, as Husserl states, "world-time, real time, the time of nature in the sense of natural science including psychology as the natural science of the psychical."[17] In other words, objective time refers to worldly events that can be measured in seconds, minutes, hours, and so forth. When I tell someone to meet me at the coffee shop between 5:00 and 5:30 p.m., I make use of objective time. I refer to a mode of temporality which is, as Sokolowski notes, "public and verifiable," and which allows me to organize my temporal experience of the object-world in discrete, mathematical intervals: 60 seconds in a minute, 60 minutes in an hour, 24 hours in a day, etc.[18] Like the object-world more generally, Husserl argues that objective time is not a fundamental datum. Although we generally take objective time as given, it is in fact constituted by consciousness. Objective time is a *theoretical* layer applied to temporal experience, and must therefore be excluded as a basis for understanding the origins of temporality.

In point of fact, Husserl argues that objective time is constituted within a second temporal mode: immanent time, which applies to subjective components of experience—e.g., feeling, hearing, experiencing, and remembering. Husserl gives the example of a melody: "The evidence that consciousness of a tonal process, a melody, exhibits a succession even as I hear it is such as to make every doubt or denial [of immanent time] appear senseless."[19] To elaborate upon Husserl's example, consider the musical technique of *arpeggio*, in which the notes of a chord are played in sequence rather than altogether. In the "tonal process" of an *arpeggio*, one hears a certain defined musical pattern wherein one note follows another. The pattern of the arpeggio is temporal, built around a *progression* from one note to the next, but the experience of the *arpeggio* is not measured primarily in terms of objective time; there is a specific sense of what notes come *before* and *after*, but it does not matter how many seconds each note of the *arpeggio* is held. Similarly, feelings cannot be measured in terms of objective time. When I feel fear upon seeing a bear, there is a temporal sequence—I see the bear *and then* I become afraid—but the "before" and "after" of fear are not measured in seconds or minutes. Fear is not an objective occurrence; it is a lived experience. The temporality of fear is, then, an immanent temporality, inextricably connected to the "flow of consciousness."[20]

Additionally, it is only within immanent time that objective time has any sense: "The phenomenological data are the apprehensions of time, the lived experiences in which the temporal in the objective sense appears." Just as the object-world gains its objectivity through noetic processes, so also objective time gains its objectivity through immanent temporality. The regularities of immanent time—the experience of a day, for example—may be reckoned in terms of units of objective time—24 hours, in this case— but the "objectivity" of that time is grounded in a repeated and widely available lived experience. The objective time of 24 hours makes no sense apart from the lived experience of a day. So Husserl claims:

Objectivity [*Objectivität*] belongs to "experience," that is, to the unity of experience, to the lawfully experienced context of nature. Phenomenologically speaking, Objectivity is not even constituted through "primary" content but through characters of apprehension and the regularities [*Gesetzmässigkeiten*] which pertain to the essence of these characters.[21]

Objective time is constituted in immanent time by apprehending (in the mode of objectification) various regularities in live experience. As Sokolowski notes, "Worldly things can be measured by clocks and calendars, and can be experienced as enduring, only because we experience a succession of mental activities in our subjective life. If we did not anticipate and remember, we could not organize the processes that occur in the world into temporal patterns."[22] Objective time therefore has its origin in immanent time.

Within immanent time, Husserl distinguishes a third level of temporality: time-consciousness. First, Husserl notes that one can speak of immanent temporal objects in themselves: "We can make self-evident assertions concerning the immanent Object in itself, e.g., that it now endures, that a certain part of the duration has elapsed, that the duration of the sound apprehended in the now . . . constantly sinks back into the past."[23] So, for instance, if I am afraid upon seeing a bear, I can make assertions about the "way in which [I am] conscious of it as actually past or present": I saw the bear *and then* I was paralyzed by fear.[24] Second, one may speak of the way in which the "before" and "after" of immanent time is constituted: "We can also speak of the way in which we are 'conscious of' all differences in the 'appearing' of immanent sounds and their content duration."[25] That is, one can view immanent temporal objects as phenomena in themselves, or one can view them as *products* of consciousness. This suggests two levels of immanent time: the bare flux of immanent time, where temporal objects flow from the now to the past, and the *consciousness* of immanent time. Husserl distinguishes these two levels of immanent time in the following way: "[The object] we cannot term a form of consciousness (any more than we can call a spatial phenomenon, a body in its appearance from one side or the other, from far or near, a form of consciousness). 'Consciousness,' 'lived experience,' refers to an object by means of an appearance in which 'the object in its modal setting' subsists."[26] In other words, the "lived experience" of temporal objects refers back to consciousness as the constitutive source of temporality.

In the 1905 lectures, Husserl locates time-consciousness *within* immanent time: "It is indeed evident that the perception of a temporal object itself has temporality, that perception of duration itself presupposes duration of perception, and that perception of any temporal configuration whatsoever itself has its temporal form."[27] Husserl later argues that the 1905 lectures involved an infinite regress, for if time-consciousness is situated in time, then what accounts for the temporality of time-consciousness? Thus in later works collected in the Bernau Manuscripts (*Husserliana* XXXIII)—some of which are appended to *The Phenomenology of Internal Time-Consciousness*—and the C-manuscripts (*Husserliana-Materialien* VIII), Husserl locates time-consciousness outside of time: "Subjective time is constituted in absolute, timeless consciousness, which is not an object."[28] On the latter view, time-consciousness is the timeless flux of primal impressions—"timeless" because no extended duration is possible in an infinite ever-changing flux. Yet although time consciousness has no duration—i.e., no time of its own—it is not without change: "consciousness changes insofar as that of which it is conscious changes temporally. A temporal change can appear within consciousness only by way of a change of consciousness."[29] Consciousness is always in flux. The question, for Husserl, is: how is the flux of consciousness, as the constitutive source of immanent and Objective time, structured?

The "source-point" within the flux of conscious for the generation of temporal objects is, according to Husserl, the "primal impression," which may be thought of as the now-phase of consciousness, though it never occurs in isolation: "The actual [*liebhafte*] tonal now is constantly changed into something that has been; constantly, an ever fresh tonal now, which passes over into modification, peels off."[30] The now of the primal impression is not a single point, but always runs off into the past (retention) and portends a future (protention). As William James states, "The practically cognized present is no knife-edge, but a saddle-back, with a certain breadth of its own on which we sit perched, and from which we look in two directions into time."[31] The primal impression, as the now-phase of consciousness, slides off into a retentional phase, in which consciousness is directed toward that which has just elapsed, and a protentional phase, in which consciousness is directed toward that which is about to occur.

Husserl is clear that retention is "an actual existent." In reference to sound, Husserl states, "While [retention] itself is actual (but not an actual sound), it is the retention of a sound that has been."[32] This is a crucial point: retention does not retain, or recall, some past state of a temporal object (in the way that a memory does), but it retains the living present that has just elapsed—more specifically, it retains the living present *as elapsed*. The retained living present is, in turn, made up of another primal impression accompanied by retention and protention; this second retention similarly retains in itself an earlier living present. As Sokolowski notes, "In the living present we have a retention of retentions of retentions. We never have an atomic living present all by itself."[33] To put it differently, retention is not a singular *act* performed on a past temporal object; rather, retention is a *structural element* that pervades the temporal flux in all of its phases—past, present, and future. The following figure illustrates the roles played by retention and protention within the temporal flux.

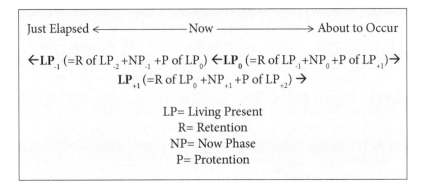

Just Elapsed ←————————— Now —————————→ About to Occur

$$\leftarrow LP_{-1}\ (=R\ of\ LP_{-2}+NP_{-1}+P\ of\ LP_0)\ \leftarrow LP_0\ (=R\ of\ LP_{-1}+NP_0+P\ of\ LP_{+1})\rightarrow$$
$$LP_{+1}\ (=R\ of\ LP_0+NP_{+1}+P\ of\ LP_{+2})\rightarrow$$

LP= Living Present
R= Retention
NP= Now Phase
P= Protention

Retention is the *structure* of the flux in its past-directedness. Similarly, protention is the structure of the flux in its future-directedness. As Dan Zahavi puts it, "[protention] intends the phase of the object about to occur thereby providing a future-oriented temporal context for the primal impression."[34] Together, the three temporal aspects of consciousness constitute the temporal structure of all lived experience: retention—primal impression—protention.

Husserl differentiates retention and protention, as structural features of the temporal flux of consciousness, from memory and expectation, as acts of consciousness. In the 1905 lectures, Husserl distinguishes between retention, as "primary remembrance" and recollection, as "secondary remembrance." Retention, on the one hand, is a structural feature of experience; Husserl calls it a "comet's tail" of just elapsed experiences attached to actual perception.[35] Secondary remembrance, on the other hand, is something totally different. As an example, Husserl considers the memory of a melody heard in childhood:

We remember a melody, let us say, which in our youth we heard during a concert. Then it is obvious that the entire phenomenon of memory has, *mutatis mutandis*, exactly the same constitution as the perception of the melody. Like the perception, it has a favored point; to the now-point of the perception corresponds a now-point of the memory, and so on. We run through a melody in phantasy; we hear "as if" [*gliechsham*] first the first note, then the second, etc.[36]

In primary remembrance (i.e., retention) the temporal object that has just elapsed is still "present" to consciousness as that which has just passed—present as that which has become absent. In secondary remembrance (i.e., recollection) the object falls outside of the temporal field of current lived experience, and must be *re*-presented to consciousness through memory. Thus, as the preceding quotation illustrates, recollection has a structure similar to perception: like perception, recollection involves a temporal object that is "present," though in recollection the object has the quality of being presented *as if it were present*. As Toine Kortooms puts it, "A melody may be intuitively presented in recollection, but the melody does not appear as present itself, it is *as if* I hear this melody. This character of the memory-presentation is expressed in the term 'representation' (*Vergegenwärtigung*). In recollection, something that is not actually present to consciousness is presented *as if it were present*."[37] Primary memory, or retention, is a mode of perceptual consciousness, while recollection is a mode of representational consciousness; thus, for Husserl, memory is similar to phantasy-consciousness, though the former is posited as a past lived-experience while the latter is not necessarily connected to actual lived-experience.[38] In the end, Husserl distinguishes between retention and memory in the following way:

> Nun, die grundwesentliche Differenz springt in die Augen. In der Phantasie erscheint selbst ein Jetzt uns vor Augen, nur als vergegenwärtigtes Jetzt. Der eben vergangene Ton in der Wahrnehmung steht aber in keiner Weise selbst als Jetzt vor Augen, und zwar als vergegenwärtigtes Jetzt, sondern als nicht vergegenwärtigtes Vergangen. Der ganze Charakter und Habitus des Phänomens ist ein anderer.

> Now, the fundamental difference springs into view. In phantasy, a now manifests itself, standing before our eyes, but only as a

represented now. The tone that just elapsed in perception does not stand before us as now in any way, including as a represented now; rather, it stands before us as a *not* represented past. The whole character and *habitus* of the phenomenon is different.[39]

Retention, for Husserl, applies to the perceptual lived experience that has just passed. Memory presents a previously lived experience not in the mode of perception, but in the mode of representation.

Similarly, Husserl distinguishes protention from expectation. Protention is a mode of perceptual consciousness, while expectation is a different intentionality altogether. Like remembrance, which is a mode of phantasy-consciousness that "offers me the vivid reproduction of the expiring duration of an event," expectation is a mode of phantasy-consciousness that offers not a reproduction, but "an intuitively *productive* 'image.'"[40] Husserl distinguishes expectation from memory as an inversion of the same intentional structure: "Expectational intuition is an inverted memorial intuition, for the now-intentions do not go 'before' the process but follow after it."[41] In remembrance, what is re-presented as "now" is an event that happened before the process of remembering; in expectation, what is presented as "now" is an event that will happen *after* the process of expecting.

The main difference between memory and expectation is their manner of fulfillment. Memory is fulfilled by re-presenting past events, which permits "only the confirmation of the uncertainties of memory and their improvement by being transformed in a reproduction in which each and everything in the components is characterized as reproductive."[42] In other words, to confirm a memory we ask questions like: Am I sure that I am remembering the experience correctly? Did my real experience match my current re-presentation of the experience? The fulfillment of memory has to do with the quality and validity of the re-presentation. Alternately, expectation is fulfilled in perception: "It pertains to the essence of the expected that it is an about-to-be-perceived."[43] That is, to confirm an expectation, we wait until the expected future event is perceived in the present, then ask questions like: Is my perception what I expected it to be? Does my experience match my expectation? Expectation is thus confirmed in present lived experience.

Having adumbrated Husserlian time-consciousness, we may now ask whether Husserl's notion of time "fits" the eschatological temporality envisioned by Paul. On the one hand, Husserl's idea of time, like Paul's, does not rely on a simple present; past, present, and future are interwoven in lived experience. One the other hand, there are two major divergences between Husserl's time-consciousness and Paul's apocalyptic eschatology. First, in expounding the "retention—primordial impression—protention" structure of the temporal flux of consciousness, Husserl privileges perception. Retention, primordial impression, and protention are all modes of consciousness that apply to the lived experience of perception. So, for example, Husserl speaks of retention as "a comet's tail which is joined to actual perception."[44] Consequently, Husserl's most fundamental temporality (time-consciousness) is schematized in terms most appropriate to perceptual experience. Memory and expectation (non-perceptual categories) are viewed as particular intentionalities which can be differentiated categorically from fundamental temporality, but which always refer back (or forward) to the perceptual temporal flux.

Alternatively, for Paul, memory and expectation (as the "already" and "not yet") are fundamental modes of temporality. The *expectation* of an imminent "new age"—as a fulfillment of the eschatological event that *already* occurred in Christ's life, death, and resurrection—forms the temporal structure of lived experience in Paul's apocalyptic eschatology. To put it in Husserlian terms, representation, not perception, is the fundamental temporal category that underlies lived experience: the representation of Christ in the Church, the representation of God in scripture, and the representation of sacred history in biblical narrative determine the structure of kenotic time. Additionally, remembrance and expectation in the Pauline context are not always linked to individual perception or experience. So for instance, we may never personally experience the *Parousia*, though Paul tells us to expect it anytime; and we may have had no direct individual experience of Christ, though communion is still a "remembrance" (in Reformed traditions, at least).

Second, Husserl diverges from kenotic time inasmuch as his fundamental temporality is tied to monadic perceptual consciousness. By anchoring temporality to the paradigm of conscious perception, Husserl derives his concept of time from that which is, properly speaking, intraworldly—namely, the individual egoic consciousness. Although Husserl recognizes the need to find an *original* temporality beyond any temporality constituted within the world, his commitment to monadic consciousness ultimately restricts the investigation to inherently intra-worldly categories. In other words, by the standards of the kenotic reduction, Husserl's notion of time-consciousness is not fully reduced.

7

Radicalizing Husserlian Temporality

Anticipation, Depresencing, and Representing

The previous chapter showed that Husserlian temporality is inadequate for conceptualizing kenotic time; it remains for us to suggest more appropriate phenomenological concepts. To that end, this chapter will explore two ways of radicalizing Husserl's notion of time-consciousness. First, in his work on anticipation, Jean-Yves Lacoste brackets Husserl's emphasis on perceptual experience, arguing that the fundamental category of worldly temporality is non-experience. This allows Lacoste to posit a structural connection between protention and anticipation, thereby integrating anticipation into existence itself. Consciousness, for Lacoste, is inherently anticipatory. Second, Eugen Fink argues that Husserl's notion of time-consciousness privileges the present now-phase of consciousness: past and future, as retention and protention or memory and expectation, are defined primarily with reference to the now-phase of consciousness. Inasmuch as Husserl's concept of time derives from the now-phase of consciousness, which is a *product* of constitution within the world-horizon, it is not fully reduced in the phenomenological sense. That which is properly horizonal cannot be defined primarily in terms appropriate to intra-horizonal entities (in this case, "consciousness"). Fink therefore suggests a non-presentialist, horizonal concept of time as "depresencing."

Considered together, Lacoste's and Fink's criticisms of Husserl may seem either mutually exclusive or complementary. On the one hand, Fink's notion of "depresencing" would be excluded in Lacoste's bracketing of experience, while Lacoste's concept of anticipation would be considered presentialist because the category of the "not yet" derives from an implicit "now." On the other hand, by drawing together Lacoste's non-experiential, eschatological notion of anticipation and Fink's non-presentialist, horizonal concept of time, a fully reduced treatment of kenotic time as both *escha-tological* and *horizonal* is possible. The kenōsis hymn, it will be argued, ultimately discloses a "new creation," in which space-time is defined *horizonally* as the "represencing" of God.

A. The Phenomenality of Anticipation

In his work on anticipation, Jean-Yves Lacoste calls into question the primacy that Husserl assigns to perceptual experience. For Husserl, the fundamental modes of temporality—i.e., retention, primal impression, and protention—are linked to perceptual consciousness. Expectation, or anticipation, is a secondary category—a representation (in the mode of phantasy) of events that have not yet happened. Expectation, for Husserl, has a structure similar to perception (except that expectation presents temporal objects *as if they were present*), and can therefore be broken down according to the perceptual schema of retention—primal impression—protention, which is the fundamental structure of time consciousness. In contrast, Lacoste's phenomenology of anticipation does not privilege perception as an explanatory model; thus non-perceptual and non-experiential modes of consciousness, like anticipation, are not automatically assigned a secondary status. In fact, Lacoste argues that anticipation is a fundamental structure of time-consciousness: "a consciousness that would not anticipate is evidently an unthinkable consciousness."[1]

By effectively bracketing perception, Lacoste is able to connect protention and anticipation, while Husserl draws a hard distinction between the two. Lacoste argues that anticipation is a double phenomenon:

> On the one hand, anticipation is the gesture of a consciousness that ensures the coherence and sense of its present experience by relating this experience to a pre-experience of what is not yet here but will, in time, realize [*accomplira*] what is already here. Just as the pre-perception by which the already played notes permit us to foresee the notes that will be played, so it is too with those who know what they wait for and "rehearse," by anticipation, what will (certainly, maybe, etc.) come.[2]

In this first sense, anticipation is equivalent to Husserlian protention, where the living present points to that which has not yet occurred. As in the case of an *arpeggio*, where the notes of a chord are separated and played in sequence, one tone (the "now" tone) portends the next tone, which has not yet occurred. The "now" contains within itself a pre-perception of that which is not yet.

Lacoste also envisions a second sense of anticipation: "On the other hand, all that is given to us inchoately, in the mode of a hint or promise, makes use of anticipation, for example the short visit that anticipates the long day that I will spend with a friend next month."[3] This second sense of anticipation is largely equivalent to Husserl's notion of expectation as, "the intuitive anticipation of the future."[4] Yet there is, for Husserl, a strict separation between protention, as a mode of perceptual consciousness, and anticipation, as a representational mode of phantasy-consciousness. Protention is a structural element of the living present while anticipation represents (better, pre-presents!) temporal objects as that which will soon be present. Lacoste, on the other hand, does not define temporality in terms of perceptual experience; therefore the distinction between protention (as perceptual) and anticipation (as non-perceptual or representational) breaks down. Anticipation and protention are structurally identical and foundational to time-consciousness. Put differently, anticipation as a representational mode of consciousness cannot be distinguished qualitatively from protention. Time-consciousness is inherently representational.

One of the central questions of Lacoste's work on anticipation is: how does the act of anticipation appear? In other words, what is the mode of givenness (or pre-givenness) of anticipation. "To appear," Lacoste argues, "in effect must be understood as an event."[5] And "an event" is inherently temporal: my wife, whom I did not see a few seconds ago, comes through our apartment door. The event of her arrival, her appearance in the "now," is defined by her previous absence. Similarly, the event is defined by a future absence, as that particular event gives way to other events: she comes in, takes her coat off, and has a glass of wine—her arrival, as an event, inevitably disappears. The event is, by nature, temporally bounded: "it must be the case, then, that we always deal, in the first place, with something that appears to us now, whose appearance lasts more or less time, and completes itself in a disappearance."[6] The event of appearance is flanked in both the past and future by disappearance.

Lacoste is careful to note that events are not discrete occurrences. Consciousness does not perceive one event after another in a simple ordinal sequence; rather, events can belong simultaneously to the past and present, as in the case of a memory, or present and future, as in the case of an expectation, or past and future, as in the case of a promise yet to be fulfilled. In reference to the past, Lacoste states, "We don't need to be taught that an event can belong simultaneously to our past and, by its *Wirkungsgeschichte* (history of reception), to our present. Whether represented in memory or present through the causality that it still exercises, the past defines itself as that which has disappeared but has left traces."[7] Alternately, some events leave little or no trace, or "erased traces": the people I passed on the street two weeks ago while walking to the corner market have not only disappeared, in the sense of fading into the past, but are also largely *forgotten*; they exist to my consciousness only as erased traces. In another month or so, they may be completely forgotten (this text notwithstanding). Similarly, expectations for the future can be erased: promises go unfulfilled and expectations fade. The present may hold no future whatsoever.

Given that past, present, and future run together in the interplay of the event's disappearance and appearance, one wonders whether it is possible for an event to appear fully: Can some*thing*, some*one*, or some*time* appear out of nothingness as fully present and then, perhaps, disappear into nothingness? In other words, is *Parousia* possible? For Lacoste, pure presence is proscribed by the limitations of consciousness: "To narrow consciousness only a region of being appears, primarily because it has an intuition of something. Consciousness is narrow, also, because it can perceive, remember, or imagine, but it cannot perceive, remember, and imagine simultaneously."[8] That which appears to consciousness does so as an intuition proper to a certain region of being. So, for instance, the *Mona Lisa* presents itself to visitors at the Louvre as a priceless work of art. To the curators of the Louvre, the *Mona Lisa* might also be present in a different way—e.g., as an attraction, as an object to be insured, as a means to raise funds. And to the preservationists at the Louvre, the *Mona Lisa* might appear primarily as an object to be preserved by protection from ultraviolet light, for example. The regions of being in which the *Mona Lisa* may appear are legion. Moreover, it is impossible for consciousness to perceive the *Mona Lisa* in every region of being simultaneously. All experience, Lacoste argues, "is inherently limited, and . . . human experience is in fact impossible unless it possess limits and obeys them (any other type of consciousness would certainly be an angelic consciousness)."[9] Intuitive experience is limited in scope—i.e., experience is always bordered by and suffused with non-experience. No experience is ever final.

If time is constituted in the interplay of experience and non-experience, then a full *Parousia* (which would exclude any non-experience) is only possible at the end (*eschaton*) of time: "parousia, strictly understood, probably has no place in the world. We exist in the element of the provisional, which is the element of always partial presences."[10] Lacoste illustrates this point with reference to Christ's transfiguration in Matthew 17:1–8:

> Blinded by the by the glory of Christ transfigured, the disciples believed they were witnessing the end of history—the end of their own history and of the history of Israel in the clear and distinct manifestation of the Messiah. The tents that Peter wanted to erect are a final resting place, not the dwelling place of nomads. The Transfiguration resembles the occupation of the temple of Jerusalem by the divine Shekinah. And if the disciples were right in interpreting the scene in this way (though in a confused manner, as the text of the gospel tells us), there would have been nothing left for them to see—they would have seen it all. What was given to them would have been given definitively. Now, not all has been seen, and the episode only anticipates what is still to be seen, the highest phenomenon given in history, the appearance of the risen Christ. There is more.[11]

Peter, James, and John thought that they were witnessing the full presence—the *Parousia*—of the Messiah. The "three dwellings" that Peter wanted to erect for Moses, Elijah, and Jesus represent a presumptive end to the history of Israel—a final resting place, a complete fulfillment of God's promise, an indestructible temple. Yet Peter was wrong; the transfiguration was not the *Parousia*, but an anticipation of the *Parousia*. As Lacoste says, "History would continue."[12] Ultimately, the *Parousia* is not an event, for it is not bounded by non-experience; rather the *Parousia* marks the end of time. Phenomenologically, this example serves to illustrate that non-experience (rather than experience) is the fundamental mode of temporality, for "the concept of an experience that is only an experience, not bordered by any non-experience, cannot, *a prima vista*, be rationally formed."[13] Time would not "move"; there could be no history without non-experience.

　　Anticipation is not simply one mode of non-experience, but the fundamental structure of non-experience and, thus, the fundamental structure of temporality. In basic agreement with Heidegger, Lacoste notes that consciousness is inherently future-oriented: "We cannot say who we are without . . . [recognizing] how we appropriate what by definition cannot belong to anyone, the time that has yet to pass, or how this time governs our present, the most profound determination of our relation to time."[14] If the past represents the "closing off" of possibility, the future represents the "opening up" of possibility. So, for instance, after deciding to pursue philosophy rather than science, the possibility of becoming a natural scientist was closed off to me, but all sorts of possibilities remain for me in the future: I could be an analytic philosopher, a continental philosopher; I could focus on theological issues; or, like Wittgenstein, I could abandon philosophy altogether and become a schoolteacher. (The thought has crossed my mind!) The future, up to the point of my death, constitutes the realm of my human possibilities. In my care for my own existence, I necessarily direct my attention toward future possibilities; I project myself into the future in order to evaluate (on the basis of my past experiences) the outcome of various choices I might make in the present. My very existence is anticipatory!

For Heidegger, my "care" for my future possibilities has its *telos* in death:

> Care is being-toward-death. We defined anticipatory reso-
> luteness as authentic being toward the possibility that we
> characterized as the absolute impossibility of Da-sein. In this
> being-toward-the-end, Da-sein exists authentically and totally
> as the being that it can be when "thrown into death." It does
> not have an end where it just stops, but it *exists finitely*. The
> authentic future, which is temporalized primarily by *that*
> temporality which constitutes the meaning of anticipatory
> resoluteness, thus reveals itself as finite.[15]

Lacoste argues, on the other hand, that anticipation has its *telos* not in death but in the eschatological horizon of the *Parousia*. The idea of antici-pation, as defined by Heidegger, does not suffice to explain eschatological anticipation of the Pauline sort: "Although it can shed some light on it, the excess of the possible over the real, and the future's domination of the present, cannot furnish us with an interpretive model for liturgical interpretation."[16] The reason why a general concept of anticipation will not suffice is because two modes of being are involved: "an eschatological I [*un moi eschatologique*]" and an "empirical I [*le moi empirique*]."[17] The latter, to which Heidegger's analysis mainly applies, is, "caught up in the worldly network of local and temporal relations that determine it, where God is not 'sufficient,' and where the world interposes itself between God and man."[18] And thus, while worldly anticipation shares certain features with eschatological anticipation—e.g., care and projection—there is a crucial difference with respect to worldly and eschatological modes of being: "The world is the kingdom of the non-Parousia, and it wishes for the Parousia."[19]

The eschatological I does not anticipate death (even as it accepts the empirical reality of its being-toward-death); instead it anticipates the *Parousia*. Liturgy, through which the eschatological I comes to be, effectively brackets everything that "separates man from the Parousia."[20] Therefore, "liturgical temporalization, at bottom, loses interest in every future that takes our being-toward-death as its measure."[21] Moreover, the Parousia marks an end to the possibilities of the eschatological I, but this "end" is not a negation of all possibility in the way that death is for *Dasein*; rather, the Parousia appears as "a present from which nothing is lacking . . . a present whose reality is not called into question by possibility because the final possibility, the *eschaton*, is no longer at a remove from it, because the distance that defines it finds itself neutralized."[22]

In the end, anticipation is not a double, but a triple phenomenon, encompassing Husserlian notions of protention and expectation as well as eschatological anticipation. Husserl, for his part, privileges perceptual experience and therefore distinguishes between protention as an element of perception and expectation as a *representation* of perceptual experience. Lacoste, on the other hand, brackets perceptual experience and argues that non-experience is an essential temporal category. In doing so, Lacoste is able to connect protention, worldly expectation, and eschatological anticipation as modes of non-experience. More importantly, Lacoste (following Heidegger, perhaps) integrates the triple phenomenon of anticipation into the very structure of human existence: consciousness is anticipatory. This insight resonates well with Paul's apocalyptic eschatology, in which all of existence is defined by apocalyptic anticipation of the new creation: "We know that the whole creation has been groaning in labor pains until now; and not only the creation, but we ourselves, who have the first fruits of the Spirit, groan inwardly while we wait for adoption, the redemption of our bodies" (Romans 8:22–23). Additionally, the distinction Lacoste draws between liturgical and empirical time fits with the "two ages" structure of Paul's eschatology. In short, Lacoste's phenomenality of anticipation is a promising approach to the question of kenotic time, though it remains to be seen whether anticipation represents a *fully reduced* notion of kenotic time.

B. Time as Depresencing

By the end of 1928 Husserl had assigned to his assistant, Eugen Fink, the unenviable task of editing the Bernau manuscripts, which Husserl composed during the summers of 1917 and 1918.[23] This was no small editorial project. Husserl was a prolific writer whose manuscripts (which were generally

written messily in Gabelsberger shorthand) were sometimes systematic
and well-organized, but more often fragmentary and chaotic. It was the
editorial assistant's job to organize Husserl's thoughts into a systematic
philosophical treatise, keeping in constant contact with Husserl throughout
the process. The Bernau manuscripts were particularly challenging. Not only
did Husserl consider them his "magnum opus," but the shorthand manuscripts were nearly 600 pages long! A particularly cringe-worthy anecdote
has Husserl summoning Roman Ingarden to the Black Forest, setting the
Bernau manuscript before him, and pronouncing, "That is my magnum
opus. You shall get it ready for publication for me."[24] Ingarden, who was
no longer Husserl's assistant, and who knew how difficult it had been for
Edith Stein to edit Husserl's early lectures on time, wisely declined. The job
fell to Fink, Husserl's brilliant 23-year-old doctoral student and assistant,
who had yet to finish his dissertation, and who had only recently become
Husserl's primary assistant, succeeding Ludwig Landgrebe.[25]

Husserl's editorial assistants were not subordinates, but "co-philoso-
phers." As Bruzina notes, the work of the assistants involved, "taking the
mass of these research studies and integrating them, adjusting them to
some same level of analysis, bringing their diversity to consistency and
coherence, and then making their ideas accessible by whatever tactful
rewording would retain their meaning while diminishing over-complexity
and obscurity."[26] In other words, editing Husserl's work was genuine philosophical research pursued both in concert with Husserl and on one's own.
For Fink, Husserl's manuscripts served as starting points from which to
unfold the basic philosophical problems with which Husserl was concerned.
This meant that Fink both systematized Husserl's work and pursued his
own work as a supplement to Husserl's nascent thoughts on any given
subject. Thus, in the course of editing the Bernau manuscripts, and later
the C-manuscripts, Fink came to develop his own notion of temporality
that was Husserlian in its basic trajectory, though critically opposed to
many elements of Husserl's work.

In the Bernau manuscripts, Fink notes a particular line of thought
that suggests a move beyond Husserl's earlier conception of time. Specifically, Husserl wonders how the structure of time-consciousness, as
retention—primal impression—protention, can account for consciousness's awareness of itself as a temporal flux. In other words, how does
the structure of time account for the self-perception of consciousness *as
a temporal flux*?[27] This issue arises because Husserl thinks of time in two
ways: First, he maintains that time can be understood as a temporal flow
in consciousness itself. Second, Husserl maintains that, "Andererseits ist

aber Bewusstsein in sich selbst ein Strom. Er selbst hat eine Seinsform Zeit, eben als, Strom"—"Alternately, consciousness itself is a stream; it has a temporal being-form, precisely as 'stream.' "[28] For Husserl, temporality is *both* something of which one can be conscious *and* the being-form of consciousness. How, then, can consciousness become aware of the temporal "stream" from *within* its own "streaming"?

One possibility is that temporal consciousness is aware of itself in the mode of perception: time-consciousness *perceives* itself, or "objectivates" itself. Yet if that were the case, Husserl argues, then perception of time would be constituted in time, thereby begging the question: what is the temporality of the constitutive source of the perception? According to Husserl, the perceptual model leads to an infinite regress: "Das scheint auf einen unendlichen Regress zu führen, da die Wahrnehmbarkeit dieses Prozesses wieder einen zweiten zu fordern scheint usw"—"This seems to lead to an infinite regress, since the perceptibility of these [constitutive] processes seems to require a second [constitutive source], etc."[29] Husserl therefore concludes that temporal self-awareness must be a non-objectivating, non-perceptual awareness; time-consciousness must somehow be conscious of itself *in itself*, inherently aware of its own temporal flux without presenting that flux in the mode of perception as an object in time. In other words, consciousness of time cannot involve the standard form of intentionality derived from perception.

Accordingly, Husserl proposes a new concept of the temporal flux, based not on intentional presentation (or presentification), but on *protention*, as the process through which the "not yet" becomes present. As Bruzina puts it, "Husserl now looks at the dynamic of flow in analogy to the process of filling of empty intentionality."[30] Presence and absence, on this model, have to do with a gradient of intuitive *filling* and *emptying*. The highest intuitive fulfillment is "presence," while lower intuitive fulfillment is "absence." Time, then, is a progression of intuitive filling and emptying, with two basic movements: "(1) progression toward presenting, toward 'filling,' out of a horizon of total non-presentiality—i.e., protentiality—and (2) progression away from presenting, toward 'emptying,' back into non-presentiality—i.e., retentionality."[31] Fink notices that this progression of filling and emptying implies a "horizonality of non-presence as such."[32] That is to say, the progression implies a completely empty "null state," which is essentially a horizonal complex within which intuitive filling and emptying take place.

Based upon Husserl's nascent idea of the temporal horizon, Fink inaugurates a major shift toward a notion of time as "pure horizonality."[33]

For Husserl, temporality is always defined in terms of the now-phase of consciousness. In his early work, that now-phase was the primal impression, from which protention, retention, expectation, and memory were differentiated. In the Bernau manuscripts, Husserl proposed a non-intentional notion of time as the process of filling and emptying, but temporality was still defined from the full "now," with future and past distinguished in terms of their "filling" or "emptying" motion with respect to the now. Fink, on the other hand, argues that filling and emptying take place within a horizon; thus it is the horizon that offers a true understanding of temporality. More specifically, Fink is critical of Husserl's "presentialism," which consists, "in taking the primacy of the present as fundamental, with the present taken in its double sense to mean both the here-presence of givenness and now-presentness in temporal flow."[34] The problem with Husserl's presentialism, for Fink, is that it is not a fully reduced conception of time. In privileging the present, Husserl defines the horizon of time in terms which are not properly horizonal, but which derive ultimately from an intra-horizonal entity: the egoic living present. A fully reduced treatment of time must treat the horizon of time *horizonally*, without privileging any "now" constituted *within* the horizon of time:

> Only by pushing into the time-horizons themselves can meaning be unveiled. All meaning always reaches beyond the present. Phenomenological analysis is not analysis of time because its objects are *at* a point in time, or because time is a constitutive moment in these objects, but solely because the ultimate and inmost theme of phenomenology is time itself. All phenomenological analysis is therefore always in principle a passage beyond the sphere of presence, and thus always a transgression past intuitiveness (inasmuch as one defines this as pure presence).[35]

Accordingly, the central question of a phenomenology of time is not: how do the now and not-now phases of temporal consciousness interrelate? Rather, the central question is: how can the horizon of time be defined *as a horizon*?

Beginning with Husserl's notion of time as filling and emptying, Fink characterizes the not-yet and no-longer as two modes of depresencing.[36] That is to say, the future and past share the horizonal characteristic of depresencing the "now." Such a characterization does not take us far beyond Husserl, but Fink also seeks to apply a horizonal conception of time to the present. As Bruzina notes, "That the not-yet and no-longer allow explication in terms of horizonal depresencing may be clear enough, but what about the right-now, the actually present? Is it also to be recast as *horizon*?"[37] Fink speaks of the present as a mode of spatial intentionality, or "field-intentionality." The present is that which stretches out before us spatially, as the "co-existence sphere of potential experience [*Ehrahrung*]."[38] What is present to me now—e.g., a green table, white computer, books and an empty water glass—coexists with me in space. The notions of filling and emptying, which Husserl applied to time, can also be applied to space: the present has to do with the filling and emptying of a spatial field. Fink therefore argues that the horizonality of space-time can be seen both as a flow or "stream" (as a flow from future to past) and field (as the filling and emptying of a space). Additionally, the field-horizonality of the present may be characterized as essentially "depresencing" in the same way that the flow of time may be thought of as "depresencing." Consider the field of space: we perceive various objects that are more and less full of intuitive content. Those objects closest to me may be fuller intuitively than those farthest away. My water glass, which is sitting next to me, is very full intuitively, although I cannot perceive it from every angle at once. My neighbor's apartment is less full intuitively; I have never seen it, though I am sure it looks a lot like mine. Plus, we share a wall, so some things about his apartment (his music, for example) are intuitively present for me. Less intuitively full is the surrounding city of Seattle: I see parts of the city when I look out the window, but most of it is intuitively empty until I go on a walk. Less full still—practically empty—is the intuitive content of, say, Australia, which is somewhere in the spatial field that I occupy, but is intuitively empty in its complete absence. As these examples illustrate, what makes my spatial field a "field"—i.e., what gives space its extension—is not presence, for if everything were intuitively present there could be no extension; rather, what makes space extended is the "depresencing" character of my spatial horizon. If I had a complete intuition of my water glass, for instance, perceiving it from every angle at once, then there could be no far side of the glass. Similarly, if I had a complete intuition of Australia—if Australia were completely present to me—it would make no sense to think of Australia as "the other side of the world." The world is extended, space exists for me, only through intuitive depresencing. Similarly, time moves as a flow, from not-yet to no-longer, only through the depresencing of the now. Accordingly, as Fink argues, the flow of time and the field of space are different modalities within a spatiotemporal horizon whose "horizonality" is essentially "depresencing." The egoic living present, which Husserl took as primary, is in fact constituted within the primordial spatiotemporal "swing" of depresencing.

Based on his insight into depresencing, Fink set out to write a new book on "Time and Time-Constitution," which would analyze time as the primordial horizon within which the subjective and objective moments of consciousness occur. Fink completed a manuscript of this text, but never published it, and eventually destroyed it.[39] Bruzina speculates that Fink turned away from his work because "the category of *spirit* [i.e., temporal spirit, *Geist*] may not ipso facto be the necessarily privileged one for designating the transcendentally ultimate."[40] Horizonality, for Fink, was an alternative to Husserl's presentialism, but even a concept of world-horizonality risks an "ontification" of the Absolute inasmuch as "world-horizonality" specifies what the Absolute *is*. Ultimately, for Fink, the Absolute is *meontic*; it can never be completely "ontified." What the Absolute *is* can never be specified with complete certainty. The main question, as far as the kenotic reduction is concerned, is whether Fink's notion of depresencing is sufficient to account for kenotic temporality. If depresencing turns out to be an "ontification" of the new creation disclosed in the kenotic reduction—that is, if depresencing turns out to be a temporal concept best applied to the *cosmos* and its *onta*—then the question becomes: how might "depresencing" be modified so as to be *meontic*?

C. Kenotic Time as Eschatological Horizon: The Represencing of God

Jean-Yves Lacoste and Eugen Fink offer two ways of radicalizing Husserlian temporality: First, Lacoste argues that Husserl privileges perceptual experience in his treatment of time consciousness. Consequently, Husserl draws a strict separation between the temporal structure of perception (retention—primal impression—protention) and non-perceptual modes of consciousness like memory and expectation. By bracketing experience, Lacoste uncovers the central role of non-experience in time-consciousness: anticipation of that which is not-yet pervades conscious existence. More specifically, protention, expectation, and eschatological anticipation are all modes of non-experience (though the latter is only available liturgically). The upshot, as far as the kenotic reduction is concerned, is that eschatological time is integrated into human existence in a way that Husserl never envisioned: in liturgy, the empirical I becomes an eschatological I, empirical time (the time of the *cosmos*) becomes eschatological time (the time of the new creation).

Fink provides a second way of radicalizing Husserl by bracketing the "presentialism" inherent in time-consciousness. For Fink, both Husserl's early conception of time-consciousness (as a temporal flow with the tripartite structure of retention—primal impression—protention) and Husserl's later conception of time (as the filling and emptying of intuitive content) privilege the present now-phase of consciousness. Retention and protention are both defined as modifications of the now-phase, just as filling and emptying are relative to an intuitively full present. In his work on the Bernau manuscripts, Fink moves beyond Husserlian presentialism by focusing on the horizonality of time. The idea of full and empty intuitions implies a horizon in which the filling and emptying occur. Presentialist Husserlian time-consciousness takes place within the temporal horizon and, thus, cannot serve as the *telos* of a phenomenological investigation of time. Rather, as Fink argues, a phenomenology of time must examine the horizon of time in terms of its horizonality. With respect to future and past, this is rather straightforward: both are modes of depresencing. With respect to the present, Fink introduces the idea of field-intentionality: presence is that which coexists with me in a spatial field whose "extendedness" is a mode of depresencing. Consequently, space-time may be conceptualized as "field" and "flow"—two modes of a spatiotemporal horizon whose essential horizonality is depresencing.

How do these two ways of radicalizing Husserl fit together? In one sense, Lacoste's notion of anticipation and Fink's idea of depresencing come into conflict: inasmuch as anticipation is futural and relative to a present, it is subject to Fink's critique of presentialism. Similarly, inasmuch as Fink's spatiotemporal horizon is tied to the experiential world, it is subject to Lacoste's critique of experience.[41] In another sense, Lacoste's and Fink's radicalizations of Husserl may be seen as convergent trajectories. Lacoste, on the one hand, brackets experience, bringing into view an eschatological temporality. Fink, on the other hand, brackets presentialism, opening up the idea of a temporal horizon. These two modes of *epochē* are mutually beneficial: Lacoste's critique of experience, with the resulting notion of the eschatological as inherently non-ontic, forestalls any "ontification of the Absolute." Alternately, Fink's idea of a temporal horizon might allow Lacoste's insights into non-experience to be developed into a full-blown notion of the "eschatological horizon." In other words, by bracketing both experience and presentialism, Lacoste's and Fink's notions of anticipation and depresencing together make possible a novel concept of *meontic* temporality as the "eschatological horizon."

In defining the eschatological horizon, the central question—a question on which Fink would no doubt insist—is: how might the eschatological horizon be defined according to its essential *horizonality*? Only by understanding time horizonally is a phenomenologically reduced notion of temporality achievable. For Fink, the horizonality of space-time is depresencing. Yet because as depresencing defines the world-horizon, it will not suffice in defining the eschatological horizon. There is, as Lacoste tells us, a qualitative difference between empirical (world-horizon) time and eschatological time. Consequently, the eschatological horizon must be defined (in accordance with the kenotic reduction) in the context of the new creation, not in the context of the *cosmos*. Put differently, the eschatological horizon is the horizon of the new creation; its horizonality is not the same as the horizonality of the world-horizon.

In our exploration of Paul's eschatology, we noted a number of important features of the eschatological horizon, which together suggest a *horizonal* definition of kenotic time. First, the eschatological notion of "two ages" has both historical and cosmological dimensions. In terms of salvation-history, the coming age represents a decisive break from the present age defined by sin; the new age also represents a mediated return to a primordial state in which humanity was not separated from God by sin. Thus Christ, for Paul, functions as a "new Adam" who undoes Adam's mistake: rather than bringing sin into the world, Christ inaugurates the death of sin, which is tantamount to the representing of God. Moreover, the representing of God, which has *already* begun in the life, death, and resurrection of Christ, is a process that is *not yet* complete, culminating in the pure presence of *Parousia*, which marks the end of history. In terms of cosmology, the new age inaugurates a new creation in which the sustaining and creative action of God's overflowing love is ever more present in the world, eventually resulting in a divine presence (*Parousia*) that mirrors the primordial prelapsarian divine presence. A horizonal picture of salvation-history thus emerges: an epoch defined by God's primordial presence is succeeded by an epoch of sin and divine depresencing, which is in turn succeeded by a new age or new creation defined by the "representing" of God. The final epoch, disclosed in the kenotic reduction as "new creation," is enfolded in an eschatological spatiotemporal horizon whose essential horizonality is the representing of God. In other words, a kenotically reduced understanding of kenotic time, coinciding with the cosmological and temporal/historical aspects of Pauline apocalyptic eschatology may be expressed as follows: kenotic temporality is the eschatological horizon of divine representing.

In the end, by appropriating and combining Lacoste's and Fink's radicalizations of Husserlian time-consciousness, a phenomenological concept of the "eschatological horizon" emerges, the horizonality of which is not reducible to that of the of the world-horizon. The eschatological horizon is the horizon of the new creation; its horizonality is, consequently, eschatological, reflecting the apocalyptic eschatology exemplified in Paul's disclosure of the new creation in the kenōsis hymn. Additionally, the main features of Paul's eschatology—e.g., the notion of "two ages"—suggest a horizonal (and fully reduced) characterization of kenotic space-time (disclosed as the "new age" or "new creation") as the representing of God. Considered as a whole, the kenotic reduction brackets the *cosmos*, and discloses a new creation, in which space-time is a horizon whose essential horizonality is representing.

Conclusion

A. Précis

In part I, I examined Husserlian notions of absolute science, beginning with static phenomenology, proceeding through genetic phenomenology, and ending with Fink's constructive phenomenology. In the static mode, absolute science is beholden to Cartesian categories. Absolute knowledge occurs when an intentional object (*noema*) is given in pure self-evidence to the phenomenal subject. Hence the goal of phenomenology is to bring the intentional activity of the subject into harmony with the intuitive content of the phenomenal object, culminating in a perfect adequation of intention and intuition. In the genetic mode, the notion of self-evidence is retained, though the whole process of absolute science is rooted in the life-world. Phenomenology brings its objects of investigation into self-evidence by tracing their genetic composition back to the life-world. For Fink, genetic phenomenology is problematic to the extent that it focuses on the genesis of phenomenal objects without examining the genesis of consciousness itself. By exploring the act of phenomenologizing, Fink draws a distinction between phenomenological reflection and constituting acts. The world, including consciousness and Being itself, proves to be a *constituted* reality that functions as one moment in the synthetic unity of a *meontic* Absolute encompassing constituted Being, the constitutive source of Being, and phenomenological reflection on Being. Absolute science, for Fink, is a constructive enterprise that has as its theme both the phenomenological method and phenomenal elements. It is a circular hermeneutic that begins with reflection on phenomenal elements, which leads to reflection on the phenomenological method, which in turn leads to a phenomenological clarification of the elements and further reflection on the phenomenological method, and so on. This hermeneutical process, as the life-movement of the *meontic* Absolute, is always directed toward knowledge of the Absolute, but remains radically open.

While Fink's "theory of method" goes a long way toward radicalizing Husserl's concept of absolute science, it remains incomplete inasmuch as Fink never connects the theory of method to any particular phenomenal element. Fink never *performs* absolute science. In part II, I develop an absolute science of scripture by focusing on the kenōsis hymn. Chapter 4 recounts various interpretive issues associated with the kenōsis hymn. Chapter 5 offers a phenomenological reading of the hymn as an analogy to phenomenological reduction. On the one hand, the kenotic reduction points toward a phenomenological re-reading of the hymn, which addresses the hermeneutical issues raised in chapter 4. On the other hand, the kenotic reduction points toward a radicalization of the phenomenological method in accordance with the circular hermeneutic of an absolute science of scripture. Kenōsis is not a "self-emptying" with respect to divine status or attributes, but an emptying of the *cosmos* as the source of truth and value, so that the world (creation) may be revealed as the outpouring of God's creative love. In the kenotic reduction, *cosmos* is reduced to a *new creation*, whose fundamental features are explored in chapters 6 and 7. By drawing on Fink's concept of "horizonality" and Lacoste's idea of the "eschatological I," I argue that the new creation is ultimately an eschatological horizon whose basic spatio-temporal structure is the representing of God.

To conclude, I would like to consider three lingering questions about the overall significance of this investigation: First, what would a turn to phenomenology mean for biblical studies? Second, what does the kenotic reduction reveal about the nature and purpose of Husserlian phenomenology? Third, if absolute science is radicalized through an engagement with Christian scripture, what does that mean about the relationship between phenomenology and Christianity?

B. Absolute Science and Biblical Criticism

In first chapter, I gestured toward a phenomenological critique of contemporary biblical studies based on Husserl's understanding of the "natural attitude." Biblical sciences, like all sciences grounded in the natural attitude, are not absolute in scope and therefore cannot examine scripture in all its complexity. In other words, the problem with biblical studies is not that it is overly scientific, but that it is not scientific enough. Given the preceding exploration of absolute science, we are now in a position to develop this critique of biblical studies more fully.

Husserl's exploration of various "attitudes" in *Ideas II* is particularly helpful. In that work, Husserl clarifies the notion of "natural attitude" offered in *Ideas I*. Nature, Husserl argues in *Ideas* II, "is the total spatio-temporal 'universe', the total domain of possible experience."[1] In its most basic sense, the natural attitude consists in a naïve orientation toward the world and a simple acceptance of what is given there. One may shift out this naiveté by adopting various "theoretical attitudes," which impose "ruling apperceptions" that limit the scope of nature. Speaking of the "natural-scientific attitude," Husserl claims,

> A "ruling apperception" determines in advance what is or is not a natural-scientific Object, hence what is or is not nature in the natural-scientific sense. The task is to bring that to clarity. In which respect it is evident from the outset that *all* the predicates we ascribe to things under the headings of pleasantness, beauty, utility, practical suitability, or perfection remain completely out of consideration (values, good, ends, instruments, means, etc.). These do not at all concern the natural scientist; they do not belong to nature in his sense.[2]

As a theoretical stance, the natural-scientific attitude necessarily has a ruling apperception that restricts its scope. That is to say, it "constitutes" nature in a particular way, as the sphere of "mere things," which excludes values, beauty, and so forth. None of this is very concerning. A physicist, for example, studies the physical world; no one expects her to hold forth on beauty. An ethicist studies the good; no one expects her to be an expert on quarks. (Husserl argues that beauty and the good have to do with value-objects not natural-objects.[3]) In fact, we adopt all sorts of different attitudes in the normal flow of life.

The natural-scientific attitude only becomes problematic when it degenerates into a "naturalistic attitude," which recognizes the natural world (in a very restricted sense) as the *only* domain of knowledge, truth, and value. The problem, of course, is that naturalism would exclude much of human experience from scientific inquiry: every non-physical experience would be either put out of play entirely or reduced in some way to physical reality.[4] Here one might see an analogy between the naturalistic attitude and modes of biblical studies that recognize only one domain (or one *superior* domain) of textual meaning. In nineteenth- and early-twentieth-century historical-critical scholarship, for example, it was often claimed that the meaning (or truth) of scripture could only be gained through historical methods.[5] So, for example, Charles Augustus Briggs speaks of traditional biblical interpretation as "rubbish" that must be cleaned out using historical-critical methods in order to uncover the real truths of the Bible:

> The valleys of biblical truth have been filled up with the debris of human dogmas, ecclesiastical institutions, liturgical formulas, priestly ceremonies, and casuistic practices. Historical criticism is digging through this mass of rubbish. Historical criticism is searching for the rock-bed of the Divine word, in order to recover the real Bible. Historical criticism is sifting all this rubbish. It will gather out every precious stone. Nothing will escape its keen eye.[6]

Similarly, in his introduction to David Friedrich Strauss's magisterial *Life of Jesus Critically Examined*, Otto Pfleiderer extols the singular capacity of Strauss's historical-critical method for finding the "truth" obscured in the mythic texts of scripture:

> The imaginary lights of mythological tradition must be put out, that the eye may distinguish the false from the true in the twilight of the Biblical origins of our religion. The ancient structures of belief, which the childish fancy of men has con-structed of truth and poetry, *Warheit und Dichtung*, must be taken down and cleared away, in order that a new erection of more durable materials may be raised. To all earnest seekers after truth, the *Leben Jesu* of Strauss may be helpful, not as supplying the truth ready to hand, but as stripping the bandages of prejudice from the eyes, and so enabling them clearly to see and rightly to seek it.[7]

The problem with such methods is that they limit the meaning of scripture to a very narrow domain (e.g., the natural world, original historical context, and so forth), thereby rendering biblical science incapable of addressing the full complexity of scripture. Just as the naturalistic attitude excludes much of human experience from scientific inquiry, so also historical criticism excludes much of the meaning, significance, and function of scripture from scholarly investigation. For Husserl, this is just bad science; its methods are not adequate for its object of study.

Of course, the procrustean tendencies of historical criticism will come as no surprise to those familiar with recent biblical scholarship. Many contemporary methods explicitly reject the "narrowness" of historical criticism. Reader-response theory, socio-rhetorical criticism, and other literary-critical methods are used in modern biblical studies to capture more of the significance and function of scripture than older versions of historical criticism allowed.[8] Nonetheless, even these contemporary methods fall under the scope of Husserl's broader criticism of the natural attitude. While the theoretical, naturalistic version of the natural attitude makes for bad science, the natural attitude itself proves similarly problematic.

Let us consider the natural-scientific attitude again. In *Ideas II*, Husserl argues that the natural-scientific attitude is subordinate to the "personalistic attitude," which he defines as,

> the attitude we are always in when we live with one another, talk to one another, shake hand with one another in greeting, or are related to one another in love and aversion, in disposition and action, in discourse and discussion. Likewise we are in this attitude when we consider the things surrounding us precisely as our surroundings and not as "Objective" nature, the way it is for natural science.[9]

If the natural-scientific attitude reduces nature to a sphere of mere things, the personalistic attitude constitutes nature as the world that surrounds *me*. So, for example, in the naturalistic attitude, the people I encounter in my vicinity are merely physical things—collections of cells, various combinations of molecules, and so forth. In the personalistic attitude, I encounter another person as *my* child, or *my* spouse, or *my* friend. Husserl's insight here is Kierkegaardian: the truly subjective elements of experience (*my* experience) retreat from the natural-scientific gaze. Moreover, the natural-scientific attitude and personalistic attitude are not inherently equal. Husserl argues that the natural-scientific attitude is subordinate to the personalistic because it requires us to abstract from our personal experiences in order to obtain scientific objectivity.[10] It turns out that "nature," in the natural-scientific sense, is not just there; it presumes a whole host of constituting activities that take place in the personalistic attitude.

The reliance of the natural-scientific attitude on the personalistic reflects deeper issues within the natural attitude itself. In its most basic form, the natural attitude is an opening onto the world that accepts what is given there; it is the natural state of human consciousness as it experiences the world. As Husserl puts it in the *Crisis*, the natural attitude consists in "straightforwardly living toward whatever objects are given, thus toward the world-horizon, in normal, unbroken constancy, in synthetic coherence running through all acts. This normal, straightforward living, toward whatever objects are given, indicates that all our interests have their goals in objects."[11] Phenomenological analysis reveals, however, that the object-world, which the natural attitude takes as given, is in fact constituted; there is transcendental depth underlying the world-horizon. As our investigation showed, the natural attitude gets two things wrong: First, it assumes that objects in the world are simply there, when they are actually constituted by consciousness. Second, because it takes the world as given, it cannot investigate the pre-givenness of the world-horizon. Phenomenology addresses both these issues: "In opposition to all previously designed objective sciences, which are sciences on the ground of the world, this [phenomenology] would be a science of the universal *how* of the pre-givenness of the world, i.e., of what makes it a universal ground for any sort of objectivity."[12] In other words, phenomenology can investigate both the constitution of intra-worldly phenomena and the pre-givenness of the world-horizon within the circular hermeneutic of absolute science.

This dual capacity of phenomenology exposes an important flaw in biblical studies: In all its modes, historical or otherwise, biblical criticism treats scripture as a textual object (or group of textual objects) that appears *within* the world-horizon. Because it is rooted in the natural attitude, biblical criticism is largely incapable of investigating the role that scripture plays in constituting the world-horizon. The recent profusion of interpretive methods does not correct this problem; rather, different methods tend to reflect differing assumptions about how worldly textual objects accrue meaning. So for historical critics, the meaning of scripture is governed by its original context; for reader-response critics, meaning is governed by the interpretive processes of readers; and for socio-rhetorical critics, meaning of is governed by various social structures (both ancient and modern) and rhetorical aims. In every case, scripture is treated as an intra-worldly phenomenon. Yet, for religious communities, scripture is both an object in the world-horizon and the constitutive source of horizons. That is to say, scripture is transcendentally deep; it is both given and pre-given; human and divine; it exists within horizons and gives birth to horizons.[13] The rabbis, for example, claimed that Torah existed before creation and was consulted by God in the very act of creation:

The Torah declares: "I was the working tool of the Holy One, blessed be He." In human practice, when a mortal king builds a palace, he builds it not with his own skill but with the skill of an architect. The architect moreover does not build it out of his head, but employs plans and diagrams to know how to arrange the chambers and the wicket doors. Thus God consulted the Torah and created the world, while the Torah declares, "In the beginning God created" (1:1), "beginning" referring to the Torah, as in the verse, "The Lord made me as the beginning of His way" (Prov. 8:22).[14]

This midrashic commentary attests to the transcendental depths of scripture as both intra-worldly text and pre-given constitutive origin (or *genesis*) of the world-horizon. Yet contemporary biblical criticism, which is based in the natural attitude and therefore takes the object-world as given, cannot account for the horizon generating function of scripture. That is to say, recent modes of biblical interpretation neglect the transcendental depth of scripture. In contrast, a phenomenological approach treats scripture both as a worldly textual phenomenon, which accrues meaning in various ways, and as the transcendental source of the world-horizon. Phenomenology may therefore provide a fuller understanding of what scripture is and how it functions.

C. Absolute Science and Husserlian Phenomenology

My phenomenological reading of the kenōsis hymn began with an analogy between the hymn and Husserl's phenomenological reduction. Part II expanded that analogy in an effort to clarify both the kenōsis hymn and the phenomenological reduction within the circular hermeneutic of absolute science. But let us focus, for the moment, on the initial analogy. In chapters 4 and 5, I asserted that such an analogy exists, without ever explaining *why* it exists. Some crucial questions thus confront us: Why is there an analogy between the kenōsis hymn and phenomenological reduction in the first place? Does the analogy only apply to Husserl's brand of phenomenology? Why did this project, as both a kenotic reading of phenomenology and phenomenological reading of kenōsis, work at all? And for that matter, why were such issues not resolved earlier?

These questions relate to the overarching logic of this investigation, which sought to refine and draw out the implications of a particular phenomenological hypothesis: the kenōsis hymn represents a biblical mode of reduction that is similar to, but far more radical than, phenomenological reduction. This hypothesis was generated out of two practical concerns: First, contemporary biblical scholarship is not absolute in its scope; it is not scientific enough. Second, the phenomenological notion of absolute science, inasmuch as it is primarily theoretical, is incomplete. Absolute science should be performed *in vivo*, where theoretical phenomenological reflection exists in a "synthetic unity" with the phenomena under consideration. The kenotic reduction addresses these concerns in two ways: Biblical scholarship gains an absolute scope, becoming enmeshed in a hermeneutical scientific process wherein the methods of biblical science are reformed in accordance with the scriptural phenomena at hand. Likewise, the phenomenological idea of absolute science gains real content inasmuch as theoretical phenomenological reflection exists in a "synthetic unity" with scripture itself.

In exploring the implications of the kenotic reduction, my aim has been to refine the hypothesis of the kenotic reduction to the point where it is intuitively compelling as both a demonstration of absolute science and an understanding of kenōsis. Only *after* such a radicalization of absolute science does the truth about phenomenology become clear: *phenomenology is kenotic*. The phenomenological method, when radicalized, claims no superiority over the phenomena under investigation; rather, phenomenology empties itself, adapting its methodology to the phenomena at hand in the circular hermeneutic of absolute science. Ultimately, the reason why the kenotic reduction is compelling—the reason why there is an analogy between phenomenological reduction and the kenōsis hymn—is that phenomenology is essentially kenotic. Yet this only becomes apparent *after* phenomenology is radicalized sufficiently.

One might also wonder about the necessity of the particular route taken through the works of Husserl and Fink. If phenomenology is essentially kenotic, then why should one prefer a particular articulation of the phenomenological method? Does one have to accept the philosophical baggage of a single brand of phenomenology in order to understand kenōsis? The short, if cryptic, answer is: yes and no. "Yes" in the sense that it is necessary to have some understanding of the methods and trajectory of phenomenology in order to arrive at a radicalized concept of absolute science. "No" in the sense that absolute science (if properly radicalized) always adapts its methods to the particular phenomena under consideration. Even Husserl's foundational methodological insights are subject to revision over the course of an investigation. So the kenotic reduction may diverge from Husserl's phenomenological reduction in important ways, but that is entirely appropriate. In absolute science, specific methodological machinations are less important than the phenomenological practice (*askesis*) of "nudging" phenomena to give themselves in their full transcendental depth. To paraphrase Wittgenstein, one may throw away the ladder after one has climbed up on it.[15]

D. Absolute Science and Christianity

When all is said and done, the fact remains that an absolute science of scripture, as I have developed it, is a European and Judeo-Christian form of absolute science. It takes its generative clues from phenomenology (primarily a European mode of philosophy) and the kenōsis hymn (a Christian text given to us in the letters of a messianic Jew). One wonders, then, whether radical phenomenology is essentially Judeo-Christian. If so, how can it be "absolute"? In one sense, the kenotic reduction is Judeo-Christian. The categories and concepts employed come from Christian and Jewish traditions, even if no particular piece of religious dogma predetermines the kenotic reduction. This brand of radical phenomenology may well apply outside of the Christian context but only to the extent that there are concepts analogous to kenōsis operating in other traditions (as there surely are).

It is, however, important to note that phenomenology, as radicalized in the kenotic reduction, does not attempt to universalize Christian concepts. Absolute science is not universal science, and certainly not universally Christian. If, as Fink claims, absolute science is a synthetic unity of the reflective and constitutive moments of absolute life, then phenomenological reflection is essentially linked to the life-world out of which it arises. Although phenomenologizing is a "countertendency" in the life of the Absolute, it never completely breaks from the life-world, which is generated by a whole host of processes defining a "homeworld" over and against an "alienworld," to use Steinbock's terminology. Accordingly, the kenotic reduction is a feature of an absolute science belonging to a particular homeworld, though there may be many other homeworlds (alienworlds to me), many other traditions, and thus many other forms of absolute science. Whether the kenotic reduction functions as absolute science in other homeworlds is an open question. Put differently, absolute science always exists simultaneously inside and outside of traditions— "outside" to the extent that it evaluates the generative sources of the life-world (as homeworld and alienworld), and "inside" to the extent that the goals and methods of absolute science always reflect a homeworld. Absolute science never completely separates from its homeworld in such a way that it is able to examine all homeworlds; it cannot be universal in scope, though it is hardly relativistic in a vicious sense. Kenotically radicalized phenomenology brooks none of the modernist hope for universal science. There may be an adequation between intention and intuition, but absolute science provides no last word.

Notes

Foreword

1. See Edmund Husserl, *Logical Investigations*, trans. J. N. Findlay, 2 vols. (London: Routledge and Kegan Paul, 1970), II, 784.

2. Husserl, *Logical Investigations*, I, 252.

3. See Martin Heidegger, *The Phenomenology of Religious Life*, trans. Matthias Fritsch and Jennifer Anna Gosetti-Ferencei (Bloomington: Indiana University Press, 2004), §§ 14–33.

4. See, for example, Heidegger, *Elucidations of Hölderlin's Poetry*, trans. Keith Hoeller (Amherst, NY: Humanity Books, 2000).

5. See, for example, Michel Henry, *Words of Christ*, trans. Christina M. Gschwandtner, foreword Jean-Yves Lacoste, intro. Karl Hefty (Grand Rapids, MI: William B. Eerdmans Pub. Co., 2012), Jacques Derrida, "Des tours de Babel," *Psyche: Inventions of the Other*, ed. Peggy Kamuf and Elisabeth Rottenberg, 2 vols. (Stanford, CA: Stanford University Press, 2007), I, 191–225, and Jean-Luc Marion, *God without Being: Hors-Texte*, trans. Thomas A. Carlson, foreword David Tracy (Chicago: University of Chicago Press, 1991), 95–102.

6. See, for example, Jonathan Culler, *On Deconstruction: Theory and Criticism after Structuralism* (Ithaca, NY: Cornell University Press, 1982).

7. See Derrida, *Edmund Husserl's "Origin of Geometry": An Introduction*, trans. with pref. John P. Leavey, Jr. (Stony Brook, NY: Nicolas Hays, Ltd., 1978), " 'Genesis and Structure' and Phenomenology," *Writing and Difference*, trans., intro., and notes Alan Bass (London: Routledge and Kegan Paul, 1978), *Speech and Phenomena: And Other Essays on Husserl's Theory of Signs*, trans. and intro. David B. Allison, pref. Newton Garver (Evanston, IL: Northwestern University Press, 1973).

8. See Dominique Janicaud, *Phenomenology and the "Theological Turn": The French Debate*, Part I, trans. Bernard G. Prusak (New York: Fordham University Press, 2000).

9. See Janicaud, *Phenomenology "Wide Open": After the French Debate*, trans. Charles N. Cabral (New York: Fordham University Press, 2005).

10. See Husserl, *Ideas for a Pure Phenomenology and Phenomenological Philosophy*, I: *General Introduction to Pure Phenomenology*, trans. Daniel O. Dahlstrom (Indianapolis: Hackett Pub. Co., 2014), §51 Remark.

Introduction

1. Edmund Husserl, *The Crisis of European Sciences and Transcendental Phenomenology*, trans. David Carr (Evanston, IL: Northwestern University Press, 1970), 389.
2. Martin Heidegger, *Introduction to Metaphysics*, trans. Gregory Fried and Richard Polt (New Haven, CT: Yale University Press, 2000), 28.
3. Martin Heidegger, *The Phenomenology of Religious Life*, trans. Matthias Fritsch and Jennifer Anna Gosetti-Ferencei (Bloomington, IN: Indiana University Press, 2004), 87.
4. Ibid., 7.
5. Ibid., 50.

Introduction to Part I

1. Edmund Husserl, *Logical Investigations*, vol. 1, trans. J. N. Findlay (New York: Routledge, 2001), 144.
2. Edmund Husserl, "Philosophy as a Rigorous Science," trans. Marcus Brainard, in *The New Yearbook for Phenomenology and Phenomenological Philosophy* II (2002): 293.

Chapter 1

1. Edmund Husserl, *Philosophy of Arithmetic: Psychological and Logical Investigations with Supplementary Texts from 1887–1901*, trans. Dallas Willard (The Hague: M. Nijhoff, 2003), 15.
2. Ibid. 81.
3. Robert Sokolowski, *The Formation of Husserl's Concept of Constitution* (The Hague: M. Nijhoff, 1964), 14.
4. Gottlob Frege, "Review of Dr. E Husserl's *Philosophy of Arithmetic*, trans. E. W. Kluge, in *Husserl: Expositions and Appraisals*, eds. Frederick Elliston and Peter McCormick (Notre Dame, IN: University of Notre Dame Press, 1981) 314–24.
5. Dermot Moran, introduction to *Logical Investigations*, vol. 1, by Edmund Husserl (New York: Routledge, 2001), xlii.
6. Ibid., xlii.
7. Husserl, *Logical Investigations* 1, 50.
8. Ibid., 46.

9. Ibid., 46.

10. Ibid., 47.

11. N.B., Dermot Moran rightly notes a similarity between Husserl's *Logical Investigations* and Wittgenstein's *Tractatus* regarding the *a priori* status of logical laws: "Husserl holds a view similar to Wittgenstein in the *Tractatus*—logic says nothing about the real world, the world of facts. It is a purely formal [i.e., analytic] *a priori* science." Moran, introduction to *Logical Investigations* I, xliii.

12. Husserl, *Logical Investigations* 1, 47.

13. Ibid., 51.

14. Ibid., 52.

15. Ibid., 55.

16. Matheson Russell, *Husserl: A Guide for the Perplexed* (New York: Continuum, 2006), 15.

17. Dan Zahavi, *Husserl's Phenomenology* (Palo Alto, CA: Stanford University Press, 2003), 10. Cf. Husserl, *Logical Investigations* 1, 187f.

18. Husserl never denies that meaning is context dependent. So, Zahavi: "Husserl is not denying that the meaning of an assertion can be context dependent, and that the meaning of the assertion might therefore change if the circumstances are different. His point is merely that a formal variation in place, time, and person does not lead to a change in meaning." Zahavi, *Husserl's Phenomenology*, 10.

19. Ibid., 10.

20. Husserl, *Logical Investigations* 1, 2.

21. Ibid., 169.

22. Ibid., 165.

23. Ibid., 184.

24. Husserl is clear that expressions must also function as indications when they are used in actual communication—cf. ibid., 189.

25. Ibid., 192.

26. Ibid., 197.

27. Objects of reference need not be real objects. A unicorn, for example, is a perfectly acceptable object of reference.

28. Ibid., 197.

29. Ibid., 199.

30. Ibid., 199.

31. Edmund Husserl, *Introduction to Logic and Theory of Knowledge: Lectures 1906–07*, trans. Claire Ortiz Hill (Dordrecht, The Netherlands: Springer, 2008), 137.

32. Ibid., 154.

33. Ibid., 153.

34. The connection between justification and truth is not thoroughly developed by Husserl. In *Logical Investigations*, Husserl claims that pure self-evidence is tantamount to truth, but the discussion goes no further. See: Edmund Husserl, *Logical Investigations*, vol. 2, trans. J. N. Findlay (New York: Routledge, 2001), 259–67. Husserl variously speaks of self-evidence as yielding ultimate justification and *universal* truth. Yet it is not entirely clear why apodictic certainty should be

universal. The lack of clarity on this point becomes problematic in Husserl's later work, as will be explored in the next chapter.

35. Ibid., 263.

36. Ibid., 261.

37. Ibid., 261.

38. Ibid., 264.

39. Edmund Husserl, *Ideas Pertaining to a Pure Phenomenology and to a Phenomenological Philosophy,* vol. 1, trans. F. Kersten (The Hague: M. Nijhoff, 1982), 94.

40. Ibid., 96.

41. Ibid., 96.

42. Erazim V. Kohák, *Idea and Experience: Edmund Husserl's Project of Phenomenology in Ideas I* (Chicago: University of Chicago Press, 1978), 10.

43. Husserl, *Ideas I,* 5.

44. Husserl analyzes the natural attitude (and related natural-scientific and naturalistic attitudes) in much more detail in *Ideas II.* [Edmund Husserl, *Studies in the Phenomenology of Constitution,* vol. 2 of *Ideas Pertaining to a Pure Phenomenology and to a Phenomenological Philosophy,* trans. Richard Rojcewicz and André Schuwer (Dordrecht, The Netherlands: Kluwer Academic Publishers, 1989)]. Husserl's treatment of the natural attitude in *Ideas II* will be examined in the concluding chapter.

45. Kohák, *Idea and Experience,* 11.

46. Ibid., 35.

47. Husserl, *Ideas I,* 109.

48. Ibid., 109.

49. Ibid., 110.

50. Ibid., 110.

51. Ibid., 112.

52. John D. Caputo, *Radical Hermeneutics: Repetition, Deconstruction, and the Hermeneutic Project* (Bloomington: Indiana University Press, 1987), 44.

53. Husserl, *Ideas I,* 113.

54. Ibid., 131.

55. Ibid., 132.

56. Kohák, *Idea and Experience,* 170.

57. Ibid., 170.

58. Ibid., 170.

59. Husserl, *Ideas I,* 162.

60. Ibid., 142.

61. Edmund Husserl, *The Basic Problems of Phenomenology: From the Lectures, Winter Semester, 1910–1911,* trans. Ingo Farin and James G. Hart (Dordrecht, The Netherlands: Springer, 2006), 50.

62. Ibid., 74.

63. Ibid., 75.

64. Ibid., 75.

Chapter 2

1. Edmund Husserl, *The Crisis of European Sciences*, 155.

2. Eugen Fink, *Phänomenologische Werkstatt, Teilband 2: Die Bernauer Zeitmanuskripte, Cartesianische Meditationen und System der phänomenologische Philosophie*, ed. Ronald Bruzina. (Freiburg: Verlag Karl Alber, 2008), 29.

3. Ronald Bruzina, *Edmund Husserl and Eugen Fink: Beginnings and Ends in Phenomenology, 1928–1938* (New Haven, CT: Yale University Press, 2004), 97f.

4. Edmund Husserl, *Cartesian Meditations: An Introduction to Phenomenology*, trans. Dorion Cairns (The Hague: M. Nijhoff, 1977), 78.

5. Rudolf Bernet, Iso Kern and Eduard Marbach, *An Introduction to Husserlian Phenomenology* (Evanston, IL: Northwestern University Press, 1993), 196.

6. Husserl, *Cartesian Meditations*, 66.

7. Robert Sokolowski, *The Formation of Husserl's Concept of Constitution* (The Hague: Martinus Nijhoff, 1964), 172.

8. Husserl, *Cartesian Meditations*, 77.

9. Ibid., 77.

10. Ibid., 77.

11. Ibid., 78.

12. Ibid., 79.

13. Bernet, Kern and Marbach, *An Introduction to Husserlian Phenomenology*, 201.

14. Husserl, *Cartesian Meditations*, 79.

15. Ibid., 80.

16. Husserl, *The Crisis of European Sciences*, 21.

17. On μέθεξις see, e.g., Plato, *Parmenides*, 132d–135c.

18. Husserl, *The Crisis of European Sciences*, 22.

19. Ibid., 23.

20. Ibid., 28.

21. Ibid., 29.

22. Ibid., 48f.

23. Ibid., 355.

24. It should be noted that Husserl is not actually inquiring about historical geometers. As he puts it, "The question of the origin of geometry . . . shall not be considered here as the historical-philological question, i.e., as the search for the first geometers who actually uttered pure geometrical propositions . . . Rather than this, our interest shall be the inquiry back into the most original sense in which geometry once arose . . . we inquire into that sense in which it appeared in history for the first time—in which it had to appear, even though we know nothing of the first creators and are not even asking after them." Ibid., 354.

25. Ibid., 356.

26. Ibid., 356.

27. Ibid., 360.

28. Ibid., 360.

29. Ibid., 360.

30. Ibid., 360.

31. Ibid., 360f.

32. Ibid., 367.

33. Ibid., 49.

34. Ibid., 52.

35. Ibid., 127.

36. Ibid., 59.

37. Ibid., 125.

38. Ibid., 128.

39. Ibid., 138.

40. Ibid., 138.

41. Ibid., 139.

42. Ibid., 142.

43. Ibid., 173.

44. Ibid., 152.

45. Frederick Elliston and Peter McCormick, eds., *Husserl: Expositions and Appraisals* (Notre Dame, IN: University of Notre Dame Press, 1977), 203.

46. Alfred Schutz and Maurice Alexander Natanson, *Phenomenology and Social Reality: Essays in Memory of Alfred Schutz* (The Hague: Nijhoff, 1970), 306.

47. Anthony J. Steinbock, *Home and Beyond: Generative Phenomenology After Husserl* (Evanston, IL: Northwestern University Press, 1995), 102.

48. Husserl, *The Crisis of European Sciences*, 142f.

49. Husserl also speaks of "pregivenness" in *Ideas II*, which predates the *Crisis* by almost two decades. In the context of *Ideas II*, "pre-giveness" refers to a sort of passive synthesis involved in the shift from one "attitude" (e.g., affective delight at seeing a work of art) to another (e.g., critical evaluation of the same work of art). Whenever a shift in attitude takes place, Husserl argues that the phenomenal object constituted in the prior attitude is synthesized passively into the later attitude: "If a shift of focus takes place, then the pre-giving acts . . . have already run their course in the modality of their original performance. They are now no longer active steps of the spontaneous intending and theoretical determining, of subject-positing and predicate-positing, of step-wise collecting, etc. They are alive only in an other, essentially modified, form as the 'still' having in consciousness of what has been constituted and the retaining of it" (ibid., 7f.). Alternately, in the *Crisis*, Husserl uses the term "pre-given" to characterize the life-world itself as the always-already-there horizon within which phenomenal objects appear.

50. Steinbock, *Home and Beyond*, 101.

51. Husserl, *The Crisis of European Sciences*, 151.

52. Steinbock, *Home and Beyond*, 102.

53. Ibid., 104.

54. Ibid., 112.

55. Ibid., 167.
56. Ibid., 168.
57. Ibid., 138.
58. Maurice Merleau-Ponty, *Phenomenology of Perception* (New York: Routledge, 1995), 352.
59. Steinbock, *Home and Beyond*, 158.
60. Ibid., 158. My italics.
61. Ibid., 158.
62. Ibid., 158f.
63. Ibid., 163.
64. Ibid., 171.
65. Ibid., 179.
66. Kevin Hart, *Kingdoms of God* (Bloomington: Indiana University Press, 2014), 202f.
67. Eugen Fink, *Sixth Cartesian Meditation*, trans. Ronald Bruzina (Bloomington: Indiana University Press, 1995), 40.
68. Ibid., 42.
69. Ibid., 45.

Chapter 3

1. Fink, *Sixth Cartesian Meditation*, 145.
2. Ibid., 145.
3. Ibid., 145.
4. Ibid., 145.
5. Ibid., 20.
6. Ibid., 20.
7. Ibid., 11.
8. Ibid., 23.
9. Ibid., 55.
10. Ibid., 55.
11. Ibid., 56.
12. Ibid., 39.
13. Eugen Fink, *VI. Cartesianische Meditation, Teil 2: Ergänzungsband*, eds. Guy van Kerckhoven, Husserliana Dokumente II/2 (Dordrecht, The Netherlands: Kluwer Academic Publishers, 1988), 164.
14. Ibid. 170.
15. Eugen Fink, *Studien zur Phänomenologie, 1930–1939*. Phaenomenologica 21 (The Hague: M. Nijhoff, 1966), 11.
16. Fink, *Sixth Cartesian Meditation*, 120.
17. Ibid., 40.
18. Ibid., 41.

19. Bruzina, *Husserl and Fink*, xxxviii.

20. Fink, *Sixth Cartesian Meditation*, 21.

21. Ibid., 21.

22. Ibid., 107.

23. Ibid., 21.

24. Ibid., 24.

25. Ibid., 24.

26. Ibid., 24.

27. Ibid., 13.

28. Ibid., 32.

29. Ibid., 1.

30. Many contemporary phenomenologists shy away from the transcendental extension of subjectivity proposed by Husserl and radicalized by Fink. Jean-Luc Marion, for example, argues for a transcendentally flattened concept of subjectivity, wherein subjectivity is little more than a "depthless surface," "a mere screen for lived experiences," and a "screen on which [the given] crashes." Jean-Luc Marion, *Being Given*, trans. Jeffrey L. Kosky (Palo Alto, CA: Stanford University Press), 69, 175, 265. Similarly, Claude Romano reduces subjectivity to a transcendentally shallow "self-hood," defined by "what befalls him *from* and *through* a [worldly] event." Subjectivity only arises, for Romano, as a defective form of selfhood, in which the self is no longer able to receive events, having detached itself from the events which affect it: "the term 'subject' is only appropriate for an *advenant* inasmuch as he is stripped of himself . . . an *advenant* only happens as pure 'subject' when this possibility of reception [*accueil*] is altered and closed." Claude Romano, *Event and World*, trans. Shane Mackinlay (New York: Fordham University Press, 2009) 130ff. Admittedly, some measure of suspicion regarding transcendental phenomenology is understandable. After all, pronouncements about the transcendental conditions of possibility for human being-in-the-world run the risk of a sort of colonial univocity, treating particular normative claims about humanity as universal. Moreover, transcendental phenomenology—especially, in Husserl's more Cartesian moments—carries with it a great deal of metaphysical baggage that is not always phenomenologically justifiable. Yet by abandoning transcendental subjectivity altogether, contemporary phenomenology has thrown the proverbial baby out with the bath water. In giving up the possibility of a "stretched" transcendental subject (of the type I have been advocating in my reading of Fink's *Sixth Cartesian Meditation*), phenomenology also gives up any aspirations of being an absolute science. It thereby loses much of its practical ability to address crises in the sciences, inasmuch as it is no longer able to provide a ground for the sciences in the transcendental life of subjectivity. Without the transcendental turn, phenomenology becomes little more than a philosophical language for describing various aspects of being-in-the-world and various phenomena that occur within the horizon of the world.

31. Fink, *Sixth Cartesian Meditation*, 155.

32. Ibid., 133.

33. Ibid., 133.

34. Ibid., 133.
35. Ibid., 104.
36. Ibid., 105.
37. Ibid., 105.
38. Ibid., 120.
39. Ibid., 111.
40. Ibid., 111.
41. Ibid., 111.
42. Ibid., 112.
43. Ibid., 112.
44. Ibid., 112.
45. Ibid., 112.
46. Ibid., 113.
47. Ibid., 116.
48. Ibid., 116.
49. Ibid., 118.
50. Ibid., 119.
51. Ibid., 120.
52. Ibid., 121.
53. Ibid., 121.
54. Ibid., 122.
55. Ibid., 124.
56. Ibid., 128.
57. Ibid., 129.
58. Ibid., 129.
59. Ibid., 122.
60. Ibid., 141.
61. Ibid., 141.
62. Ibid., 141.
63. Ibid., 142.
64. Ibid., 143.
65. Ibid., 147.
66. Ibid., 147f.
67. Ibid., 148.
68. Ibid., 150.
69. Ibid., 150. In a telling comment on the above quote, Husserl adds: "In addition the concepts 'mundane' and 'transcendental' [are] equivocal! Naively mundane—transcendentally mundane. Transcendental as any particular [action of] transcendental constituting. Transcendental as the total Absolute."
70. Husserl, *Logical Investigations* 2, 263.
71. Fink, *Sixth Cartesian Meditation*, 151.
72. Ibid., 151.
73. Ibid., 151.
74. Ibid., 152.

75. Ibid., 152.

76. On the relation between biology and life, see Michel Henry, *I Am the Truth*, trans. Susan Emanuel (Palo Alto, CA: Stanford University Press, 2003), 33–52. Henry argues that biology, inasmuch as it objectifies and universalizes life, never truly understands the true imminent character of life: "And in fact biology never encounters life, knows nothing of it, has not the slightest idea of it. When by some extraordinary circumstance it is biology itself that speaks . . . it pronounces a sentence on itself, declares truthfully and lucidly what it is: '*Biologists no longer study life today.*' We must take it at its word: *in biology there is no life; there are only algorithms.*" Ibid., 38.

77. Bruzina, *Husserl and Fink*, 377.

78. Fink, *Phänomenologische Werkstatt*, Teilband 2, 86.

Conclusion to Part I

1. Fink, *Sixth Cartesian Meditation*, 152.

Notes to Chapter 4:
The Life and Times of Philippians 2:5–11

1. For much of the last century, it has been generally accepted that 2:6–11 is a pre-pauline hymn. For convenience, I will refer to it as a "hymn." It should be noted, however, that scholarly consensus about the passage's hymnic status has eroded. For an overview of recent form-critical arguments, see Benjamin Edsall and Jennifer R. Strawbridge, "The Songs we Used to Sing? Hymn 'Traditions' and Reception in Pauline Letters," *Journal for the Study of the New Testament* 37, no. 3 (2015): 290–311.

2. There are, of course, other noteworthy exegetical issues. I will focus on those that are most relevant to a phenomenological reading of the hymn. For a fuller treatment, see Paul A. Holloway, *Philippians*, Hermeneia Commentary Series (Minneapolis, MN: Fortress Press, 2017).

3. Cyril of Alexandria, *Festal Letter*, 10.4.

4. See Ralph P. Martin, *Philippians* (Grand Rapids, MI: Eerdmans; London: Marshall, Morgan & Scott, 1976, 1989), 91–93. See also, O'Brien, *Commentary on Philippians* (Grand Rapids, MI: Eerdmans, 1991), 253–262.

5. O'Brien, *Commentary on Philippians*, 254.

6. "Φρονείσθω" occurs in a late revision of Codex Ephraemi (C, 04) and in the Byzantine Majority Text. "Φρονεῖτε" occurs in Codex Sinaiticus (א, 01), Codex Alexandrinus (A, 02), Codex Vaticanus (B, 03), the original version of Codex Ephraemi (C, 04), Codex Claromontanus (D, 06), Codex Augiensis (F, 010), Codex Boernerianus (G, 012), as well as other later uncials.

7. C. F. D. Moule, "Further Reflections on Philippians 2:5–11," in *Apostolic History and the Gospel*, W. Ward Gasque & Ralph P. Martin, eds. (Exeter: The Paternoster Press, 1970), 265.

8. Ibid., 265. Moule's reading is similar to Gerald Hawthorne's, except the latter prefers the inferior reading, "φρονείσθω," and expands the elliptical text in the following way: "τοῦτο φρονείσθω ἐν ὑμῖν ὃ καὶ ἐφρονεῖτο ἐν Χριστῷ Ἰησοῦ." [Gerald Hawthorne, *Philippians* (Waco, TX: Word Books, 1983), 80.] The main benefit of the inferior reading, according to Hawthorne, is that it allows one to keep the grammatical parallelism between "ἐν ὑμῖν" and "ἐν Χριστῷ Ἰησοῦ." For if "φρονεῖτε" is the preferred text, then ἐν ὑμῖν cannot mean "in you" or "in yourselves," but must mean something like "among you" or toward one another," in which case there is no parallel with "ἐν Χριστῷ Ἰησοῦ." Reading φρονείσθω, Hawthorne translates 2:5 as, "This way of thinking must be adopted by you, which also was the way of thinking adopted by Jesus Christ." (Hawthorne, *Philippians*, 81.)

9. C. H. Dodd, *The Apostolic Preaching and its Developments* (London: Hodder and Stoughton, 1944), 64f.

10. Ibid., 65.

11. Adolf Deissmann, *St. Paul: A Study in Social and Religious History* (London: Hodder and Stoughton, 1912), 169f.

12. Martin, *Philippians*, 91.

13. Rudolf Bultmann, *Theology of the New Testament*, vol. 1, trans. Kendrick Grobel (New York: Scribner's, 1951), 311.

14. Wayne Meeks, for instance, argues that the phrase "no longer male nor female" refers to a sort of "eschatological androgyny." See Wayne Meeks, "The Image of the Androgyne: Some Uses of a Symbol in Earliest Christianity," *History of Religions* 13, no. 3 (Feb. 1974): 165–208. See also Dale Martin's treatment of Galatians 3:28 in *Sex and the Single Savior* (Louisville, KY: West Minister John Knox Press, 2006), 77–90.

15. Ernst Käsemann, "A Critical Analysis of Philippians 2:5–11," trans. A. F. Carse in Robert W. Funk, ed., *God and Christ: Existence and Province* (*Journal for Theology and the Church* 5) (Tubingen: J. C. B. Mohr, 1968), 84.

16. Ibid., 86.

17. Ibid., 87.

18. Ibid., 84.

19. Martin, *A Hymn of Christ* (Cambridge: Cambridge University Press, 1967), 85.

20. Käsemann, "A Critical Analysis of Philippians 2:5–11," 84.

21. The interpretation of μορφή as a synonym for οὐσία was common among ancient interpreters. Gregory of Nyssa, for instance, in opposition to Eunomius' neo-Arian position, reads 2:6 in the following way: "The *form* of God is absolutely the same as the essence. Yet when he came to be in *the form of a slave*, he took form in the essence of the slave . . . Yet he is not thereby divorced from his essence as

God. Undoubtedly when Paul said that he was *in the form of God*, he was indicating the essence along with the form." Gregory of Nyssa, *Against Eunomius*, 3.2.147.

22. Hawthorne, *Philippians*, 83–84. Quoting: Lucien Cerfaux, *Christ in the Theology of St. Paul*, trans. G. Webb and A. Walker (New York: Herder and Herder, 1959) 305.

23. Sarah Coakley, "Kenosis: Theological Meanings and Gender Connotations" in *The Work of Love: Creation as Kenosis*, John Polkinghorne, ed. (Grand Rapids, MI: Eerdmans, 2001), 194.

24. James D. G. Dunn, "Christ, Adam and Preexistence" in *Where Christology Began: Essays on Philippians 2*, Ralph P. Martin and Brian J. Dodd, eds. (Louisville, KY: Westminster John Knox Press, 1998), 77.

25. James D. G. Dunn, *Christology in the Making: A New Testament Inquiry into the Origins of the Doctrine of Incarnation* (London: SCM Press, 1980), 119.

26. For an excellent overview of recent debates surrounding the use of "ἁρπαγμός" in the kenosis hymn, see Michael Wade Martin, "ἁρπαγμός Revisited: A Philological Reexamination of the New Testament's 'Most Difficult Word,'" *Journal of Biblical Literature* 135:1 (2016): 175–194.

27. Modern interpreters are strikingly uniform in reading "οὐχ ἁρπαγμὸν ἡγήσατο τὸ εἶναι ἴσα θεῷ" as a passive construction that may be understood in one of two ways: either Christ did not regard equality with God as something having been seized (*res rapta*) or Christ did not regard equality with God as something to be seized(*res rapienda*). In both cases, the construction is passive. In contrast, many Ancient interpreters read "ἁρπαγμός" in an active sense as "an act of robbery." In commenting on 2:6, Marius Victorinus claims, "It would be a kind of robbery If two things were not equal by nature but were forced to be made equal . . . It therefore shows great confidence and bespeaks the very nature of divinity when Paul says of Christ that he did not think it robbery to be equal with God" (*Against the Arians*, 1.23). On an active reading of "ἁρπαγμός," Christ's equality with God is not a robbery because divine equality is part of Christ's essence. C. F. D. Moule has recently revived this view. See C. F. D. Moule, "Further Reflections on Philippians 2:5–11."

28. Martin, *A Hymn of Christ*, 138.

29. Karl Barth, *Epistle to the Philippians*, trans. James W. Leitch (Louisville, KY: Westminister John Knox Press, 2002) 61.

30. Ibid., 162f.

31. Ibid., 163.

32. Martin, *A Hymn of Christ*, 138.

33. Martin, *A Hymn of Christ*, 141.

34. Jean Héring, *Le Royaume de Dieu et sa venue* (Paris et Neuchâtel: Bibliothèque théologique, 1937, 1959), 163.

35. Martin, *A Hymn of Christ*, 141.

36. Archibald. M. Hunter, *Paul and his Predecessors* (Philadelphia: The Westminster Press, 1961) 43.

37. Sarah Coakley, "Kenosis: Theological Meanings and Gender Connotations," 194.

38. Martin, *Philippians*, 100. Aristotle, *Poetics*, 1452a, 23–24. My translation.

39. Martin, *A Hymn of Christ*, 244.

40. Karl Barth's interpretation of the kenōsis hymn is an exception to this generally accepted view. Barth's interpretation of the hymn reflects Lutheran sensibilities about grace and works. Christ's exaltation cannot, for Barth, *result* from humble obedience to the Father, because that would be tantamount to claiming that Christ somehow earned the Father's grace, that Christ's exaltation was assured from the beginning, in which case nothing was truly risked in the incarnation.

41. Daphne Hampson, *Theology and Feminism* (Oxford: Basil Blackwell, 1990), 151.

42. Ibid. 152. Quoting Carter Heyward, *The Redemption of God: A Theology of Mutual Relation* (Washington, DC: University Press of America, 1982), 156.

43. Hampson, *Theology and Feminism*, 152.

44. Ibid., 152f.

45. Ibid., 153.

46. Ibid., 148.

47. Rosemary Radford Reuther, *Sexism and God-Talk* (London: SCM Press, 1983), 135.

48. Ibid., 136.

49. Ibid., 137f.

50. Hampson, *Theology and Feminism*, 155.

51. Ibid., 155.

52. Coakley, *Powers and Submissions*, 32.

53. Ibid., 11.

54. Ibid., 9.

55. Ibid., 9.

56. Coakley recognizes this. Ibid. 11.

57. Ibid., 32.

58. Ibid., 32.

59. Ibid., 34.

60. Ibid., 34.

61. Ibid., 34–35.

62. Ibid., 33.

63. Friedrich Nietzsche, *Genealogy of Morality: A Polemic*, trans. Maudemarie Clark and Alan J. Swensen (Indianapolis, IN: Hackett Publishing, 1998), 63.

64. Ibid., 63.

65. Coakley, *Powers and Submissions*, 34.

Chapter 5

1. Husserl was not particularly concerned with the idea of "phenomenological reading." It was Martin Heidegger who first became interested in the hermeneutical implications of phenomenology. See, e.g., Heidegger's reading of I and II Thessalonians (*The Phenomenology of Religious Life*, 61–89).

2. On the knight's move, as it applies to literature and art, see Viktor Shlovsky, *The Knight's Move*, trans. Richard Sheldon (Normal, IL: Dalkey Archive Press, 2005).

3. Jacques Derrida, "Des Tours de Babel," in *Difference in Translation*, ed. Joseph F. Graham (Ithaca, NY: Cornell University Press), 165–207.

4. Slavoj Žižek, *The Puppet and the Dwarf: The Perverse Core of Christianity* (Cambridge, MA: MIT Press, 2003).

5. Carol A. Newsom, *The Book of Job: A Contest of Moral Imaginations* (New York: Oxford University Press, 2003).

6. Edmund Husserl, *Erste Philosophy, Zweiter Teil: Theorie der Phänom-enologischen Reduktion*, Husserliana VIII, ed. Rudolf Boehm (The Hague: M. Nijhoff, 1959).

7. Iso Kern, "The Three Ways to the Transcendental Phenomenological Reduction in the Philosophy of Edmund Husserl," in F. Elliston and P. McCormick, eds., *Husserl: Expositions and Appraisals* (Notre Dame, IN: University of Notre Dame Press, 1977), 126–49.

8. Sebastian Luft, *Subjectivity and Lifeworld in Transcendental Phenomenology* (Evanston, IL: Northwestern University Press, 2011), 58–74.

9. Edmund Husserl, *The Idea of Phenomenology*, trans. William P. Alston and George Nakhnikian (Boston: Kluwer Academic Publishers, 1964; 1990), 2.

10. Ibid., 5.

11. Ibid., 5.

12. Ibid., 5.

13. Husserl, *Ideas* I, 110, §49. See chapter 1, above.

14. Ibid., 61 fn.

15. Ibid., 113.

16. N.B., Husserl's notion of consciousness bears some similarity to Wilhem Wundt's, whose lectures Husserl attended at the University of Leipzig. Husserl criticizes Wundt's psychologism, but largely retains Wundt's idea of consciousness as "inner experience." See Wilhelm Wundt, *Principles of Physiological Psychology*, trans. Edward Bradford Titchener (New York: MacMillan, 1904).

17. Luft, *Subjectivity and Lifeworld in Transcendental Phenomenology*, 65.

18. Husserl, *The Crisis*, 203.

19. Ibid., 203.

20. Ibid., 210.

21. Ibid., 171.

22. Ibid., 172.

23. Ibid., 173.

24. For further explanation of Fink's position, see chapter 3.

25. Fink, *Sixth Cartesian Meditation*, 94.

26. My reading of the kenōsis hymn is indebted to Kevin Hart's work on the synoptic gospels—particularly the parables—in which he identifies a reduction from world (*cosmos*) to kingdom (*Basileia*). See, e.g., Kevin Hart, "Absolute Fragment or the Impossible Absolute," *Christianity and Literature* 59, no. 4 (Summer 2010). See

also Hart's *Kingdoms of God*. The Pauline kenotic reduction is very similar, though the concept of *Basileia* is not as operative for Paul (in the undisputed letters) as the concept of "καινὴ κτίσις" ("new creation."). The small differences between Hart's basilaic reduction and my kenotic reduction are entirely appropriate given that the two versions of phenomenological reduction derive from different biblical sources. Hart focuses on Jesus's parables, where *Basileia* is a central concept, while I focus on Paul's kenōsis hymn, where the apocalyptic idea of a "new creation" is more relevant. If we take "absolute science" seriously, then the methods of phenomenology must reflect the phenomena under consideration—different phenomena require different methods. Of course, there are significant similarities between Paul's eschatology and Jesus' eschatology, which would suggest a link between the kenotic reduction and the basilaic reduction, but establishing that link would take us too far afield.

27. Fink, *Sixth Cartesian Meditation*, 40.

28. Ibid., 47.

29. Ibid., 94.

30. *Book of Steps*, XII.1.

31. *Book of Steps*, XXI.9.

32. *Book of Steps*, XII.2.

33. Fink, *Sixth Cartesian* Meditation, 42.

34. Ibid. 41.

35. Ibid. 41.

36. Fink, *Sixth Cartesian Meditation*, 77. Fink's idea of an epistemic exaltation is gnostic in character. By contrast, the exaltation of Christ in the kenosis hymn is involves more than exalted *gnosis*; it is the exaltation of all creation. A kenotic transformation of phenomenology must also transform Fink's gnostic and idealistic tendencies.

37. Ibid. 120.

38. On demythologization, see Rudolf Bultmann, "The New Testament and Mythology," trans. Reginald Fuller, in *Kerygma and Myth*, ed. Hans Werner Bartsch (New York: Harper and Row, 1961).

39. Plato, *Symposium*, 200a–e. In *Plato in Twelve Volumes*, vol. 9, trans. Harold N. Fowler (Cambridge, MA: Harvard University Press; London: William Heinemann, Ltd., 1925.)

40. Aristotle, *Nichomachean Ethics*, 1158b. In *Aristotle in 23 Volumes*, vol. 19, trans. H. Rackham (Cambridge, MA: Harvard University Press; London: William Heinemann Ltd., 1934.)

41. Warren Zev Harvey, *Physics and Metaphysics in Hasdai Crescas* (Amsterdam: J. C. Gieben, 1998), 109.

42. Coakley, *Powers and Submissions*, 34.

43. Robert C. Solomon, *Living with Nietzsche* (Oxford: Oxford University Press, 2003), 94–95.

44. Hampson, *Theology and Feminism*, 155.

45. I am not claiming that Crescas's work gives *historical* insight into Paul's letters; rather, Crescas's criticsm of *eros* is a helpful hermeneutical tool for under-

standing Paul's use of kenōsis. A version of this summary of Crescas also appears in my article, "A Tree with Many Branches: Abrahamic Approaches to Interreligious Dialogue," which is forthcoming in *Studies in Interreligious Dialogue*.

46. Zev Harvey, *Physics and Metaphysics in Hasdai Crescas*, 110.

47. Hasdai Crescas, *Light of the Lord*, trans. Warren Zev Harvey (*Physics and Metaphysics in Hasdai Crescas* [Amsterdam: J. C. Gieben, 1998]), II, 6, 1.

48. Zev Harvey, *Physics and Metaphysics in Hasdai Crescas*, 111.

49. Crescas, *Light of the Lord*, II, 6, 1.

50. Crescas, *Light of the Lord*, I, 3, 5.

51. Zev Harvey, *Physics and Metaphysics in Hasdai Crescas*, 113.

52. Fink, *Sixth Cartesian Meditation*, 144.

53. Ibid., 148.

54. Translation modified.

Chapter 6

1. Paul Hanson, *The Dawn of Apocalyptic* (Philadelphia: Fortress Press, 1975), 29–30.

2. Albert Schweitzer, *The Mysticism of Paul the Apostle*, trans. William Montgomery (New York: MacMillan, 1960), 11.

3. Ibid., 11.

4. Ibid., 54.

5. Hanson, *The Dawn of Apocalyptic*, 160.

6. Martin C. de Boer, "Paul and Apocalyptic Eschatology" in *Continuum History of Apocalypticism*, ed. Bernard McGinn, John J. Collins, and Stephen J. Stein (New York: Continuum, 2003), 176.

7. Ibid., 176.

8. Ibid., 177.

9. Ibid., 181.

10. Ibid., 181.

11. John J. Collins, *The Apocalyptic Imagination The Apocalyptic Imagination* (Grand Rapids, MI: Eerdmans, 1998), 268.

12. Ibid., 267.

13. Husserl's thought on temporality is extraordinarily complex. Not only did his views on the subject change throughout his life but his writings on time were collected from various lectures and edited into longer texts by a number of assistants: Edith Stein, Martin Heidegger, Ludwig Landgrebe, and Eugen Fink. To fully assess Husserl's work on time one must take into account the evolution of Husserl's thought, as well as the editorial activity of Husserl's assistants. For a full treatment of time-consciousness in Husserl, see: Toine Kortooms, *Phenomenology of Time: Edmund Husserl's Analysis of Time-Consciousness* (Dordrecht, The Netherlands: Kluwer Academic Publishers, 2002). This section will not treat time-consciousness

in full detail, but will offer a summary of Husserl's concept of time-consciousness. The goal is to assess whether Husserlian temporality is sufficient to characterize kenotically reduced time.

14. Edmund Husserl, *The Phenomenology of Internal Time-Consciousness*, trans. James Churchill (Bloomington, IN, and London: Indiana University Press, 1964), 22.

15. Robert Sokolowski, *Introduction to Phenomenology* (Cambridge: Cambridge University Press, 2000), 130.

16. Husserl, *Phenomenology of Internal Time-Consciousness*, 22.

17. Ibid., 23.

18. Sokolowski, *Introduction to Phenomenology*, 130.

19. Husserl, *Phenomenology of Internal Time-Consciousness*, 23.

20. Ibid., 23.

21. Ibid., 27.

22. Sokolowski, *Introduction to Phenomenology*, 132.

23. Husserl, *Phenomenology of Internal Time-Consciousness*, 47.

24. Ibid., 46.

25. Ibid., 46.

26. Ibid., 47.

27. Ibid., 42.

28. Ibid., 150.

29. Bernet, Kern, and Marbach, *Introduction to Husserlian Phenomenology*, 109.

30. Husserl, *Phenomenology of Internal Time-Consciousness*, 50.

31. William James, *The Principles of Psychology*, 2 vols. (New York: Henry Holt and Company, 1918), 1:609.

32. Husserl, *Phenomenology of Internal Time-Consciousness*, 50.

33. Sokolowski, *Introduction to Phenomenology*, 137.

34. Dan Zahavi, "Inner (Time-)Consciousness," *On Time: New Contributions to the Husserlian Phenomenology of Time*, eds. Dieter Lohmar and Ichiro Yamaguchi (Dordrecht, The Netherlands: Springer, 2010), 321.

35. Husserl, *Phenomenology of Internal Time-Consciousness*, 57.

36. Ibid., 57.

37. Toine Kortooms, *Phenomenology of Time*, 68. My italics.

38. Husserl, *Phenomenology of Internal Time-Consciousness*, 74.

39. Edmund Husserl, *Einleitung in die Logik und Erkenntnistheorie. Vorlesungen 1906/07*, ed. Ullrich Melle (The Hague: Martinus Nijhoff, 1985), 257f. My translation.

40. Husserl, *Phenomenology of Internal Time-Consciousness*, 79. My Italics.

41. Ibid., 79.

42. Ibid., 80.

43. Ibid., 80.

44. Ibid., 57.

Chapter 7

1. Jean-Yves Lacoste, "The Phenomenality of Anticipation" *Phenomenology and Eschatology: Not Yet in the Now*, eds. John P. Manoussakis and Neal DeRoo (Farnham, Surrey, and Burlington, VT: Ashgate Publishing, 2009), 32. This article is an English translation of the chapter by the same name in Lacoste's *La Phénoménalité de Dieu* (Paris: Cerf, 2008), 133–57. I will quote from the English translation.

2. Lacoste, "The Phenomenality of Anticipation," 15.

3. Ibid., 15.

4. Husserl, *Phenomenology of Internal Time-Consciousness*, 80.

5. Lacoste, "The Phenomenality of Anticipation," 16.

6. Ibid., 16.

7. Ibid., 17.

8. Ibid., 19.

9. Ibid., 19f.

10. Ibid., 27.

11. Ibid., 27.

12. Ibid., 27.

13. Ibid., 20.

14. Jean-Yves Lacoste, *Experience and the Absolute: Disputed Questions on the Humanity of Man*, trans. Mark Raftery-Skeehan (New York: Fordham University Press, 2004), 57.

15. Martin Heidegger, *Being and Time*, trans. Joan Stambaugh (Albany: State University of New York Press, 1996), 303.

16. Lacoste, *Experience and the Absolute*, 57.

17. Ibid., 57–58.

18. Ibid., 58.

19. Ibid., 58.

20. Ibid., 58.

21. Ibid., 58.

22. Ibid., 59.

23. Bruzina, *Edmund Husserl and Eugen Fink*, 14–15.

24. Ibid., 15.

25. Ibid., 17.

26. Ibid., 258f.

27. Ibid., 265.

28. Edmund Husserl, *Die Bernauer Manuskripte Über Das Zeitbewusstsein*, Husserliana Band XXXIII, eds. Rudolf Bernet and Dieter Lomar (Dordrecht, The Netherlands: Kluwer Academic Publishers, 2001), 45.

29. Ibid., 191.

30. Bruzina, *Edmund Husserl and Eugen Fink*, 267.

31. Ibid., 268.

32. Ibid., 267.

33. Eugen Fink, *Phänomenologische Werkstatt, TeilBand 2*, 39.

34. Bruzina, *Edmund Husserl and Eugen Fink*, 303.

35. Eugen Fink, *Phänomenologische Werkstatt, Teilband 1: Doktorarbeit und erste Assistenzjahre bei Husserl*, ed. Ronald Bruzina (Freiburg: Verlag Karl Alber, 2006), 168.

36. Bruzina, *Edmund Husserl and Eugen Fink*, 276.

37. Ibid., 276.

38. Fink, *Phänomenologische Werkstatt Freiburg, Teilband 2*, 102.

39. Bruzina, *Edmund Husserl and Eugen Fink*, 310.

40. Ibid., 311.

41. Lacoste would also presumably object to Fink's gnostic tendencies.

Conclusion

1. Husserl, *Ideas II*, 3.

2. Ibid., 4.

3. Ibid., 29.

4. Think, for instance, of the many recent neurological studies of prayer. See, for instance, Uffe Schjoedt, et al., "Highly religious participants recruit areas of social cognition in personal prayer," *Social Cognitive and Affective Neuroscience* 4, no. 2 (Feb. 2009): 199–207.

5. While I am focusing on the nineteenth- and early-twentieth-century origins of the historical-critical method, it should be noted that historical criticism is still very influential. As Dale Martin notes, "One would have to say that in spite of recent innovations and moves away from teaching only historical criticism, that method is still the dominant one taught to students training to be ministers. They may be taught to go beyond the historical meaning of the text, but that historical meaning is nonetheless predominant or foundational in the education of most clergy." Dale B. Martin, *Pedagogy of the Bible: An Analysis and Proposal* (Louisville, KY: Westminster John Knox, 2008), 3.

6. Charles Augustus Briggs, *General Introduction to the Study of Holy Scripture: the Principles, Methods, History, and Results of its Several Departments and of the Whole* (New York: Charles Scribner's Sons, 1899), 531.

7. Otto Pfleiderer, introduction to David F. Strauss, *The Life of Jesus Critically Examined*, trans. George Eliot (New York: MacMillan & Co., 1892), vi.

8. For a good summary of contemporary methods of biblical interpretation, see Steven L. McKenzie and Stephen R. Haynes (eds.), *To Each Its Own Meaning, Revised and Expanded: An Introduction to Biblical Criticisms and Their Application* (Louisville, KY: Westminster John Knox, 1999).

9. Husserl, *Ideas II*, 192.

10. Husserl, *Ideas II*, 193.

11. Husserl, *The Crisis of European Sciences*, 144.

12. Husserl, *The Crisis of European Sciences*, 146.

13. Jean-Louis Chrétien makes a similar remark about scripture's ability to transform human subjectivity by existing simultaneously inside and outside of experience. See Jean-Louis Chrétien, *Under the Gaze of the Bible*, trans. John Marson Dunaway (New York: Fordham University Press, 2015.

14. Genesis Rabbah, *Bereshith, par. 1:1*, on Genesis 1:1. *Midrash Rabbah*, trans. H. Freedman and Maurice Simon (London: The Soncino Press, 1939), 1. Formatting modified. Similarly, in the Gospel of John, the *Logos* exists before creation (John 1:1).

15. Ludwig Wittgenstein, *Tractatus Logico-Philosophicus* (New York: Harcourt, Brace, and Co., 1922), 189.

Bibliography

Adams, Edward. "The 'coming of God' tradition and its influence on New Testament parousia texts." In *Biblical Traditions in Transmission*. Leiden: Brill, 2006: 1–19.

Aristotle. *Nichomachean Ethics*. Translated by H. Rackham. In *Aristotle in 23 Volumes*. Cambridge, MA: Harvard University Press, 1934.

Barth, Karl. *Epistle to the Philippians*. Translated by James W. Leitch. Louisville, KY: Westminister John Knox Press, 2002.

Benson, Bruce Ellis, and Norman Wirzba. *Words of Life: New Theological Turns in French Phenomenology*. New York: Fordham University Press, 2010.

Bernet, Rudolf, Iso Kern, and Eduard Marbach. *An Introduction to Husserlian Phenomenology*. Evanston, IL: Northwestern University Press, 1993.

Bostock, Gerald. "Origen's Exegesis of the Kenōsis Hymn (Philippians 2:5–11)," *Origeniana Sexta: Origine et la Bible/Origen and the Bible: Actes du Colloquium Origenianum Sextum Chantilly, 30 août-3 septembre 1993*. Louvain: Peters, 1995.

Briggs, Charles Augustus. *General Introduction to the Study of Holy Scripture: The Principles, Methods, History, and Results of its Several Departments and of the Whole*. New York: Charles Scribner's Sons, 1899.

Bruzina, Ronald. *Edmund Husserl and Eugen Fink: Beginnings and Ends in Phenomenology 1928–38*. New Haven, CT; London: Yale University Press, 2004.

Bultmann, Rudolf. "The New Testament and Mythology." Translated by Reginald Fuller. In *Kerygma and Myth*. Edited by Hans Werner Bartsch. New York: Harper and Row, 1961.

———. *Theology of the New Testament*. Vol. 1. Translated by Kendrick Grobel. New York: Scribner's, 1951.

Cairns, Dorion, Edmund Husserl, and Eugen Fink. *Conversations with Husserl and Fink*. Phaenomenologica. Vol. 66. The Hague, The Netherlands: Martinus Nijhoff, 1976.

Caputo, John. *Radical Hermeneutics*. Bloomington and Indianapolis, IN: Indiana University Press, 1987.

Cerfaux, Lucien. *Christ in the Theology of St. Paul*. Translated by G. Webb and A. Walker. New York: Herder and Herder, 1959.

Chrétien, Jean-Louis. *Under the Gaze of the Bible*. Translated by John Marson Dunaway. New York: Fordham University Press, 2015.

———. *The Unforgettable and the Unhoped For*. Translated by Jeffrey Bloechl. New York: Fordham University Press, 2002.

Coakley, Sarah. "Kenosis: Theological Meanings and Gender Connotations." In *The Work of Love: Creation as Kenosis*. Edited by John Polkinghorne. Grand Rapids, MI: Eerdmans, 2001. 192–210.

———. *Powers and Submissions: Spirituality, Philosophy and Gender*. Oxford: Blackwell, 2002.

Collins, Adela Yarbro. *Cosmology and Eschatology in Jewish and Christian Apocalypses*. Boston and Leiden: Brill, 1998.

Collins, John J. *The Apocalyptic Imagination*. 2nd Edition. Grand Rapids, MI: Eerdmans, 1998.

———. "Prophecy, Apocalypse and Eschatology: Reflections on the Proposals of Lester Grabbe." In *Knowing the End from the Beginning: The Prophetic, The Apocalyptic and their Relationships*. Edited by Lester Grabbe and Robert Haak. New York: Continuum, 2003. 44–53.

Crescas, Ḥasdai. *Sefer Or Adonai (Light of the Lord)*. Farnsborough, UK: Gregg, 1969.

Crisp, Oliver D. *Divinity and Humanity*. Cambridge: Cambridge University Press, 2007.

Dalferth, Ingolf U. *Becoming Present: An Inquiry into the Christian Sense of the Presence of God*. Leuven: Peeters, 2006.

De Boer, Martin C. "Paul and Apocalyptic Eschatology." In *Continuum History of Apocalypticism*. Edited by Bernard McGinn, John J. Collins, and Stephen J. Stein. New York: Continuum, 2003. 166–94.

———. "Paul, theologian of God's apocalypse." *Interpretation* 56, no. 1 (Jan., 2002): 21–33.

Deissmann, Adolf. *St. Paul: A Study in Social and Religious History*. London: Hodder and Stoughton, 1912.

Derrida, Jacques. *The Problem of Genesis in Husserl's Philosophy*. Translated by Marian Hobson. Chicago: University of Chicago Press, 2003.

———. *Speech and Phenomena and Other Essays on Husserl's Theory of Signs*. Translated by David B. Allison. Evanston, IL: Northwestern University Press, 1973.

———. *Writing and Difference*. Translated by Alan Bass. Chicago: University of Chicago Press, 1978.

Dodd, C. H. *The Apostolic Preaching and its Developments*. London: Hodder and Stoughton, 1944.

Dunn, James D. G. "Christ, Adam and Preexistence." In *Where Christology Began: Essays on Philippians 2*. Edited by Ralph P. Martin and Brian J. Dodd. Louisville, KY: Westminster John Knox Press, 1998. 74–95.

———. *Christology in the Making: A New Testament Inquiry into the Origins of the Doctrine of Incarnation*. London: SCM Press, 1980.

Edsall, Benjamin, and Jennifer R. Strawbridge. "The Songs We Used to Sing? Hymn 'Traditions' and Reception in Pauline Letters." *Journal for the Study of the New Testament* 37, no. 3 (2015): 290–311.

Evans, C. Stephen, Ed. *Exploring Kenotic Christology: The Self-Emptying God*. Oxford: Oxford University Press, 2006.

Falque, Emmanuel. *Dieu, La Chair Et l'Autre: D'Irénée à Duns Scot*. Paris: Presses universitaires de France, 2008.

Fink, Eugen. *VI. Cartesianische Meditation, Teil 2: Ergänzungsband*. Husserliana Dokumente II, 2. Edited by Guy van Kerckhoven. Dordrecht, The Netherlands: Kluwer Academic Publishers, 1988.

———. *Phänomenologische Werkstatt, Teilband 1: Die Doktorabeit und erste Assistenzjahre bei Husserl*. Edited by Ronal Bruzina. Freiburg: Verlag Karl Alber, 2006.

———. *Phänomenologische Werkstatt, Teilband 2: Die Bernauer Zeitmanuskripte, Cartesianische Meditationen und System der phänomenologische Philosophie*. Edited by Ronald Bruzina. Freiburg: Verlag Karl Alber, 2008.

———. *Sixth Cartesian Meditation*. Translated by Ronald Bruzina. Indianapolis, IN: Indiana University Press, 1995.

———. *Studien zur Phänomenologie, 1930–1939*. Phaenomenologica Vol. 21. The Hague: The Netherlands: Martinus Nijhoff, 1966.

Freedman, H., and Maurice Simon, trans. *Midrash Rabbah*. London: The Soncino Press, 1939.

Frege, Gottlob. "Review of Dr. E Husserl's *Philosophy of Arithmetic*." Translated by E. W. Kluge. In *Husserl: Expositions and Appraisals*, eds. Frederick Elliston and Peter McCormick. (Notre Dame, IN: University of Notre Dame Press, 1981), 314–24.

Gibbs, John G. "Relation between creation and redemption according to Phil 2:5–11." *Novum Testamentum* 12, no. 3 (July 1970): 270–83.

Gorman, Michael J. *Inhabiting the Cruciform God: Kenōsis, Justification, and Theosis in Paul's Narrative Soteriology*. Grand Rapids, MI: Eerdmans, 2009.

Grabbe, Lester. "Prophetic and Apocalyptic: Time for New Definitions—and New Thinking." In *Knowing the End from the Beginning: The Prophetic, The Apocalyptic and their Relationships*. Edited by Lester Grabbe and Robert Haak. New York: Continuum, 2003. 107–33.

Hampson, Daphne. *Theology and Feminism*. Oxford: Basil Blackwell, 1990.

Hanley, Catriona. *Being and God in Aristotle and Heidegger: The Role of Method in Thinking the Infinite*. Lanham, MD: Rowman & Littlefield Publishers, 2000.

Hanson, Paul. *The Dawn of Apocalyptic*. Philadelphia: Fortress Press, 1975.

Hart, Kevin. "Absolute Fragment or the Impossible Absolute." *Christianity and Literature* 59, no. 4 (Summer 2010).

———. *Kingdoms of God*. Bloomington: Indiana University Press, 2014.

Harvey, Warren Zev. *Physics and Metaphysics in Ḥasdai Crescas*. Amsterdam Studies in Jewish Thought, Vol. 6. Amsterdam: J. C. Gieben, 1998.

Hawthorne, Gerald F. *Philippians*. Waco, TX: Word Books, 1983.

Heidegger, Martin. *Basic Concepts of Aristotelian Philosophy*. Bloomington: Indiana University Press, 2009.

———. *Being and Time: A Translation of Sein Und Zeit*. Translated by Joan Stambaugh. Albany: State University of New York Press, 1996.

────. *Introduction to Metaphysics*. Translated by Gregory Fried and Richard Polt. New Haven, CT: Yale University Press, 2000.

────. *The Phenomenology of Religious Life*. Translated by Matthias Fritsch and Jennifer Anna Gosetti-Ferencei. Bloomington: Indiana University Press, 2004.

Henry, Michel. *I Am the Truth: Toward a Philosophy*. Translated by Susan Emanuel. Palo Alto, CA: Stanford University Press, 2003.

────. *Material Phenomenology*. Translated by Scott Davidson. New York: Fordham University Press, 2008.

Héring, Jean. *Le Royaume de Dieu et sa venue*. Paris et Neuchâtel: Bibliothèque théologique, 1937, 1959.

Heyward, Carter. *The Redemption of God: A Theology of Mutual Relation*. Washington, DC: University Press of America, 1982.

Hodge, Joanna. *Derrida on Time*. New York: Routledge, 2007.

Holloway, Paul A. *Philippians*. Hermeneia Commentary Series. Minneapolis, MN: Fortress Press, 2017.

Hunter, Archibald M. *Paul and his Predecessors*. Philadelphia: The Westminster Press, 1961.

Husserl, Edmund. *The Basic Problems of Phenomenology: From the Lectures, Winter Semester, 1910–1911*. Translated by Ingo Farin and James G. Hart. Dordrecht, The Netherlands: Springer, 2006.

────. *Die Bernauer Manuskripte Über Das Zeitbewusstsein*. Husserliana Band XXXIII. Edited by Rudolf Bernet and Dieter Lomar. Dordrecht, The Netherlands: Kluwer Academic Publishers, 2001.

────. *Cartesian Meditations: An Introduction to Phenomenology*. Translated by Dorion Cairns. The Hague, The Netherlands: M. Nijhoff, 1977.

────. *The Crisis of European Sciences and Transcendental Phenomenology*. Translated by David Carr. Evanston, IL: Northwestern University Press, 1970.

────. *Einleitung in die Logik und Erkenntnistheorie*. Vorlesungen 1906/07. Edited by Ullrich Melle. The Hague, The Netherlands: Martinus Nijhoff, 1985.

────. *Erste Philosophie (1923/24)*. Zweiter Teil. Husserliana Band VIII. Edited by Rudolf Boehm. The Hague, The Netherlands: Martinus Nijhoff, 1959.

────. *The Idea of Phenomenology*. Translated by Lee Hardy. Dordrecht, The Netherlands: Kluwer Academic, 1999.

────. *Ideas Pertaining to a Pure Phenomenology and to a Phenomenological Philosophy*. Translated by F. Kersten. The Hague, The Netherlands: M. Nijhoff, 1982.

────. *Introduction to Logic and Theory of Knowledge: Lectures 1906–07*. Translated by Claire Ortiz Hill. Dordrecht, The Netherlands: Springer, 2008.

────. *Logical Investigations*. Vol 1. Translated by J. N. Findlay. New York: Routledge, 2001.

────. *Logical Investigations*. Vol 2. Translated by J. N. Findlay. New York: Routledge, 2001.

────. *Phantasy, Image Consciousness, and Memory (1898–1925)*. Translated by John B. Brough. Dordrecht, The Netherlands: Springer, 2005.

────. *The Phenomenology of Internal Time-Consciousness*. Translated by James Churchill. Bloomington: Indiana University Press, 1964.

———. *Philosophy of Arithmetic: Psychological and Logical Investigations with Supplementary Texts from 1887–1901*. Translated by Dallas Willard. The Hague, The Netherlands: Martinus Nijhoff, 2003.

———. "Philosophy as a Rigorous Science." Translated by Marcus Brainard. *The New Yearbook for Phenomenology and Phenomenological Philosophy* II (2002): 249–95.

———. *Psychological and Transcendental Phenomenology and the Confrontation with Heidegger (1927–1931): The Encyclopaedia Britannica Article, the Amsterdam Lectures, "Phenomenology and Anthropology," and Husserl's Marginal Notes in being and Time, and Kant and the Problem of Metaphysics*. Dordrecht, The Netherlands: Kluwer Academic, 1997.

———. *Studies in the Phenomenology of Constitution*, vol. 2 of *Ideas Pertaining to a Pure Phenomenology and to a Phenomenological Philosophy*. Translated by Richard Rojcewicz and André Schuwer. Dordrecht, The Netherlands: Kluwer Academic Publishers, 1989.

James, William. *The Principles of Psychology*. 2 Vols. New York: Henry Holt and Company, 1918.

Käsemann, Ernst. "A Critical Analysis of Philippians 2:5–11." Translated A. F. Carse. In *God and Christ: Existence and Province*. Edited by Robert W. Funk. Tubingen: J. C. B. Mohr, 1968. 45–88.

Koch, Klaus. *The Rediscovery of Apocalyptic*. London: SCM Press, 1972.

Kohák, Erazim V. *Idea and Experience: Edmund Husserl's Project of Phenomenology in Ideas I*. Chicago: University of Chicago Press, 1978.

Kortooms, Antonie Johannes Maria. *Phenomenology of Time: Edmund Husserl's Analysis of Time-Consciousness*. Dordrecht: Kluwer Academic, 2002.

Lacoste, Jean-Yves. *Experience and the Absolute: Disputed Questions on the Humanity of Man*. Translated by Mark Raferty-Skehan. New York: Fordham University Press, 2004.

———. *Note Sur Le Temps: Essai Sur Les Raisons De La Mémoire Et De l'Espérance*. Théologiques. Paris: Presses universitaires de France, 1990.

———. *La Phénoménalité de Dieu*. Paris: Cerf, 2008.

———. *Présence et parousie*. Genève: Ad Solem, 2006.

Lawlor, Leonard. *Derrida and Husserl: The Basic Problem of Phenomenology*. Bloomington: Indiana University Press, 2002.

Lohmar, Dieter, and Ichirō Yamaguchi, eds. *On Time: New Contributions to the Husserlian Phenomenology of Time*. Dordrecht, The Netherlands: Springer, 2010.

Lohmeyer, Ernst. *Kyrios Jesus: Eine Untersuchung zu Phil. 2,5–11*. Heidelberg: Winters, 1928.

Longenecker, Richard. *Biblical Exegesis in the Apostolic Period*. Grand Rapids, MI: Eerdmans, 1999.

———. " 'Faith of Abraham' theme in Paul, James and Hebrews: a study in the circumstantial nature of New Testament teaching." *Journal of the Evangelical Theological Society* 20, no. 3 (1997): 203–12.

MacDonald, Paul S. *Descartes and Husserl: The Philosophical Project of Radical Beginnings*. Albany: State University of New York Press, 2000.

Manoussakis, John P., and Neal DeRoo, Eds. *Phenomenology and Eschatology: Not Yet in the Now*. Farnham, Surrey, and Burlington, VT: Ashgate Publishing, 2009.

Marion, Jean-Luc. *Being Given: Toward a Phenomenology of Givenness*. Translated by Jeffrey Kosky. Palo Alto, CA: Stanford University Press, 2002.

———. *Reduction and Givenness: Investigations of Husserl, Heidegger, and Phenomenology*. Translated by Thomas A. Carlson. Evanston, IL: Northwestern University Press, 1998.

Martin, Dale B. *Pedagogy of the Bible: An Analysis and Proposal*. Louisville, KY: Westminster John Knox, 2008.

———. *Sex and the Single Savior*. Louisville, KY: West Minister John Knox Press, 2006.

Martin, Michael Wade. "ἁρπαγμός Revisited: A Philological Reexamination of the New Testament's 'Most Difficult Word.'" *Journal of Biblical Literature* 135, no. 1 (2016): 175–94.

Martin, Ralph P. *Carmen Christi: Philippians ii. 5–11 in Recent Interpretation and in the Setting of Early Christian Worship*. Cambridge: Cambridge University Press, 1967; Downers Grove, IL: InterVarsity Press, 1983, 1997.

———. *Philippians*. New Century Bible Commentary. Grand Rapids, MI: Eerdmans; London: Marshall, Morgan & Scott, 1976, 1989.

McKenzie, Stephen L., and Stephen R. Haynes, Eds. *To Each Its Own Meaning, Revised and Expanded: An Introduction to Biblical Criticisms and Their Application*. Louisville, KY: Westminster John Knox, 1999.

Meeks, Wayne. "The Image of the Androgyne: Some Uses of a Symbol in Earliest Christianity." *History of Religions* 13, no. 3 (Feb. 1974): 165–208.

Moran, Dermot. "Fink's Speculative Phenomenology: Between Constitution and Transcendence." *Research in Phenomenology* 37 (2007): 3–31.

Moule, C. F. D. "Further Reflections on Philippians 2:5–11." In *Apostolic History and the Gospel*. Edited by W. Ward Gasque and Ralph P. Martin. Exeter, UK: The Paternoster Press, 1970. 265–76.

Neill, Stephen, and N. T. Wright. *The Interpretation of the New Testament, 1861–1986*. 2nd Edition. Oxford: Oxford University Press, 1988.

O'Brien, Peter T. *Commentary on Philippians*. Grand Rapids, MI: Eerdmans, 1991.

O'Keefe, John, and R. R. Reno. *Sanctified Vision*. Baltimore, MD: The Johns Hopkins University Press, 2005.

Plato. *Symposium*. Translated by Harold N. Fowler. In *Plato in Twelve Volumes*. Vol. 9. Cambridge, MA: Harvard University Press, 1925.

Plevnik, Joseph. *Paul and the Parousia: An Exegetical and Theological Investigation*. Peabody, MA: Hendrickson Publishers, 1997.

Protevi, John. *Time and Exteriority: Aristotle, Heidegger, Derrida*. Lewisburg, PA: Bucknell University Press, 1994.

Roberts, J. J. M. "Myth Versus History." *Catholic Biblical Quarterly* XXXVIII, 1976: 1–13.

Reuther, Rosemary Radford. *Sexism and God-Talk*. London: SCM Press, 1983.

Rudavsky, Tamar. *Time Matters: Time, Creation, and Cosmology in Medieval Jewish Philosophy*. Albany: State University of New York Press, 2000.

Russell, Matheson. *Husserl: A Guide for the Perplexed*. New York: Continuum, 2006.

Sanders, E. P. "The Genre of Palestinian Jewish Apocalypses." In *Apocalypticism in the Mediterranean World and the Near East: Proceedings of the International Colloquium on Apocalypticism*. Edited by David Hellhom. Tubingen: J. C. B. Mohr, 1983. 447–59.

Schleiermacher, Friederich. *The Christian Faith*. Edinburgh: T & T Clark, 1989.

Schjoedt, Uffe, et al. "Highly religious participants recruit areas of social cognition in personal prayer." *Social Cognitive and Affective Neuroscience* 4, no. 2 (Feb 2009): 199–207.

Schrijvers, Joeri. *An Introduction to Jean-Yves Lacoste*. New York: Routledge, 2016.

Schweitzer, Albert. *The Mysticism of Paul the Apostle*. Translated by William Montgomery. New York: MacMillan, 1960.

Schweizer, Eduard. *Erniedrigung und Erhöhung bei Jesu und seinen Nachfolgern*. Zurich: Zwingli, 1955.

Shlovsky, Viktor. *The Knight's Move*. Translated by Richard Sheldon. Normal, IL: Dalkey Archive Press, 2005.

Sokolowski, Robert. *Eucharistic Presence: A Study in the Theology of Disclosure*. Washington, DC: Catholic University of America, 1994.

———. *The Formation of Husserl's Concept of Constitution*. The Hague, The Netherlands: M. Nijhoff, 1964.

———. *Introduction to Phenomenology*. Cambridge: Cambridge University Press, 2000.

———. *Presence and Absence: A Philosophical Investigation of Language and Being*. Bloomington: Indiana University Press, 1978.

Solomon, Robert. *Living with Nietzsche*. Oxford: Oxford University Press, 2003.

Steinbock, Anthony J. *Home and Beyond: Generative Phenomenology After Husserl*. Evanston, IL: Northwestern University Press, 1995.

Stone, Michael. "Lists of Revealed Things in Apocalyptic Literature." In *Magnalia Dei*. Edited by Frank Moore Cross. New York: Doubleday, 1976. 414–52.

Strauss, David F. *The Life of Jesus Critically Examined*. Translated by George Eliot. New York: MacMillan & Co., 1892.

Thomasius, Gottfried. "The Person of the Mediator." Translated by Claude Welch. In *God and Incarnation in Mid-Nineteenth Century German Theology*. Edited by Claude Welch. Oxford: Oxford University Press, 1965.

Vielhauer, P. *Aufsätze zum Neuen Testament*. Munich: Kaiser, 1965.

Watson, Francis. *Paul, Judaism and The Gentiles*. Grand Rapids, MI: Eerdmans, 2007.

Wittgenstein, Ludwig. *Tractatus Logico-Philosophicus*. New York: Harcourt, Brace, and Co., 1922.

Wolfson, Harry Austryn, and Hasdai Crescas. *Crescas' Critique of Aristotle: Problems of Aristotle's Physics in Jewish and Arabic Philosophy*. Cambridge: Harvard University Press, 1929; 1957.

Wundt, Wilhem. *Principles of Physiological Psychology.* Translated by Edward Brad-
    ford Titchener. New York: MacMillan, 1904.
Zahavi, Dan. *Husserl's Phenomenology.* Stanford, CA: Stanford University Press, 2003.

Index

Ricoeur, Paul, xii

Scheler, Max, xii
Schutz, Alfred, xii
Schweitzer, Albert, 120–121
scripture
  historical criticism (*see* historical
    criticism)
  phenomenology of (*see under*
    phenomenology)
  theological turn (*see under*
    phenomenology)
sedimentation, 30, 35–36
self-evidence. See *Evidenz*
sign, 13–15
Sixth Cartesian Meditation, 52–72,
  103
Sokolowski, Robert, 10, 124, 125, 126,
  128
static phenomenology. *See under*
  phenomenology
Steinbock, Anthony, 39–48, 157
Stoicism, 120

theological turn in phenomenology.
  See under phenomenology
time-consciousness, 124–130, 134–135,
  140–141, 145
  expectation, 131, 134–135, 142 (*See
    also* anticipation)
  field and flow, 143, 145
  filling and emptying, 141–143, 145
  memory, 129–131, 142
  protention, 127–128, 134–135, 140,
    142, 145
  retention, 127–129, 134, 140, 142, 145
transcendental onlooker. *See*
  phenomenologizing I
transcendental subjectivity, 9, 17, 20–23,
  28, 40, 46, 47, 48, 52–59, 61–65, 66,
  67, 68, 70, 102, 106, 116
transcendental theory of elements. *See
  under* phenomenology
transcendental theory of method. *See
  under* phenomenology

Zahavi, Dan, 12, 128